NED CHRISTIE

NED CHRISTIE

THE CREATION OF AN
OUTLAW AND
CHEROKEE HERO

DEVON A. MIHESUAH

UNIVERSITY OF OKLAHOMA PRESS : NORMAN

This book is published with the generous assistance of the Wallace C. Thompson
Endowment Fund, University of Oklahoma Foundation.

Epigraph 1: "About the Bad Man: Some Strange Facts Concerning Indian
Territory Outlaws," *Chicago Daily Tribune*, November 7, 1894.

Epigraph 2: Peter Clines, *The Fold* (New York: Crown, 2015), 93.

Library of Congress Cataloging-in-Publication Data

Name: Mihesuah, Devon A., 1957– author.
Title: Ned Christie : the creation of an outlaw and Cherokee hero / by Devon A. Mihesuah.
Other titles: Creation of an outlaw and Cherokee hero
Description: Norman, OK : University of Oklahoma Press, [2018] | Includes
    bibliographical references and index.
Identifiers: LCCN 2017028436 | ISBN 978-0-8061-5910-2 (hardcover : alk. paper)
Subjects: LCSH: Christie, Ned, 1852–1892. | Cherokee Indians—Biography. |
    Cherokee Indians—History—19th century. | Cherokee Indians—Government
    relations. | Outlaws—Indian Territory—History. | Indian Territory—Biography.
Classification: LCC E99.C5 C65575 2018 | DDC 973.04/975570092 [B] —dc23
LC record available at https://lccn.loc.gov/2017028436

1 2 3 4 5 6 7 8 9 10

TO NEDE WADE CHRISTIE'S FAMILY,
ESPECIALLY ROY HAMILTON, WHO PASSED AWAY
AS THIS BOOK WENT TO PRESS

*This is the story of the bad man the killer,
as he blossoms in the Indian Territory. He is truly an entertaining
creature. His ways are interesting and variously vile.*

CHICAGO DAILY TRIBUNE, November 7, 1894

....

*"I think," Bob said, "that a person can always find what they're looking for,
whether it's there or not. They'll just see what they want to see."*

PETER CLINES, *The Fold*, 2015

CONTENTS

ILLUSTRATIONS

ACKNOWLEDGMENTS

Much of the information here about Ned's family life comes from Roy Hamilton, Ned's great-great nephew, collector of Christie stories, and president of the Cherokee Arts and Humanities Council. Roy heard stories about Ned mainly from Ned's great-nieces; his mother, Jewell Dean, known to everyone as Juki; and Roberta Reynolds Teague, his mother's cousin, called "Aunt Bertie," who lived a quarter mile from Ned's home. Roy listened to reminiscences as the women talked and washed clothes in the same creek fed by the spring used by Ned and Nancy a hundred years prior.

Roy lived within walking distance of Ned's homeplace, the spring, the site where the stone lookout stood on "Ned's Mountain," the old Wauhillau Trading Post, the deteriorating house of Ned's nephew Watt A., as well as Ned's final

Roy Hamilton, June 2015, in front of the spring used by Ned and Nancy and subsequent generations of Ned's descendants. *Photo by author.*

resting place in the Watt Christie Cemetery. Roy spent his childhood here and attended the small school across the street from the trading post. He recalled playing barefoot in the creek and walking the old wagon trail to Tahlequah, the same road taken by Ned when he traveled to council meetings. Roy lived in a place of history, surrounded by memories of family and tribe. It is indeed an enviable situation for a person to live among one's ancestors. Family roots are crucial, as Roy told me: "I love my Cherokee family. They mean a great deal to me, those living and my beloved departed. I miss my elders so much. But they left me with memories that will be a part of me forever." Roy's statements about family are pivotal to this exploration of Nede Wade and it has been a joy to converse with him.

I also thank the following: Stacy Leeds, dean of Law School, University of Arkansas; Jerry Akins and Emily Lovick at the Fort Smith National Historic Site; Victoria Sheffler, Delores Sumner, Ashley Stoddard, and Darren Tobey at the John Vaughan Library, Northeastern State University; Elisabeth Branam, Jacquelyn Reese, and Kristina Southwell at the Western History Collections, University of Oklahoma; Meg Hacker, director, National Archives at Fort Worth; Elizabeth Bass, editor of the *Chronicles of Oklahoma*; Mallory Covington, Jennifer Day, J. A. Pryse, Angela Spindle, William Welge at the Oklahoma Historical Society; Susan Burch, American Studies Program, Middlebury College; Jerry "Catcher" Thompson, archivist, and Gene Norris, genealogist, Cherokee National Historical Society; John Reinhardt, supervisor, Operations and Reference Section, Illinois State Archives; Mary Frances Ronan and Mark Mollan at the National Archives in Washington, D.C.; Sandra Zimdars-Swartz, Christopher Forth, Marti Proctor, and Claire Marie Wolnisty at the University of Kansas; Matthew Bokovoy, University of Nebraska Press; Billie Conway, Interlibrary Loan at Watson Library, University of Kansas; Ethan Hartzell, student at Pittsburg State University in Kansas. Great thanks to my family—Joshua, Toshaway, and Ariana—for their endless support and patience. And many thanks to Bonnie Lovell, who carefully and professionally copyedited the manuscript, and to Sarah C. Smith and Steven Baker, who kept the book moving through editing and proofing.

Excerpts from chapters 1 through 8 appear in "Nede Wade 'Ned' Christie and the Outlaw Mystique," *Chronicles of Oklahoma* 93, no. 3 (Fall 2015): 260–89.

FAMILY TREES

Throughout these family trees, dates following commas after a spouse name are marriage dates; years and year spans in parentheses are birth and death dates. Solid lines denote descendants, and dashed lines denote marriages.

These family trees are constructed using Hamilton, *Ned Christie*; personal communication with Hamilton; 1880 Cherokee Census and Index, Schedules 1–6, 7RA-07, rolls 1–4; 1890 Cherokee Census (no index), schedules 1–4, 7RA-08, rolls 1–4; Index to the Five Civilized Tribes, Final Dawes Roll, M1186, roll 1; and Enrollment Cards, Five Civilized Tribes, 1898–1914, M1186, rolls 2–15, cards 1–11132, at the National Archives, Fort Worth.

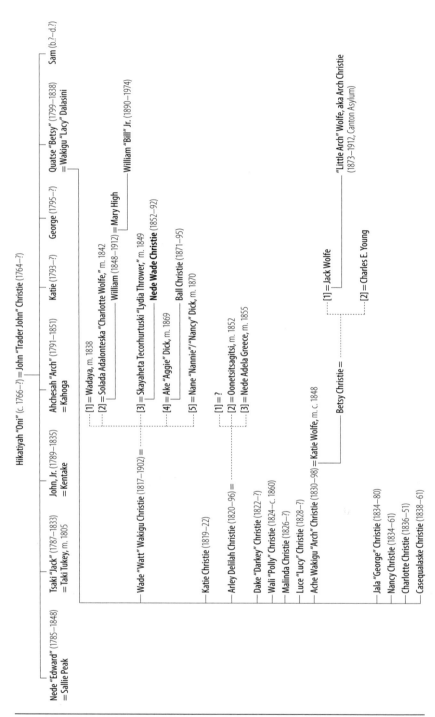

Descendants of Oni and John Christie

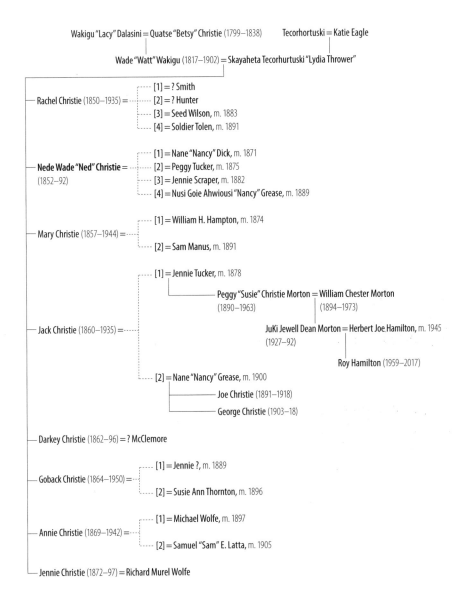

Wakigu "Lacy" Dalasini = Quatse "Betsy" Christie (1799–1838)   Tecorhortuski = Katie Eagle

Wade "Watt" Wakigu (1817–1902) = Skayaheta Tecorhurtuski "Lydia Thrower"

Rachel Christie (1850–1935) =
- [1] = ? Smith
- [2] = ? Hunter
- [3] = Seed Wilson, m. 1883
- [4] = Soldier Tolen, m. 1891

Nede Wade "Ned" Christie = (1852–92)
- [1] = Nane "Nancy" Dick, m. 1871
- [2] = Peggy Tucker, m. 1875
- [3] = Jennie Scraper, m. 1882
- [4] = Nusi Goie Ahwiousi "Nancy" Grease, m. 1889

Mary Christie (1857–1944) =
- [1] = William H. Hampton, m. 1874
- [2] = Sam Manus, m. 1891

Jack Christie (1860–1935) =
- [1] = Jennie Tucker, m. 1878

Peggy "Susie" Christie Morton = William Chester Morton
(1890–1963)   (1894–1973)

JuKi Jewell Dean Morton = Herbert Joe Hamilton, m. 1945
(1927–92)

Roy Hamilton (1959–2017)

- [2] = Nane "Nancy" Grease, m. 1900
  - Joe Christie (1891–1918)
  - George Christie (1903–18)

Darkey Christie (1862–96) = ? McClemore

Goback Christie (1864–1950) =
- [1] = Jennie ?, m. 1889
- [2] = Susie Ann Thornton, m. 1896

Annie Christie (1869–1942) =
- [1] = Michael Wolfe, m. 1897
- [2] = Samuel "Sam" E. Latta, m. 1905

Jennie Christie (1872–97) = Richard Murel Wolfe

Descendants of Wade "Watt" Wakigu and Skayaleta Tecorhurtuski "Lydia Thrower." Note that Ned Christie's descendants are not listed here but separately in the following family tree.

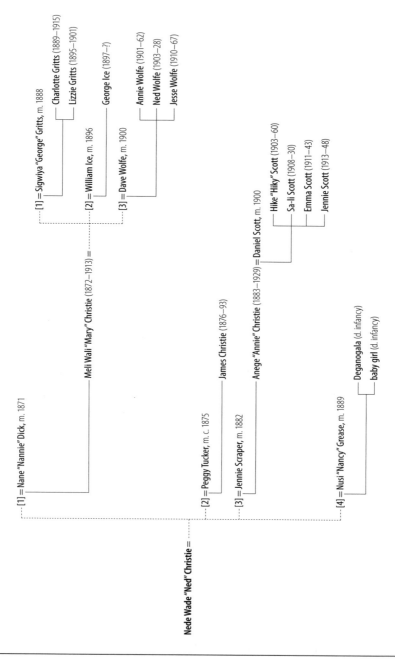

Descendants of Nede Wade "Ned" Christie

Nede Wade "Ned" Christie =

[1] = Nane "Nannie" Dick, m. 1871

Meli Wali "Mary" Christie (1872–1913) =

[1] = Sigwiya "George" Gritts, m. 1888

Charlotte Gritts (1889–1915)

Lizzie Gritts (1895–1901)

[2] = William Ice, m. 1896

George Ice (1897–?)

[3] = Dave Wolfe, m. 1900

Annie Wolfe (1901–62)

Ned Wolfe (1903–28)

Jesse Wolfe (1910–67)

[2] = Peggy Tucker, m. c. 1875

James Christie (1876–93)

[3] = Jennie Scraper, m. 1882

Anege "Annie" Christie (1883–1929) = Daniel Scott, m. 1900

Hike "Hiky" Scott (1903–60)

Sa-li Scott (1908–30)

Emma Scott (1911–43)

Jennie Scott (1913–48)

[4] = Nusi "Nancy" Grease, m. 1889

Deganogala (d. infancy)

baby girl (d. infancy)

NED CHRISTIE

INTRODUCTION

HOW WE KNOW ABOUT NED CHRISTIE

Until prosperity brought higher ideals of amusing diversion, the
public appetite for pleasure fed on the escapades of the desperado. . . .
They prefer tales of outlawry and border ruffianism to stories
of successful agriculture, and are inclined to shut their ears
to all stories save those that thrill the imagination.
ATLANTIC MONTHLY, 1900

Most Oklahoma Cherokees and Wild West literature aficionados know about Nede Wade "Ned" Christie, the Cherokee Keetoowah, national councilman, and advisor to Chief Dennis Bushyhead.[1] In May 1887, Deputy U.S. Marshal Daniel Maples traveled from his Bentonville, Arkansas, home to Tahlequah, Cherokee Nation, in northeastern Indian Territory to investigate the burgeoning whiskey problem. Christie also happened to be in town to attend the early-May session of the Cherokee National Council. During the evening of May 4, the day Maples arrived, Christie and his uncle Nede Grease had been seen in the vicinity of Maples's camp next to what is known today as Seminary Spring. Bystanders also noticed other men around the camp: Bub Trainor, John Parris, Charley Bobtail, John Hogshooter, and Looney Coon. After sunset, someone shot Maples. He died the next day.

Some of the men witnesses swore they observed in the area were indicted by the U.S. Court of the Western District of Arkansas at Fort Smith, and those men declared their innocence to Judge Isaac Parker. No witness saw who killed Maples, although they testified that the suspects told them who did the shooting. Bub Trainor and Charley Bobtail both swore that John Parris pulled the trigger. Despite those accusations, and even though Trainor and Parris had multiple charges and convictions in their history, they, along with Bobtail, were released.

Christie feared Judge Isaac Parker and refused to travel to Fort Smith to defend himself. This momentous decision began a chain of events that led directly to his death.

Christie spent the last five years of his life evading capture by posses sent from Fort Smith, and details of those years are still being told with embellishments, fictional scenarios, and omissions of facts. Murders and robberies committed by others in the territory were attributed to Christie, and his reputation as an outlaw spread across the country. Judge Isaac Parker authorized a reward for him, and Christie remained alert to anyone who might try to accost him at his home in Wauhillau. Posses did confront Ned several times at his home, most notably in 1889, when they burned his house and injured his left eye. Three years later, deputy U.S. marshals used dynamite to drive Christie from his newly built cabin and they shot him when he emerged from the fiery building. The posse roped Ned's body to a wooden door and took him to Fort Smith, where he lay on the door for three days, available to photographers and gawkers. His family then brought him home to Wauhillau for burial.

Editors want fantastic storylines to market their publications, and for over a century the Christie saga has offered prime opportunities for libelous aggrandizement. Armed with their imaginations, late-nineteenth-century newspapermen began crafting the image of Christie as a drinker and unrepentant killer who sold whiskey, robbed stores, and killed U.S. marshals and innocent bystanders. Exciting stories created by newspapermen about the murder of a white lawman amid the backdrop of an already violent land increased readers' fascination.

A few papers published derogatory pieces about Christie in December 1887, seven months after the death of Maples and after the court at Fort Smith heard the testimonies of the men who were seen in the vicinity of Maples's camp the night of the killing. A few more writers created tales in February 1888, after Christie was accused (and exonerated) of killing Bear Grimmett; then hundreds more stories followed. The majority of stories about Christie appeared after his death in 1892, when newspapers tried to associate his name with prominent criminals and lawmen in order to satisfy readers' desires for exciting tales from Indian Territory and Oklahoma. Local residents loved to talk about Christie and to impart fantastical scenarios in which they knew him, were wounded by him, or shot him. Newspapers included interviews with lawmen who told tales about Christie ranging from partial truths to outright fabrications. Later interviewees who newsmen assumed to be informed voices about Christie took their cues from previous stories, pretty much repeating them, and all follow the basic formula of good triumphing over evil. Modern article, book, and website writers sometimes copy verbatim from those old newspapers and present those yarns as truth.

During the decades of the most unfavorable descriptions of Christie—especially 1890 through the 1960s—Indians were not in positions of power to create their own images in the media, books, and entertainment industry. All of the libelous stories told about Christie were, and still are, told without fear of reprisal and without regard for the feelings of Christie's family and, certainly without considering that he might be innocent.

Fervent imaginations combined with lack of fact-checking among writers and news editors past and present has resulted in the popular image of Ned Christie as "one of the worse cases in the whole Territory,"[2] a "bad Indian . . . who is perhaps as desperate a man—white, red or black—as was ever produced in any country,"[3] "the most distinguished outlaw within the Territory,"[4] his family and friends are "a gang of desperadoes,"[5] "He developed into one of the worse cases in the whole Territory,"[6] "the most sought-after man that ever lived in the Territory," "notorious outlaw and terror of the Indian Territory," "notorious outlaw and desperado," "reckless," "surly," "possessed a deadly hatred for Deputy Marshals,"[7] "notorious bandit,"[8] "in his day murdered more men than the celebrated Tom Starr,"[9] "horse thief," "one of the most desperate outlaws in the nation," "last of the old school of outlaws,"[10] "the most notorious outlaw that ever roamed the wilds of the Cherokee Nation,"[11] "common thief and a whiskey seller,"[12] and "one of the Territory's most savage outlaws."[13] The most overwrought description comes from the March 18, 1906, *Daily Oklahoman*, asserting that Christie was "a man who had fought a greater number of battles with the officers of the government than any other outlaw known to civilization."[14]

Alongside these depictions of Christie was the ever-changing list of people he supposedly killed and injured: "two deputy marshals, three Cherokee Indians and has wounded three other deputies and over a dozen law abiding citizens,"[15] "one deputy marshal, three other men and wounded a score of others."[16] A variation on this last one is "one deputy marshal, three Cherokee Indians, wounded three deputies and over a dozen law-abiding citizens,"[17] "two or three Cherokees, wounded numerous others," and during the last two years of his life robbed "no less than four stores,"[18] "eight Cherokees, one deputy marshal and wounded three others,"[19] "six deputy marshals, four express messengers, and ten other men,"[20] "fourteen men, women and children during a robbery in Arkansas."[21] Erin H. Turner's *Rotgut Rustlers* and Robert Barr Smith's "The Two Faces of Ned Christie: Hero or Villain" both include this uncited passage (Smith copied directly from Turner): "Eleven murders were credited to Christie. Among his victims were two officers, an Indian woman, and a half-breed boy. He was born a killer, cold blooded, ruthless; no one knew when or where he would strike next. Along the isolated paths to the lonely cabins of settlers he stalked relentless in his maniacal hatred."[22]

Ramon Adams makes a pertinent truism about this kind of mythical Wild West literature: "Just as burrs under the saddle irritate a horse, so the constant writing of inaccurate history irritates the historian. And nowhere has research been so inadequate or writing so careless as in accounts of Western outlaws and gunmen. Indeed, many chroniclers seem to delight in repeating early sensational and frequently untrue stories without any real attempt to investigate the facts."[23]

What Adams also says about the myriad works about Billy the Kid is also true about Ned Christie: "Writers follow one another blindly without any effort to verify what their predecessors wrote."[24] It is indeed easier to copy what others have published than it is to check references. However, many writers like what has been written about Christie. They have no desire to engage in research because further investigation might require alteration of those accepted "facts."

Robert G. Athearn wrote that "The myth is an essential part of the Western past."[25] Western narratives usually include common components for compelling storytelling, each aspect exaggerated and crafted to form rousing, larger-than-life tales: the passing of the frontier, honor, justice, vengeance, violence, and manliness.[26] The Christie saga includes all those elements and more: Indians, horses, a murdered deputy U.S. marshal, liquor, women (present to bolster the masculine narrative), political arguing, inter- and intratribal factionalism, forbidding wilderness, cannons, dynamite, beheadings, tarring and featherings, racism, and discrepancies over criminal jurisdiction in a multicultural land belonging to tribes rapidly overrun with white intruders. Hundreds of vicious crimes were committed in the territory each year. After the Civil War, especially, murder, larceny, rapes, whiskey peddling, and stock rustling were commonplace. Many troublemakers who settled there illegally wanted tribal resources and were often sly and dishonest in how they got them. Christie lived in the violent world of postwar Indian Territory and it was not difficult to imagine him behaving like the criminals who also inhabited the region.

If we are to believe the Wild West stories, Christie was more formidable than the average lawbreaker, his family matched his violent nature, his home stood as an almost impregnable fortress, and lawmen were forced to traverse a dangerous and forbidding landscape to get him. There was, and still is, an underlying motive for this portrayal, and the goal was never to find the truth. Many Wild

West writers and their fans need Christie to remain guilty so that the righteous and white masculine entities—lawmen—can be celebrated as heroic vanquishers of the evildoer. Christie's image as a hulking, dangerous desperado continues to appear in stories that focus on the men who were incapable of making errors in judgment and who never failed to dispatch the bad guy.

Those who have access to Christie familial remembrances can provide clarifications of events, sociopolitical aspects of his Cherokee family, and insight into what might have crossed Christie's mind. As Roy Hamilton tells us, Christie "was like us all, full of dreams, hopes and fears.[27] Most people, however, get their information about Christie from writings authored by those who molded him into the image of what they want him to be. For sure, family stories can be embellished. But what overshadows any oral or written testimonies by Christie's descendants are the tales in the media.

Comparison of hundreds of newspapers, articles, books, and interviews with provable timelines and Christie family stories reveals that the wellspring of information about Christie emanates from three main sources. The first is newspapers. Mid- to late-nineteenth-century newspaper editors were eager to garner readers and they realized that one way to get paying customers was to diversify the content, including social, religious, and sports stories. International news, opinion pieces, and stock market reports began to appear in many papers, as did eye-catching stories from around the United States.[28] Publishers knew that readers wanted news, but they also were aware that in order to sell copies headlines had to grab readers' attention. In theory, it was the job of newspapermen to publish truthful stories. Like today, some writers attempted to publish facts, while others either voiced the biases of their editors or aimed to be as sensationalistic as possible to sell copies.

In the late nineteenth century, newspaper editors were well aware of how captivated the public was by stories of the exploits of men and women who defied society's mores, how they managed to elude lawmen in creative ways, but ultimately lost to the forces of good and met their deaths by bullet or rope. Belle Starr, Jesse James, and Blue Duck are among the most well-known criminals, and there were hundreds of crimes committed each year by other individuals who provided fodder for larger-than-life stories.[29]

Will Wright, in his book *Sixguns and Society*, states that film "is the medium that the Western has taken on its uniquely mythical dimensions."[30] Movies give us facial expressions, noise, movement, and color. Obviously, late-nineteenth and early-twentieth-century news stories about Christie give readers none of that. Many of those stories are merely snippets of information with readers left to imagine sights and sounds. Movies, newspapers, and Wild West literature have a few things in common, however, one being that all are commercial products, shrewdly crafted to give audiences what they want. Even films claiming to be "based on actual events" often altered the stories to make them more exciting and adventurous. After all, most media and entertainment entities were, and still are, in business to make money.

Reporters often were paid low wages, yet they often received bonuses for marketable stories.[31] Therefore, in order to make deadlines and please their bosses they worked long hours and sometimes gussied up old story lines, which is why some stories about Christie have been rehashed time and again, saying basically the same things only varying the adjectives and the numbers of people Christie supposedly killed. Facts were eschewed in favor of stories that were "dressed up and high spiced" with "all sorts of imaginary conversations and episodes."[32] Often papers published stories that had originally been printed in other papers just a few days before with editors adding their own spin. For example, on November 5, 1892, the *Lawrence Daily Journal* in Kansas reiterated the same information as did dozens of other papers around the country about the two sieges on Christie's home and his death, yet this paper created a particularly attention-grabbing headline that forces one to focus on it like an optometrist's eye chart (see figure, opposite page).

Readers bought newspapers in Indian Territory, New York, North Dakota, and other states where newspaper editors followed Christie's stories as they were wired to them. Like today, readers far from the scene of action relied on the news to tell them accurately about current events. A disconnection remained, however, between reality and what readers were told. Biased, exaggerated, and patriotic stories about Indian-white encounters were often written by white males with miniscule knowledge about Indians.[33] Writings about outlaws and lawmen appealed to those readers looking for escapist tales but who knew little about Indian Territory and the western part of the United States. Most nineteenth-century Americans could not differentiate between tribes and did not know much about Indians in general except that they were perhaps uncivilized marauders. "Indian Territory" conjured images of tipis and feathers. Most readers outside of the territory (and some within its bounds) would not know about the diversity of cultures within the region, much less about the factionalism within the Cherokee Nation or about the complexity of Ned Christie.

The first of the Wild West authors to take advantage of sensational stories in

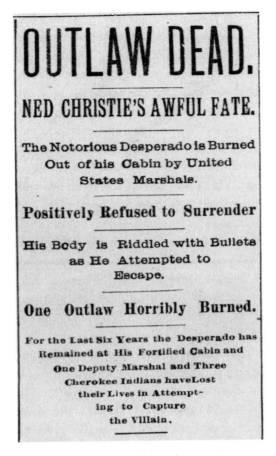

OUTLAW DEAD.

NED CHRISTIE'S AWFUL FATE.

The Notorious Desperado is Burned Out of his Cabin by United States Marshals.

Positively Refused to Surrender

His Body is Riddled with Bullets as He Attempted to Escape.

One Outlaw Horribly Burned.

For the Last Six Years the Desperado has Remained at His Fortified Cabin and One Deputy Marshal and Three Cherokee Indians haveLost their Lives in Attempting to Capture the Villain.

Lawrence Daily Journal, November 5, 1892, p. 1.

nineteenth-century newspapers is S. W. Harmon. His still-popular book, *Hell on the Border* (1898), is replete with Harmon's use of newspaper stories that he copied verbatim about lawmen and outlaws (guilty and innocent), including Christie, who had connections with Judge Parker at Fort Smith. Harmon may have copied from newspapers, but he also edited those stories to achieve the context he needed to provide thrilling adventures.[34]

After 1918, Christie had two public images: guilty outlaw and innocent martyr. In 1917, a story emerged in the *Tulsa World* that attempted to exonerate Christie. That was followed by a letter to the editor pointing out mistakes in the story; then a year later the *Daily Oklahoman* basically copied the contents of the letter and published a fanciful piece brimming with unsubstantiated evidence.

The premise for these claims is that a man named Humphreys came forward twenty-five years later to say that he watched another man shoot Dan Maples. As discussed in chapter 8, it is easy to discredit both stories and the letter; nevertheless, many writers today cling to the *Daily Oklahoman* story as the basis for Christie as an innocent man and they construct their books and articles around that information. Regardless of the stories' validity, many Wild West writers proceed with their principle of Christie as guilty outlaw and do not even mention the *Tulsa World* and *Daily Oklahoman* publications.

In the 1930s, hundreds of residents of Oklahoma were interviewed by Works Progress Administration (WPA) workers and those interviews appear in the *Indian-Pioneer Papers* oral history collection. Some of the interviewees had no association with Christie and were over eighty years old at the time that they imparted their dubious tales to untrained interviewers. Testimonies also were recorded in the 1960s as the Doris Duke oral histories. Many of the statements of older residents of Oklahoma are best described by Ramon F. Adams: "Perhaps the most charitable view is that most of them are elderly, their minds are hazy, and their memory of what they did and what they heard as rumor or conjecture is so mixed that they really do not know when they depart from the truth. Characteristically, they are careless with facts; they spell the names and places by ear; and dates have little significance for them."[35]

It is understandable that one might want to agree with these testimonies, to want them to be true. My great-great-grandfather Charles Wilson served the Choctaw Nation in many capacities, including lighthorseman, Sugar Loaf County (Moshulatubbee District) sheriff and treasurer, and later as a deputy U.S. marshal. His father was a headman of the Okla Hannali District in the southeast prior to the tribe's forced removed to Indian Territory and he signed the 1830 removal treaty. Wilson too is the subject of fanciful stories, such as the time my heroic forebear caught twenty-two men led by Dixon Booth, all of whom were eventually found guilty and eleven were executed.[36] Even more stirring is the legend that Wilson killed a gang of cattle rustlers singlehandedly by making them "all kneel down and [he] shot them one at a time."[37] These highly unlikely yet stimulating vignettes illustrate the type of folklore that opportunistic writers will use as absolute truth.

Dates, places and names associated with Christie do not mesh with other documentation and testimonies are confused, obviously exaggerated, or completely made up. A few people testified in the 1930s that they knew Ned and they did in fact live near him. Their statements have been used in previous works about

Christie, but because they have proven inaccurate, Christie family members have urged caution in using them. Other "Indians and Pioneers" alter information taken directly from the *Daily Oklahoman* story to suit their preferred beliefs and later writers then cite those embellished interviews, as opposed to citing the earlier newspaper source.

Despite their mythical nature, stories that emanate from the 1930s have influenced later writers. For example, a full-blood Cherokee named Eli Wilson grew up in the Wauhillau area and was nine years old in 1887 when the thirty-six-year-old Ned Christie had been accused of killing Maples. Fifty years later, in 1937, Wilson recalled that Christie told him that he killed Maples. Wilson also said that he and his brothers regularly gathered empty shell casings after Ned had shoot-outs with posse men, then a jovial Christie engaged the kids in neighborly banter, as if lethal gunfire occurred on a daily basis on Christie's property. In addition, Wilson testified that Christie bought a new Winchester .44 from him believing that "he would be able to live a little longer with his family by being able to kill a few more of those marshals."[38] The problem with utilizing testimonies such as Wilson's should be obvious: first, it is difficult to believe that that Ned bought a rifle from a preteen. More far-fetched is the claim that Christie told a nine-year-old that he had committed murder. Despite these invented happenings from Eli Wilson's youth, some writers, notably Bonnie Speer, use some of Wilson's statements as cornerstones of their theories about Christie.[39]

The *Chronicles of Oklahoma* are important sources of information, but, like the *Indian-Pioneer Papers*, one needs to carefully consider statements made by the authors. In 1929, the *Chronicles* published "Bits of Interesting History," by W. C. Riggs, a white man who came from Alabama with his parents in 1878. Riggs claimed that in 1883 a group of men dubbed "The Christie Gang" plotted to rob the Missouri-Kansas-Texas (MKT) passenger train while it watered at the Reynolds tank, five miles north of Limestone Gap on the property of Captain Charles LeFlore, who happened to be a Choctaw lighthorseman. According to Riggs, LeFlore and twenty-five men foiled the robbers by hiding and waiting for the Christie Gang to appear, then opened fire. Two of LeFlore's group were shot, and several of Christie's group were killed and wounded, then taken by train to "federal authorities" to be charged with mail robbery and other crimes.[40] For sure, this is an interesting piece and it has been copied numerous times, but there are no newspaper reports of this incident, nothing in court documents, nor does it appear within the *Indian-Pioneer Papers*. Riggs, who was only five years old at the time of the alleged train incident, does not tell us what happened to the "Christie" in this action-packed account and neither does anyone else who rehashes this one uncorroborated source. Further, shortly after this alleged train incident Ned Christie joined the Cherokee National Council and Chief Bushyhead would not have approved the appointment of a scoundrel.

From the time of Christie's death in 1892 to the 1950s, Christie was not always the focal point of Wild West stories that prominently featured his name. To be sure, lawmen faced some awful criminals who killed, raped, and stole. Marshals and their deputies had to be brave, competent, and they needed some understanding of human nature. But lawman were not the supermen some claimed them to be. Newspapers featured interviews with elderly lawmen who were associated with criminal activity in Indian Territory. Aided by crafty editors, retired lawmen spun eyebrow-raising tall tales of personal heroism and used as a prop the fanciful image of a fiercely murderous Christie with whom they all vigorously tangled. Alongside those imagination inflations, letters to the editors from Indian Territory and Oklahoma residents claimed knowledge about Christie and they ranged from sympathetic (though not always accurate) to hostile and wholly outlandish.

Wild West literature created in the 1950s, such as found in *True West, Real West*, and other sensationalist publications, took from all the previous stories and added outrageous details. The wild fantasies can be a kick to read, but as viable sources of data—besides illustrating the marketability of outlaw stories—they are often useless. Writers did not bother to look beyond the papers, ignored the Cherokee and Fort Smith court transcripts, and constructed tales about Christie according to the magazines' standards. If the realities of Christie's situation were not to their liking, writers simply created scenarios. Former president of the Western History Association Robert G. Athearn recalled his stint in what he calls "the never-never land of western fiction." A New York editor wanted, and got, "the blood and guts that he imagined to be the authentic (or marketable) thing when recounting western history to the masses. An obedient colonial took the proffered money and bowed to the East."[41] It is curious, however, that many other editors who published codswallop about Christie lived and worked in the same vicinity as their subject. Despite having access to more information than writers who lived outside of Indian Territory and Oklahoma, they persisted in composing untruths. Frank Richard Prassel's quote about outlaws—"He comes to us through mists of facts and fiction"—is indeed true. The irony is that Prassel writes only one sentence about Christie and it is from a faulty source.[42]

Glenn Shirley's aforementioned *Law West of Fort Smith* appeared in 1957. Known for his fictionalized western writings based on real people, Shirley had a penchant for taking newspapers at their word without cross-checking facts. Although he includes references and a bibliography, he does not cite his passages about Christie, including this gripping, yet erroneous vignette: "The most dangerous outlaw the marshals had to go after was Ned Christie. A full-blooded Cherokee, Christie had served as one of the tribe's executive councilors, but soon found the life of bandit, horse thief, whisky peddler, and killer more exciting. He fought a greater number of battles with government officers than any other outlaw in the history of Judge Parker's court."

Clearly unaware of the Wauhillau geography, Shirley also writes that "Christie's fort stood high against a steep wall, commanding every approach up the canyon." He presents events out of order, stating that Christie inexplicitly turned bad and "ambushed one of Parker's deputies, likable Dan Maples," and subsequently encountered marshals who pursued him for his various crimes. Considering the number of accounts of Christie's ordeal that appeared from 1892 to 1957, it is rather astonishing that Shirley fumbled the sequence of happenings. Unless, of course, he did it on purpose in order to make Christie appear more of a career criminal.[43] Shirley does not mention the other men who were initially accused of killing Maples—John Parris, Charles Bobtail, Bub Trainor, and John Hogshooter; instead, he focuses entirely on Christie, as if he were the only one involved.

Building on all this previous libel, Phillip Rand composed his over-the-top 1958 *Wild West* story, "Blood in the Cookson Hills," referring to Christie as a "terror," "cutthroat," and "psychotic killer." According to Rand, Christie "only comes when there is somebody to kill." When citizens of Tahlequah protested after Christie "took over Tahlequah," they were "shot down in cold blood."[44] Rand depicts Christie's family and friends as "a band of cutthroats" and "psychotic killers" who would "ambush farmers, riddle their bodies with bullets, and drive away in their wagons. They struck at one town after another, more interested in spilling blood than robbing." No doubt Rand felt comfortable adding his own vilifying descriptors because others had already manufactured Christie's image as a brigand.

In 1963, Joe Pride outdid Rand's claims in his story, "The Battle of Tahlequah Canyon," in which he states that the final attempt to take Christie "outdid the O.K. Corral Battle in the way of savagery and destruction." According to Pride, Christie stayed in "the hills" except for sorties against Wells Fargo, banks, railroads, and horse herds." Ned's father, Watt, continually tried to no avail to convince his "rebellious son" to give himself up. In this piece, Christie is portrayed as more animal than human and "never used the same tactics twice, never struck the same town, bank, Wells Fargo stage, or railroad more than once." And he never returned to his hideout from the same direction by which he left. The tale continues, with Pride describing Christie's "gang" as having to meet the criteria of "being young, possess two fast horses, a good rifle, a six-gun, an over-supply of recklessness and the ability to carry out orders under fire." Pride's concocted story continues in the same vein when describing the numerous attempts to capture Christie by deputy U.S. marshals, of whom the indefatigable John Wayne, then at the height of his popularity, was the very embodiment.[45]

Two years later, the University of Oklahoma Press published Arrel Gibson's *Oklahoma: A History of Five Centuries*. Gibson chose Christie to illustrate the "famous bad men" in the Indian Nations: "Most notorious was the 'Cherokee Bandit,' Ned Christie. His career in crime began in 1885 when he shot a federal deputy marshal at Tahlequah. Shortly thereafter he collected a group of followers, and the Christie gang became a terror on the border. Christie's escapades became legendary among the Cherokees. So great was his daring that deputy marshals dreaded receiving an assignment to search for him."[46]

This account is interesting because in no other place do we see Christie called "Cherokee Bandit." Gibson does not tell readers what "border" Christie allegedly terrorized, he has the date of Maples's death incorrect, and there are no Cherokee legends about Christie's "escapades" as described by Gibson.

In 1967, Doubleday published freelance writer C. H. McKennon's *Iron Men*, aptly subtitled *A Saga of the Deputy United States Marshals Who Rode the Indian Territory*. In his account, McKennon used the same sources everyone else had up to that point, and inserted his own inventive conversations between Christie and his wife, between Christie and lawmen, in addition to interjecting Christie's thoughts into various scenarios as they unfolded. McKennon hoisted Christie to six foot four inches tall and this physical characteristic is repeated in countless publications. He lifted passages directly from newspapers, and his unsupported statements about Christie's height, criminal antics, and unpleasant personality, as well as the farfetched adventures of the resolute lawmen who killed him, are the original sources used by later writers.

In 1978 Wayne T. Walker authored another version of Christie in *Real West*, "Ned Christie: Terror of the Cookson Hills." The story begins with discussion about the alcohol problem in the Cherokee Nation—true enough—but as one can guess from the title, quickly digresses into the same thrilling fictionalizations common to this genre. In Walker's version, Nancy Shell (a bona fide whiskey runner) was known to many law enforcement officers. Maples confronted drunken men who emerged from Shell's house, then he was shot by one of them. Walker claims that Sam Maples, son of the murdered Dan Maples, killed Christie even though Sam was not present during the final siege on Christie's home in 1892. Christie did not "roam" the Cookson Hills. Rather, his activities took place around the foothills of the Ozarks. Nor did he live in Rabbit Trap, as many other publications also claim.[47]

It was inevitable that the image of Christie would appear in a movie. While still at school, I recall my father talking enthusiastically about a movie planned on the life of Ned, starring Creek actor Will Sampson and western movie staple Ben Johnson. This movie was to be produced by Ralph Powell and staffed by members of the Tulsa-based American Indian Talent Guild. The movie was to start filming in 1980, but was never made.[48] The song "His Eye Is on the Sparrow" by Houston singer Mickey Newbury was to be the theme music.[49] A movie with Christie did emerge, however. The 1980 made-for-television movie *Belle Starr* included Elizabeth Montgomery as Belle and Fred Ward as Christie. In this imagining, Christie is a close friend of a veritable array of outlaws: Belle, the James and Dalton brothers, Blue Duck, and Cole Younger. The inclusion of Christie in this story does not make sense considering that by the time Christie was accused of killing Maples in 1887, Belle's outlaw career had all but stopped and the bulk of the story takes place in Eufaula, 120 miles from Christie's residence in Wauhillau. Eight years later, Christie was featured on the television show *America's Most Wanted*.[50]

One of the best-known western novels, *True Grit* (1968) by Charles Portis, takes place amid the violence of the nineteenth-century Choctaw Nation. Some claim that the villain in the movie, Lucky Ned Pepper, was patterned after Christie, but Portis has not said that. W. David Baird, in *The Story of Oklahoma*, writes, "People call him Lucky Ned because he always managed to evade Judge Parker's marshals and deputies," but that nickname rarely appears in written documentation.[51] Neither Robert Duvall nor Barry Pepper, the two actors who portrayed Ned Pepper in the two movie versions, remotely resemble Christie.

Others did the best they could with what they found. In 1974, Daniel F. Littlefield, Jr., and Lonnie E. Underhill published "Ned Christie and His One-Man Fight with the United States Marshals" in the *Journal of Ethnic Studies*. The short article is an outline of Christie's saga that includes the basic source material, much of it dubious. Still, the piece is notable because the authors do not embellish their essay in order to bolster any bias they may have had, nor do they manipulate data like future writers would.[52]

A goal of this project is to uncover the fabrications, the purposeful changing of informants' quotes, data misuse, and changing of events and names in order to make Christie appear either guilty or innocent. One can see this kind of deliberately deceptive writing in newspapers, articles, and books, but two modern works stand out in particular because the writers had ample opportunity to present their works honestly and with integrity and did not. The first is Philip Steele's *The Last Cherokee Warriors* (Pelican, 1987) and the other is Bonnie Speer's *The Killing of Ned Christie: Cherokee Outlaw* (Reliance Press, 1990). These two books are important because they are the tomes that most readers interested in Christie read, but even more so because of the magnitude of their errors and fabrications.

In *The Last Cherokee Warriors*, Steele devotes half his book to Christie and the other half to another Cherokee Keetoowah, Zeke Proctor, a man who writers also like to portray as an outlaw. Steele includes a bibliography, but does not cite his text and makes unsubstantiated assertions about both men based on earlier, unconfirmed stories, many taken directly from McKennon. Steele also states that much of the information for the Christie portion of his book comes from one Cecil Atchison who obtained his knowledge from Deputy Hugh Harp (d. 1958), a man with no connection to Christie that can be ascertained other than that he placed his rifle in the deceased Christie's hands for the requisite Dead Outlaw photograph.

Steele also says that "a major portion of the information" for his book came from Bill Christie, Jr., the son of William Christie, a half-brother to Ned, and the son of Watt Christie and Charlotte Wolfe. Bill Jr. did not speak English and lived in a nursing home at the time that a translator served as a go-between for Steele in 1970. While it is always desirable to talk to family members of the subject, in this situation we see more than simply a case of "lost in translation." Steele states that Bill Christie, Jr., "vividly recalls his uncle" and that "he was in or around Ned's home when marshals would attack, and he remembers having to run and dodge to stay out of the line of fire." Steele then states that Bill Jr. was "the only living person who actually lived in Ned's home during his trouble with the law" and that he has "been invaluable in an effort to separate fact from fiction."[53] These claims reflect the sort of writing one can expect from Steele because Bill Jr. was only two years old when Ned Christie was killed in 1892.[54]

In addition, Steele states that Bill Jr. told him (supposedly through a translator) that Watt Christie had multiple wives and that Ned slept with a different woman every night. Christie is also described as "uncommonly handsome" and so is his father, Watt. Steele informs us that numerous women flocked to both of them because of their looks and no doubt their sexual prowess.[55] According to family,

Bill Jr. would never have made such statements. In addition, Steele connects his assertion about Ned's height (six foot four) to Bill Jr., when actually McKennon is the first one to state that Christie stood that tall.[56] Here we see a strategy at work: include many "facts" in one paragraph, then attribute everything in that paragraph to one source.[57] In this case, Steele cleverly attributes the source of confirmation of Christie's impressive height to a Christie family member when his size actually was concocted by a freelance writer.

On the heels of Steele's book came Bonnie Speer's *The Killing of Ned Christie: Cherokee Outlaw.* Speer, the late adjunct professor of journalism at the University of Oklahoma, authored *The Art of Self-Publishing* (Reliance, 1997) and *Miss Little Britches: Story of a Girl's Struggle to Accept a Homely Horse and Win a Title in a Junior Rodeo* (Reliance, 1999). Unlike almost every other book about Christie, Speer expended some energy looking in archives. The concern is not with the legitimate information she may have unearthed; rather, the problem is with how she chose to utilize that data.

This book came from the publishing house Reliance Press, which happened to be owned by Speer. That means there was no peer-review process prior to publication, although she did contact Christie's family. They told Speer about mistakes, mainly dealing with familial connections. She took offense, thereafter refused to speak to them, and the errors—plus a myriad more—remain.[58] Investigation into her references reveals that the book contains misquoted, untraceable, fabricated, and incomplete sources, incorrect sequences of events, interviews with unidentified persons, data manipulation, as well as other faulty sources that Speer claims are the "most reliable" and "well founded." Several of her chapters are based entirely on incorrect newspaper stories, and key statements are attributed to documents that do not exist. Speer did exactly what Adams complained about: she writes "inaccurate history that irritates the historian," and she does not even bother to change what are clearly flawed testimonies. Adams wrote, "Although it is rather tragic that later writers follow these old timers without question, our quarrel is not with them, but with current writers who do nothing to correct the mistakes of these old men with their garbled facts."[59] Adams takes to task many writers of inaccurate Wild West stories and says he is not suggesting that they are liars. But there are enough bad stories about Christie to prove that some writers *do* lie.

Many positively review Steele's and Speer's books because they declared Christie innocent of killing Maples. It could be that Christie did not kill Maples, but that is not the point. The ethical problem is that both Steele and Speer forced that conclusion with narrative trickery that diminishes their stories. The irony is that addressing the content of their accounts may not even matter because their writings are agreeable to many who support Christie's innocence.

The late Cherokee writer Robert Conley authored *Ned Christie's War* (St. Martin's, 1990), a faulty yet reasonable fictional account of Christie's last years. Conley mused about Christie and others mentioned in this book—Bill Pigeon, Zeke Proctor, and Charlie Wickliffe—in *The Witch of Goingsnake and Other Stories* (University of Oklahoma, 1988) and *Cherokee Thoughts: Honest and Uncensored* (University of Oklahoma, 2008).

Larry McMurtry and Diana Ossana's *Zeke and Ned* (Simon and Schuster, 1997) is a purely fictional tale of the two men as friends and even as brothers-in-law, and the book is assessed by Ned's family as "terribly wrong on every part of Nede's life." More recently, Robby McMurtry (my husband's cousin) created an intriguing and beautifully illustrated graphic novel, *Native Heart: The Life and Times of Nede Christie, Cherokee Patriot and Renegade* (2009) and Lisa C. LaRue wrote the slight *He Was a Brave Man: The Story of an Indian Patriot* (2010). Both are considerate albeit brief outlines of Ned's life that use information from prior writings.[60] They portray Christie as a defender of tribal sovereignty and a staunch opponent of Oklahoma statehood, tribal land allotment, and railroad construction. They consider that many of his views made him a thorn in the side of Progressive Cherokees and an enemy of the intruders who wanted Cherokee lands and resources who all wanted him silenced.

Most stories about Christie focus only on him, his male relatives, and the lawmen who killed him, as if no one else were involved. Indeed, foundational elements of the Christie saga are the masculine strength and shooting skills of Christie and of the manly marshals who pursued him. Tales about Christie are typically misogynist, the kind of male-oriented writing that Athearn calls "hairy-chested literature."[61] The assumption was that white men and Indian men held power positions within their societies. Women were not so important and therefore often merely serve as plot devices.

The *Cherokee Advocate* newspaper in Tahlequah mentioned women and children in their stories about Christie, whereas other papers either ignored them or threw women into the mix only on occasion. Ned's wife, Nancy, who survived him by twenty-nine years is rarely mentioned by name, nor is she referred to as his wife. Instead, she is an "old squaw," one of his "two wives," or simply a woman in the house.[62] Christie did not survive for those almost five years by himself. Nancy in all probability held their daily life together. Food preparation, mending clothes, hauling water, starting cooking fires, and garden cultivation were all important, but so was emotional support. Until recently there appears to be no attempt on the part of writers to discover if Christie had a mother or wife, much less a daughter, aunts or sisters. Philip Steele portrays Ned and his father, Watt, as Lotharios, but that is hardly a respectable portrayal of those men, or the women they married. Male family members are mentioned in papers because they wielded guns and because of their relation to their alleged wayward relation, Ned Christie. One can say the same about the wives of lawmen. We might learn about them in the men's biographies, but there is almost nothing in the newspapers about what they were doing when their lawmen spouses were away taking care of lawbreakers.

Indeed, this story cannot just be about Nede Wade Christie. With few exceptions, the most notable being Roy Hamilton's *Ned Christie* (2004), the lives of the people who meant the most to Ned and who suffered in the aftermath of his death have been ignored by writers. After the death of Maples, Ned's wife, Nancy, not only had to contend with the constant stress of impending attacks by lawmen, but her cousin George was found dead on Christmas Day in 1887. After Ned's passing in November 1892, the family had to struggle with his loss as well as the fate of Ned's cousin Arch Wolfe and another young man Charles Hair, a family friend who had been burned in the destroyed house. Both were charged with assault with intent to kill by a representative of the posse who proved relentless in their persecution of Christie's associates, even if one was a teenager and the other a preteen.

Still reeling from these events, just eight months after Ned's passing, the family grieved over the murder and mutilation of sixteen-year-old Jim Christie, the son of Ned and his second wife, Peggy Dick. A few years after that, Arch Wolfe, after eighteen months in prison, was sent to the Government Hospital for the Insane in Washington, D.C. Arch's file reveals letters of distress from his worried family, but there are no symptoms of insanity mentioned in his ward notes. Nevertheless, in what appears to be a purely political move, in 1903 he was sent to the notorious Canton Asylum for Insane Indians in South Dakota. After living nine years in misery, he died there in 1912 and is buried alongside 120 other inmates from various tribes in the cemetery of unmarked graves situated between the fourth and fifth holes of the Hiawatha Golf Course. The mistreatment of Arch Wolfe, the emotional suffering his distressed family endured while he lingered at the disreputable Canton Asylum, and his untimely death is a travesty that perhaps surpasses what happened to his cousin Ned. Nancy, as well as Ned's father, brothers, sisters, daughter, and other relatives, survived all of this, but we can only venture to guess at what cost to their emotional well-being.

Among Cherokees not related to him, Christie is not viewed as an outlaw, thief, and killer of lawmen whose life in the western genre spans only five years from the time Maples was shot to when Ned died at the hands of those seeking revenge. To Cherokees, Christie's life and how he died mean more than providing fodder for entertainment or a folklore symbol of immorality generated to bolster reputations of the lawmen who dispatched him.

Christie was thirty-five years old when Maples died in 1887, and to that point Christie led a busy social and political life, but we do not find many reports about those years. At the time of Dan Maples's death, Ned Christie held a place of high esteem in the tribe. Papers and western stories do not address the enormous amount of time Christie spent as a National Council member, nor do writers acknowledge that he had to be literate and informed about the Constitution, laws, and happenings in not only the Cherokee Nation but also in other Indian Territory tribal nations and in the United States. Lengthy written transcripts of National Council meetings reveal that meetings took up much of his time and the seriousness of the agendas required his full attention. He had to be punctual and to understand the formal protocol of the meetings, which included drafting acts and laws. His father, Watt, also served on the tribal council for decades, and his half-brother Jim was a senator from the Flint District. Most members of the Christie family were Keetoowahs, traditional Cherokees who valued and promoted Cherokee culture and sovereignty and stood against allotment and Oklahoma statehood. Christie's views on U.S. policies did not endear him to the Progressive faction of the Cherokee Nation, nor to those intent on taking tribal lands, and that aspect of his life is missing from Wild West stories.

This book also explores the "Humphrey Theory," the claim that Christie did not kill Maples. That viewpoint is important, but we cannot simply declare Christie "not guilty" because we want it to be so and leave it at that. I did not set out to prove Christie's innocence of murdering Deputy Dan Maples. In fact, before starting this project I thought it possible that Christie did shoot Maples. However, after hearing family stories and scrutinizing hundreds of newspaper and magazine articles, government documents, Fort Smith criminal files, Cherokee House, Senate, and Council records, textualized oral testimonies, and after piecing together political maneuverings, it looks fairly obvious that the shooter was another man.

Although it appears to me that someone besides Christie killed Maples, that does not mean Ned lived as a teetotaling pacifist. Christie lived in turbulent times and was capable of violent behavior as were members of his family. In 1871, nineteen-year-old Ned shot a man for bothering a woman at a dance. He shot and killed William Palone in 1884, stood trial for the murder of Bear Grimmett in 1888, and he shot lawmen who confronted him at his home. His half-brother William was associated with Blue Duck in the death of Samuel Wyrick in 1884. Another half-brother brother, Ball, was indicted for whiskey peddling and murder and, another half-brother, Levi, was accused, then acquitted, of killing William Lovett in 1886. Ned's second cousins Jim and French shot each other in 1887 and are buried side by side in the Watt Christie cemetery. Such was life in post–Civil War Indian Territory.

A final chapter analyzes Christie's position within the genre of "outlaw versus lawmen" western literature and how he got there. The opposing images of Christie as the wild, crazed, and guilty outlaw and Christie as the innocent martyr serve various purposes for various people. As we shall see, perspective is everything. Was, and is, Christie considered an outlaw, a hero, or a bit of both? It could be that analyzing the "Christie as Violent Outlaw" myth and debunking it, along with questioning the sometimes curiously amazing exploits of stouthearted lawmen, will not change many minds. As Meyer points out, "Folk and popular conceptions of outlaws, whatever their degree of separation from abstract and sacrosanct 'truth,' do continue to exist, and furthermore, one presumes, to be believed."[63]

Despite the plethora of tales about Christie, I concede that all this data is still not enough information to tell his complete story. Christie remains in large part an enigma because of his silence in written records. Even with a plethora of commentary about Christie, there are some obvious voices missing from the historical record. Either news reporters did not approach Christie, or they tried to talk to him and he rebuffed them, or he did give interviews and those documents have been lost. Christie did not leave behind letters or journals. With few exceptions, his family did not speak to reporters. There is a reason for that. The day after Ned's death, dozens of newspapers from the around the country published stories about the killing of "the notorious outlaw" and these stories recounted in embellished detail his life as a criminal. Interest in Ned and where he lived was at a high point in the 1890s and no doubt the anguished family feared more retaliation for the death of Maples. After the indictment of Arch Wolfe and Charles Hair, and the death of Ned's son Jim Christie in 1893, Jim's grandfather (and Ned's father) Watt, visited a Cherokee doctor (that is, a medicine man) in an attempt to protect the remainder of Ned's family. The ritual performed was designed to keep outsiders from learning anything about them for one hundred years. There are, therefore, no reliable testimonies revealing Christie's perspective besides the stories told to descendants and today Roy Hamilton is the keeper of the few narratives that exist.

Ned Christie lived in a fast-changing, violent, and complicated world. The nineteenth-century Indian Territory population ranged the spectrum of racial, social, economic, and religious backgrounds. Tribes with varying languages, religions, appearances, and values settled in the territory after being forcibly removed from their traditional homelands. Some members of the tribes remained staunchly traditional and attempted to avoid contact with whites and their cultures. Others, especially some members of the "Five Tribes" (Cherokees, Choctaws, Chickasaws, Muscogees [Creeks], and Seminoles) of eastern Indian Territory, were more amenable to acculturation. After removal to Indian Territory in the 1830s, schools were built across the Five Tribes' lands. Few Americans outside of Indian Territory knew about the advanced curriculums of some of the schools and the impressive wealth of some tribal members.[64]

The Cherokee Nation has a vibrant and multifaceted history. During Christie's lifetime (and indeed, even today) the Cherokee Nation was enmeshed in political factionalism and value differences regarding Christianity, education, intermarriage, and freedmen. Disagreements sometimes resulted in murder. In addition, the natural world, with dense forests, rivers, rich soils, underground resources, and an abundance of game animals, attracted thousands of intruders. Cherokees and other Native peoples clashed with settlers, criminals, unscrupulous politicians, and speculators of many ethnic backgrounds intent on taking their resources. Nationalists and Progressives within tribal nations argued about railroads, intruders, citizenship, resource depletion, wealth inequity, allotment, and statehood. All tribes had groups who strongly resisted severalty and all were concerned about loss of tribal control over laws and criminal jurisdiction. Nede Wade Christie played a role in determining how all of these concerns would impact his tribe and the stances he took may have contributed to his death.

The *Chicago Daily Tribune* made a true statement in 1894: "It is a land of many strange contradictions, this Indian Territory."[65] Not only did Nede Wade Christie live and die in the midst of this paradoxical and complex land, one can argue that his images fit that description as well.

CHAPTER 1

FAMILY, FRIENDS, AND HOME

This son will be my greatest joy and greatest sadness.
SKYAHETA "LYDIA" CHRISTIE,
mother of Nede Wade

From an early age, Nede Wade Christie listened to family stories of Cherokee life before removal. He learned about promises made and broken, the desire that non-Indians had for what Cherokees possessed, and just how far they would go to take those resources. He heard about the horrors of the removal trail, about the death of his relatives, and what the future might hold for the Cherokee Nation. Ned also knew just how much his own family lost. Those realities molded his attitudes towards the federal government.

Ned's ancestors were well established in the East. Nede Wade Christie's grandmother Quatse "Betsy" was the daughter of Hiketiyah, a Cherokee, and Dutch trader John Christie. Ned's grandfather Wakigu "Lacy" Dalasini (also known as "Sugar Tree" and "Step-a-long") was the son of Tsatsi Dalasini. They lived at the base of the Smoky Mountains in the forested Tahquohee District of the Cherokee Nation, in the village of Turtletown. Their son, who became Nede Wade's father, Wade "Watt" Wakigu, was born in 1817 and he grew up in the same area.[1]

Nede Wade's great-uncle Edward (Betsy's brother), who also was known as "Nede," and his wife, Sallie Peak Christie, lived on a productive farm on the north side of the Hiwassee River, in modern-day Murphy, North Carolina, less than twenty miles from Turtletown. Great-uncle Edward "Nede" and Sallie were not wealthy, but they lived comfortably in a seventeen-by-seventeen two-story log home with plank floors, a chimney made of sticks and clay, and an attached shed. Also on the property were a smaller log home with a chimney, a smokehouse, two large cornhouses, corncribs, stables and an old hill house. The Christies' most valuable assets were the sixty-five acres of cultivated land with almost two hundred peach, cherry, and large and small apple trees. They also had a son they named Watt (like Ned's father) who was born in 1812 and later farmed at the mouth of the Valley River.[2]

The Cherokee Nation encompassed over 120,000 square miles of northern Alabama, northwestern Georgia, northwestern South Carolina, southwestern North Carolina, western Virginia, and eastern Tennessee and Kentucky.[3] The areas around the Hiwassee River and its tributaries were fertile and abundant with iron ore and gold, which were greatly desired by intrusive white settlers whose hunger for the resource-rich Cherokee lands resulted in methodical reductions of the Cherokee land base. Between 1721 and 1785, the tribe lost more than half their lands. Then in 1785, after the Revolutionary War, the Treaty of Hopewell with the United States guaranteed the protection of the remaining Cherokee lands; however, over the next thirty years, more treaties were signed and the tribe lost two-thirds of the lands that were supposed to be protected.[4]

Lacy and Betsy witnessed the land reduction and no doubt worried they would lose more, if not all of it. By the beginning of the nineteenth century, the stream of white intruders onto Cherokee lands had increased. In response to the persistent whites who wanted tribal lands, the government kept pressure on the Cherokees to move. Understanding that they would inevitably have to move anyway, almost 3,000 of the 15,000 Cherokees moved to Arkansas Territory in 1818. These "Old Settlers" were later forced to sign a treaty in 1828 requiring them to move farther west to northeast Indian Territory.[5]

A declining land base was not the only stressor in the Cherokee Nation. The Christie family also paid close attention to how Americans influenced their traditional system of governance and social organization. Non-Indian men, such as the Dutchman John Christie, entered into the Cherokee territory and often married Cherokee women. By the late eighteenth century, the Cherokees' association with Irish, English, German, and other European traders, artisans, and merchants resulted in a significant population of mixed-bloods who adhered to the value systems of their non-Native fathers. Factionalism resulted between those Cherokees who desired wealth, to become Christians, and to leave the old ways behind, including the matriarchal system (that is, tracing descent and clan membership through one's mother's female line) and seeking advice from tribal doctors (medicine men and women). But some intermarried whites like John Christie (Ned's great-grandfather) respected the Cherokees' social organization and traditional system of governance, and their families continued to adhere to

Lacy Christie, Watt's father and Ned's grandfather. *Roy Hamilton Collection.*

Cherokee mores. The Christies continued to trace their Bird Clan line through the traditional way.[6]

In 1828, gold was discovered on Cherokee land in Dahlonega, an hour north of modern-day Atlanta, resulting in a renewed fervor for tribal land.[7] Georgians were determined to take Cherokee property even though the tribe had created a government and declared itself a sovereign nation. The Georgia legislature abolished the Cherokee government and laws and prepared to take the tribal property and give it to white citizens. In 1830, Congress passed the Removal Act that authorized President Andrew Jackson to negotiate removal treaties with tribes.[8]

Two factions emerged among the Cherokees: those who believed there was no choice but to remove west to Indian Territory and those who vowed to fight leaving. Mixed-blood Guwisguwi, also known as John Ross, led the anti-removal National Party. The educated Ross campaigned tirelessly against removal,

Watt Christie, father of Ned, in Civil War uniform.
Roy Hamilton Collection.

including confronting Congress for compensation for Cherokee grievances in 1824. The tribe elected him chief in 1828 and he remained in that position until his death in 1866.[9] The leader of the Removal Party, Degatada, also known as Stand Watie, served as speaker of the Cherokee National Council and worked as a businessman and lawyer. His brother Gallegina Uwati, also known as Buck Watie, attended the Foreign Mission School in Cornwall, Connecticut, and while there converted to Christianity and married a white woman. He changed his name to Elias Boudinot and continued to argue for Cherokee acculturation.[10] A prominent leader of the pro-removal Treaty Party was the wealthy plantation owner and slaveholder Nunnehidihi, or Ganundalegi, best known as Major Ridge or The Ridge.[11]

Chief John Ross, whom Ned's father, Watt, knew well, sought an injunction with the Supreme Court arguing that Georgia had no constitutional rights to take

Cherokee lands and Georgia laws violated the Cherokee Nation's sovereign rights. In *Cherokee Nation v. Georgia* (1831), the Supreme Court ruled that it lacked the authority to hear claims of Indian nations because they are not foreign nations, but are dependent nations within the United States.[12] The state of Georgia then passed a law requiring citizens who wanted to reside within the bounds of the Cherokee Nation to obtain a license. A missionary named Samuel Worcester, who established the newspaper *Cherokee Phoenix* with Elias Boudinot and who translated the Bible into Cherokee, refused to purchase a license and as a result Georgia tried and convicted him. The Supreme Court heard the case and ruled in *Worcester v. Georgia* (1832) that Georgia's license law was unconstitutional; only the United States had power to negotiate terms of Indian lands. This ruling had virtually no effect. Georgia and President Jackson ignored it and the removal commenced.[13]

Even before these Supreme Court cases, the Cherokee Nation took steps to prevent the further loss of land. In 1829 the National Council revitalized a Cherokee law condemning to death any tribal member who sold lands without permission of the council.[14] Despite the seriousness of that law, Stand Watie, Elias Boudinot, and Major Ridge signed the Treaty of New Echota in 1835 anyway, thus committing the entire tribe to removal. Knowing full well what he had done, Major Ridge told Thomas L. McKenney after signing that "I expect to die for it."[15] And indeed he did, on June 22, 1839, at the hands of those furious at his deception.

It did not matter that only a small portion of the tribe committed the entire Cherokee Nation to move. Thirteen detachments of Cherokees started west between January and March 1839.[16] In the 1930s, numerous Cherokees interviewed for the *Indian-Pioneer Papers* oral history collection recounted what their grandparents told them. Stories range the spectrum of horrors: starvation, disease, hypothermia, injuries, and theft of personal property.[17] Russell Thornton estimates that almost eight thousand Cherokees died as a result of removal. Some died en route to Indian Territory, although the majority of those who perished did so after arrival, from malnutrition, sickness, disease, and hypothermia. Choctaws, Chickasaws, Muskogees, and Seminoles underwent similar removals, resulting in thousands more deaths.[18]

The Christie family managed to survive, except for Ned's great-grandmother Betsy who perished from cold and hunger on the trail.[19] The Christies arrived in Indian Territory in 1839 during the winter and like other traditionalist families, they settled away from well-traveled roads. Watt and his first wife, Wadaya, established their home in Wauhillau, twelve miles east of Tahlequah on the banks of the Barren Fork in the Goingsnake District and this is where Nede Wade was born.[20] "Wauhillau," a word that comes from the Cherokee *awa'hili*, meaning "eagle," is named for Ned's mother's mother, Katie Eagle, who is also known as Wahila, or Goback.[21] Other Cherokee families such as the Adairs, Sanders, Squirrels, and Wolves also established homesteads in the area.[22]

In 1917, the *Tulsa World* published a story about thief Bob Davis, "notorious Oklahoma outlaw" who robbed the Bank of Canehill in Arkansas. Davis and his partner-in-crime fled into Oklahoma, heading for Rabbit Trap, a small community five miles from Wauhillau, an area the paper referred to as a "notorious rendezvous" site for "desperados."[23] The paper also described the Rabbit Trap area as "the principal rendezvous of the Union Indians . . . [a] deep and narrow valley . . . strewn with great boulders and masses of rock [that] was regarded as all but impregnable."[24] The reputation of Rabbit Trap as a destination for criminals and as a defensible hideout might account for why most writers incorrectly claim that the Christie family settled in Rabbit Trap and that Ned was born, raised, and died there.[25]

Wadaya, like so many other Cherokees, had been weakened by the removal ordeal and died in 1842. Watt then married Skyaheta Tecorhurtuski, also known as Lydia Thrower, in 1849.[26] Steele states in his *Last Cherokee Warriors* that Christie's father, Watt, had "eight wives" and that those "various wives" bore him eleven children. Steele indulges in more stereotypical fiction by adding, "Watt was a strikingly handsome Indian and soon collected a harem of the most beautiful Indian maidens in the territory."[27] The reality is that Watt married five women, but only because he became a widower four times. Besides, in 1825, the National Council passed a law stating that no man, white or Cherokee, could have more than one wife.[28]

Travelers from California stopped at the Wauhillau Trading Post—one of the few trading posts at that time—and camped by nearby Caney Creek on their way east to Fort Smith and west to California. If short on money, customers might pay for goods with livestock.[29] Many Christies, including Wadaya and Nede Wade, are buried in the Watt Christie cemetery next to the still-standing old stone Wauhillau Trading Post.

After arrival in the territory, Watt immediately began building a log home, filling in chinks between logs with clay, and established a garden and livestock pens. Some Cherokees had dirt floors, and others puncheon floors. Most had one bedroom, a kitchen—although some families preferred to do their cooking outside—and a smokehouse either adjoining the main house or a separate structure.

The old Wauhillau Trading Post still stands. The cemetery is behind the building.
Photo by author.

Instead of a smokehouse, some dug a hole in the floor to store food. Windows and doors were made of little poles two feet long and fastened with bark and strips of hide for hinges.[30]

Much of their new territory resembled the bountiful East. Nede Wade's Wauhillau land is uneven, with 800-foot-high hills and sloping valleys crossed by streams and creeks and during his lifetime covered with timber, edible plants, and teeming with wildlife. In 1885, the *Cherokee Advocate* described the Goingsnake District as being "beautifully supplied with the purest water that flows from its many hillsides in sparkling springs."[31]

During Ned Christie's time, the foliage grew so densely that geologist Charles Newton Gould stated that "a person may ride all day and scarcely be out of the woods." There is a variety of timber, with oaks and hickories the most common, followed by walnut, cedar, pecan, dogwood, elms, redbud, sycamore, maples, pawpaw, chinaberry, locust, crabapple, hawthorn, and others.[32] The Christies were surrounded by much seasonal food, such as blackberry, raspberry, dewberries, strawberries, grapes, huckleberries, and plums. Tributaries of the Illinois River provided an abundance of fish; a favorite way to catch them was what residents referred to as "poisoning" the water by using powdered root of the buckeye tree or the crushed roots of the white snakeroot (*Ageratina altissima*), also known as the devil's shoestring, to stun fish so they could easily be caught.[33] Although much of the land has been cleared for farming and livestock grazing, today it still retains much of the nineteenth-century flora and fauna. Canoeing, rafting, and kayaking the stretch of the Illinois where Ned lived is a peaceful way to photograph the wildlife and lush vegetation, although poison ivy pervades the area.

The Christies also had ample animal foods: bear, deer, raccoons, opossums, beavers, ducks, geese, prairie chickens, quail, wild pigeons, muskrats, squirrels, and rabbits. Residents of that period recall seeing deer in droves, and turkeys roosted in trees right outside of houses. Squirrels, a favorite food of Ned's, were sometimes so populous that they destroyed corn crops. Copperheads and rattlesnakes inhabited the hillsides while cottonmouths lived along the streams and creeks. Wild and garden foods were usually plentiful except during times of drought, although some affluent residents who could afford to purchase foods from trading posts had changed their traditional ways of eating to the extent that white flour, coffee, and sugar appeared at every meal.[34] Most residents, including the Christies, had what many called a "milch-cow" and chickens. They raised corn, beans, potatoes, and pumpkins and traded with neighbors for peanuts, sweet potatoes, watermelons, black-eyed peas, and honey from their apiaries.[35]

A gristmill was built on the creek close to the Wauhillau Trading Post; then in the early 1880s another took its place one hundred yards to the southeast and became known as "Bidding" Mill, named after Dr. Nicholas Bitting, who settled there in 1876. This name later changed to Golda's Mill, after Golda Unkefer, who operated the mill until 1900. The name Bitting was initially misnamed and now the church and creek are named "Bidding." The Christie family, however, has always called Bidding Creek by the name "Goback Creek" and others refer to it as Bitting Spring, Goingsnake Creek, and Ned Christie Springs.[36]

It was amid the developing Cherokee Nation and growing Indian Territory that Ned was born into the Bird Clan, on December 14, 1852. Lydia gave birth to Ned on a cold, dark evening while her Wauhillau neighbors stood outside the cabin by the fires, the women softly singing. Lydia's mother, Solada ("Charlotte" in English), smoked and blessed the house, then braided her daughter's hair. Wahila, a tall, imposing woman with long silver hair she kept piled atop her head, served as Lydia's midwife. Dick Keyes, known as "Backfoot" because when he walked a sound like another foot behind him kept pace, played the fiddle on the front porch. After Ned emerged into the world, Wahila buried the afterbirth on the east side of the cabin.[37]

Nede Wade grew up amid a large extended family who spoke mainly Cherokee. Watt and Lydia had eight children: Rachel, born in 1850; Ned (1852); Mary

(1857); Jack (1860); Darkey (1862); Goback (1864); Annie (1869); and Jennie (1872). When old enough, Ned went to the small Caney school located next to the Caney graveyard. This school became known as Christie School, sometimes as Sugar Mountain School, and his cousin Katie later taught there.[38] Ned spoke, read, and wrote in Cherokee as well as in English. He learned Cherokee manners, traditions, and politics from all his relatives, but notably from his uncle Goback Eagle.

In 1852, the year of Ned's birth, thousands of Cherokees could speak English and learned to read.[39] Many adults already could read and write in Cherokee because in 1821, the silversmith Sequoyah (also known as George Gist or George Guess) created the Cherokee syllabary.[40] Prior to their move to Indian Territory, the Cherokees began publication of the *Cherokee Phoenix* newspaper with columns in both English and in Cherokee. After their arduous removal from the East in the 1830s, they started printing the *Cherokee Advocate* with College of New Jersey (now Princeton) graduate William Potter Ross as the first editor. Ross was the nephew of Chief John Ross, leader of the antiremoval faction of Cherokees.[41] By the 1820s, many Cherokees, mixed-bloods mainly, made it clear they wanted a system of education for their children and they approved many missionary-run schools such as the American Board's Dwight Mission.[42] The constant push for education continued long after removal.

The Progressive Cherokees were those who spoke mainly English, had converted to Christianity, strived for material wealth, and wanted to compete economically with the surrounding whites. They continued to believe the way to accomplish their goal was to regulate their own schools and curricula. In so doing, they would educate Cherokee youth in their way of thinking, believing that after graduation they would then become savvy enough to maintain control over tribal politics.[43] The most prominent Cherokee schools were the two boarding schools, Cherokee Female Seminary at Park Hill (where the Cherokee Historical Society is now located) and its counterpart, the Cherokee Male Seminary (located southwest of Tahlequah), which were established by the tribal council with the intention of educating their children in the ways of white society. The seminaries did not teach Cherokee students about their culture. The first female teachers came from Mount Holyoke in South Hadley, Massachusetts, and the male teachers from Yale. The tribe spent $60,000 apiece on the seminaries, creating institutions that were large, spacious, and equaled, if not surpassed, the best eastern schools.[44]

Ned was born a year after the seminaries opened but he never attended the male seminary. Although he was cognizant that the seminaries were not intended to be cultural schools, he supported them because they were an avenue for students to understand the white world that surrounded them. He hoped that students would acquire knowledge of Cherokee culture from their families, and to learn English and how to negotiate the changing political and cultural landscape at the seminaries.[45]

Ned remained a staunch traditionalist. The Christie family belonged to the Keetoowah Society, the religious organization determined to preserve Cherokee culture and sovereignty, which included objecting to the influx of white intruders into tribal nations, white men intermarrying with Cherokee women, the allotment of their lands, and Oklahoma statehood. They were also antislavery and advocated for the tribe's rights as per the treaties with the United States. Ned's grandfather Lacy and his father, Watt, served as chiefs of the Keetoowah ceremonial ground located on the Wauhillau family grounds.[46] As a future council member, Ned retained his traditionalist beliefs and concerns and preferred to speak Cherokee, yet his ability to read and write in English and knowledge of the U.S. federal government enabled him to make crucial political, social, and economic decisions that impacted the Cherokee Nation.

Ned learned gun- and metalsmithing from his father, Watt, who maintained his reputation as a skilled smith through the decades. The *Cherokee Advocate* wrote that citizens took their plows and hoes to Watt Christie because "he never fails to put them in order, no odds how rough they may be, and rough they are, as everyone knows who has ever been in their district."[47]

Ned's brother, named Goback like his uncle, became a respected metal and gunsmith too. Neighbor George Keys recalled that "he could make anything he wanted. Didn't make any difference what it was. He could make it. He could make a pocketknife and blades. The only difference between it and the factory was it didn't have no lettering on it." Goback also made wagon rims, plows, and watch springs and his arrowpoints and fish gigs were "works of art."[48] In addition, the gregarious Goback was an artist and belonged to the Masonic lodge.[49] Not only was Goback a "master in working metals, wood and stone . . . [but] his gift of knowledge of the use of herbs and plants in treating the sick was known far and wide," and he knew enough about healing to successfully set a compound fracture. And he served as a "confidant to those in trouble." According to Goback's son Amos Christie (and grandson of Watt), his father was considered "one of the best known and most loved of all the Cherokees of his time."[50]

Goback learned about healing from his maternal grandmother, a medicine woman. His older sister's husband, Seed, was a medicine man.[51] One of the most

Ned's brother Goback with one of the many chairs he made. *Roy Hamilton Collection.*

serious consequences of Indian removal was the inability of the tribal doctors to immediately locate the traditional medicinal plants needed for ceremonies and healing, and Goback quickly filled an urgent need. Another brother, Jack, lived near Hungry Mountain and made a living at sharpening mill burrs, among other things. He took after his father, for he too was deemed "a natural mechanic" who "could do almost anything."[52]

Ned's happy childhood was disrupted by the Civil War. Prior to the start of the war in 1861, members of the antiremoval Ross faction and the Treaty Party maintained resentments and the advent of the war brought forth the old Cherokee factionalism. The majority of Ross's followers were Keetoowahs, at that time also known as "Pin Indians." They had no loyalty to the Confederacy or to white southerners; instead, they pledged allegiance to John Ross.[53] His Company E is the regiment that Ned's father, Watt (age forty-one), joined, along with Watt's brother Arch (thirty), and Watt's son and Ned's brother James (twenty).[54] There are no stories about Ned's participation in the Civil War since he was barely nine years old when the war began.[55] John Ross spent the last years of the war in Washington, D.C., and when he died on August 1, 1866, Watt Christie served as one of his pallbearers.[56]

The war soon spread to Indian Territory and the aftermath resulted in more loss of tribal lands, loss of life, property damage, and societal upheaval with unprecedented violence spreading throughout the tribal nations. Residents recall having plenty to eat and wear prior to the war. With the corn, pumpkins, wild berries, fruits, honey, and game, together with gardens and wild fowls, "the Indians before the war, were living good," yet the troops came through and "they simply stripped us of everything." Troops burned barns, houses, and cribs after taking furniture and driving off cattle. The tribal properties look as "hopeless as can be conceived," wrote Indian agent Proctor.[57]

After the war the Indian population, especially full-bloods, decreased, while the numbers of non-Indians and mixed-bloods increased. The federal government saw an opportunity to seize more tribal lands. The western half of Indian Territory was renamed Oklahoma Territory and served as home for Southern Plains tribes from Kansas and Nebraska. "Agreements" for these moves were not exactly honest. For example, Kickapoos learned that government agents had accepted a ten-year-old's signature on their agreement to move to Oklahoma. Tribes also had to acquiesce to the intrusion of railroads and the loss of lands as rights-of-way.[58]

The Christies worked to find normalcy after the war. Ned learned to play a fiddle that he purchased by mail order. The Wauhillau community had regular music gatherings where Ned played and neighbors danced. Roy recalls that when he was a child the tradition of music parties held at his great-uncle John's, with plenty of "food, music, lots of laughing, sometimes games of horseshoes, chunky, or shooting contest (cans on the fence)." Ned's last fiddle eventually found a home with one of Nancy Christie's sons, but it disappeared after Ned's death.[59] Christie developed into a skilled marble player, a popular game among peoples around the world including Natives of many tribes. Cherokees call marbles *digadayosdi*. Using rolled clay or polished river stones about the size of today's billiard balls, players attempt to toss the marbles into five holes in the proper sequence while knocking opponents' marbles out of the way.[60]

Ned's father and the men who visited his shop taught young Christie how to shoot pistols and rifles. A preteen carrying a weapon at that time was not surprising. By necessity, most people in Indian Territory were forced to learn to shoot and even more acquired guns to protect themselves after the Civil War. White and Indian murderers, rapists, whiskey peddlers, and thieves inhabited the western portion, especially the Union Agency that included the Cherokee, Chickasaw, Choctaw, Creek, and Seminole Nations. In 1866, Allen Wright, chief of the Choctaw Nation directly to the south of the Cherokee Nation, stated that "every species of lawlessness, violence, robbery and theft" pervaded his tribal lands.[61] The number of murders would not subside in part because of the railroad construction and the volume of transient criminals passing through the territory. Christie also learned the time-consuming task of making ammunition, a potentially dangerous project using hot liquid metal. He had a steady hand and good eye and his widow, Nancy, later recalled that he would "draw his guns so fast you would never see them leave his holster; but, there they were, having magically jumped into his hands.[62] Watt gave Ned the guns he used in the war, .44-caliber cap and ball pistols. Using what he learned in his father's smithy, Ned transformed the guns into five-shot pistols.

In his October 1859 annual address to the nation, Chief John Ross had already discussed the dire need for jails to curb the increasing violence. Cherokees had passed laws in 1852 addressing gambling and carrying weapons. The tribe had its own three-story sandstone national jail, and a gallows outside. In 1884, the jail housed twenty prisoners who wore zebra-striped suits and who were assigned to chop wood and to work on buildings and roads.[63]

Considering the number of cases in which noncitizens living in the tribal nations were accused of serious crimes, the federal government had to know something needed to be done even before the Civil War started. In 1851, Congress authorized the federal court for the Western District of Arkansas in Van Buren, Arkansas, jurisdiction over the western counties in Arkansas and all of the Indian Territory.[64] In 1871, William Story was appointed as judge but resigned in 1874 after corruption charges. His replacement, thirty-six-year-old Isaac Parker had served as a Missouri City attorney, a circuit attorney and circuit judge, in addition to serving in the U.S. House of Representatives. During his tenure as judge, he tried an impressive 13,490 cases, with 344 of those capital crimes.[65] Tribal courts only heard cases involving tribal members. If one party was Indian and the other white, or if a crime occurred in which the victim and perpetrator both were white, then the case was heard at the U.S. court in the western district of Arkansas. Cherokees became involved in many crimes, either as victims or perpetrators, and Nede Wade Christie soon became familiar with Judge Parker's reputation and how the court system worked.

Ned matured amid these postwar changes. He grew to resemble his half-blood grandmother Quatie Christie. He had the bone structure of his Cherokee forebearers, and the wavy hair with auburn and red highlights of Quatie and her father, Trader John Christie, which he usually wore down. Ned related well to children, and females apparently found him captivating. In 1871, nineteen-year-old Ned met his first wife, Nani Digi, also called Nannie Dick, at a dance where he played the fiddle. During that dance, a drunken man grabbed Nannie's arm, causing her to fall. That man wanted a dance with her and Ned told him to back off. The inebriated man pulled a knife, then Ned hit him in the nose and put the barrel of his pistol to the man's forehead. "Hadn't you rather go home than die?" Ned asked him. The man stood, Ned put away his gun, but then the man drew his pistol. In response, Christie quickly shot him in the arm. There is no word on what happened to the would-be suitor.[66] Ned and Nannie married and the next year had a daughter, Mele or Wali, also known as Mary, who witnessed her father's death in 1892.

The year Mary was born, the Cherokee Nation contended with yet another violent episode: a gunfight at the Goingsnake Courthouse, an event that shaped Ned's perception of federal authority over crimes in the Cherokee Nation. The event spotlighted Cherokee Ezekiel "Zeke" Proctor, a mixed-blood Keetoowah who survived the removal trek and has long been labeled by writers as an outlaw associate of Christie.

In 1872, a Fort Smith posse attempted to accost and take Zeke to trial at Fort Smith for killing, albeit accidentally, Polly Hildebrand. Polly's first husband, Stephen, was the uncle of Zeke's wife, Rebecca. After his death she married James "Jim" Kesterson (also seen as Chesterson). On February 27, 1872, Zeke went to talk to Jim, possibly because of a dispute over cattle. An argument ensued, Zeke attempted to shoot Jim, and hit Polly instead. Zeke immediately surrendered to Goingsnake District sheriff Blackhawk Sixkiller. Because Zeke and Polly were Cherokees, Cherokee lawmen were determined uphold the law and keep Proctor's trial in a Cherokee court, but Fort Smith men wanted him tried at Fort Smith because they argued that Zeke had attempted to kill Jim, who was a white man. They forced the issue in trying to take Zeke during his trial and the result was the Goingsnake Massacre that left ten men dead and many wounded.[67]

This confrontation occurred only four miles from the Christie home and the aftermath certainly impacted Ned. All Cherokees, including Keetoowahs, paid close attention to how the federal government responded as the situation grew more volatile. The U.S. district attorney of the Western District of Arkansas believed that by resisting the marshals' attempts to take Proctor, the Cherokees were purposely defying U.S. authority.[68] After the shootings, Zeke made himself scarce in the hills of Wauhillau along with Sixkiller, members of the Cherokee Senate, and almost fifty supporters. Proctor garnered the reputation as an unrepentant killer outlaw who spent his days raiding and murdering. Like Ned Christie, Zeke Proctor's reputation underwent character defamation for the sake of selling newspaper copies. For examples, *Pomeroy's Democrat* in Chicago wrote, "It is said, on good authority, that Proctor has killed twenty-three men and two women during his pilgrimage here on earth."[69] Zeke eventually turned himself in, as did other members of the Senate who were also wanted. Ultimately, their charges were dismissed. Surviving members of the posse who attempted to arrest Zeke at the Goingsnake Courthouse left the territory even though they had warrants against them.

Zeke has been the subject of fabricated stories and is portrayed as either a murderous outlaw (he killed twenty-one men and wore a steel breastplate)[70] or, like Christie, whom Steele calls one of the "Last Cherokee Warriors," a valiant defender of Cherokee sovereignty. Despite all the negative publicity, the Cherokees knew the reality and Zeke was appointed to the Cherokee National Council, along with Ned's father, Watt, and uncle Nede Grease. A few years later Cherokees showed their continued confidence in him by electing him a Cherokee senator.[71] He also became a successful rancher, cultivated large amounts of produce on his farm, and later served the Cherokee Nation as a sheriff. Except for a few gossipy sentences, newspapers did not connect Christie and Proctor together, mainly because they never were together except perhaps in group settings. Zeke's family settled ten miles from the Hildebrand-Beck Mill along Flint Creek, about thirty-six miles from where Ned's family lived in Wauhillau. While the two men knew of each other, if there was any socialization going on, it would have been conducted between Watt Christie and Proctor, not Nede Wade and Proctor. In 1872, Zeke was forty-one and Nede Wade twenty-one years old and the latter had just married. Christie focused on his new family, not on outlaw escapades with a man twice his age.[72]

Amid the turmoil in the Cherokee Nation, Nannie took Mary and left Ned in 1874; she later married Ned's father, Watt, thereby becoming Ned's ex-wife and stepmother. All remained friendly. Nannie reportedly was shot and killed around 1882 by a man named Booger Sanders who wanted to stop her from testifying against him in court. There are no news reports about this incident, although there is mention of Sanders being shot dead by William Madden on November 9, 1901, as the "result of an old feud."[73]

In 1874, when Ned was twenty-two, he and Watt traveled to Tahlequah to meet Watt's friend Toyanisi "Bug" Tucker, who had arrived with his daughters Peggy and Jennie. The smaller woman, Peggy, with long, dark hair and eyes caught Ned's attention. They wed two years later and her sister, Jennie, married Ned's brother Jack. In 1876 Peggy bore a son, James, usually known as Jim.[74] Their happy marriage was short-lived for around 1880 Peggy became ill and died sometime in 1881. She was buried in the Thornton Family Cemetery alongside her mother, Millie, and sister, Jennie Tucker Christie.[75]

Ned then married Jennie Scraper, the daughter of his friends Otter and Sallie Scraper, in 1881, and they had a daughter, Annie. The outspoken Jennie had no qualms about debating politics with Ned and she did not approve of him drinking. She divorced him in 1882. Ned's descendants recall how proud he was of his daughter Annie, once telling some friends while riding in a wagon with her, "Don't look gentlemen. I have the most beautiful woman in the world riding with me today. One look and you will surely be blinded." He and ex-wife Jennie remained on good terms and he continued to visit Annie and bring her Jennie's other children by her new husband, Lou Johnson, candy and other gifts. Ned referred to all of the children as "his girls" and they were just as fond of him. Jennie passed away after 1918.[76]

Ned married for the last time, probably in 1886. Nusi Goie Ahwiousi "Nancy" Grease was Ned's cousin, the daughter of Ned's aunt Arley Christie Grease (often seen as "Greece"). Ned and Nancy rediscovered each other one spring while both were in the woods, Nancy looking for firewood and Ned hunting. She asked him to come to her home for supper and they never parted after that. He called her Nusi Goie.

Nancy had previously been married at age thirteen to William "Will" Adair and they had two children: Albert, and a girl who died shortly after birth. Nancy was not happy in this marriage, so after the death of her daughter she let Will know the marriage was over by setting his belongings outside the front door. Albert then lived with her and Ned. Roy Hamilton grew up communally with another of her sons, John (his great-uncle, "Uncle John"), whom she had with the man she married after Ned died, Ned's brother Jack Christie.[77] Nancy's leaving the disgruntled Adair would later have consequences for the fate of Christie and his cousin Arch Wolfe.

Ned and his half-brother James "Jim," c. 1880. The latter's parents are Watt and
Charlotte Christie. *Courtesy of the Cherokee National Historical Society, Tahlequah, Oklahoma.*

The marital upheavals raise the question of why two of Ned's wives left him.
Jennie did not like him drinking, but no one has mentioned anger issues. Descendant Roy Hamilton believes that Ned's wives left him because "his devotion and
passion to government was stronger than his devotion to the wives. . . . Nancy said
the only fight they ever had was over him giving so much of his life to the Cherokee
people and their right to be a sovereign Nation. She hoped he would devote his
life to her and their daughter and their children (though their children died in
infancy); but, he was obsessed with his people's rights and the Cherokee Nation.
But, she did love him dearly."[78]

Nede Wade, Nancy, Albert, and Jim (Ned's son with Peggy) made their home
at the top of a heavily treed hill along modern-day E0790 Road in Wauhillau.
They utilized a spring a short distance down the hill from their home. Ned gardened as he had learned from his parents, cultivating beans, corn, squashes, and
potatoes. A rail fence kept the horses and cows contained. Some full-bloods in
the vicinity lived in smaller homes with barely adequate cribs, but they tended to
be communal and helpful to each other. Most of the families owned a wagon and

Nancy Grease, Ned's last wife. After his death, she married his brother Jack.
Roy Hamilton Collection.

horses and the "very social and hospitable" full-bloods liked to visit friends, what Indian agent Owen called "loafing," but what Cherokees called socializing.[79] The Keetoowahs, including Ned Christie, continued to gather together to mull over the future of their nation.

Ned and Nancy did not have much money, but they had what they needed to survive comfortably and they were happy. At least until Dan Maples died.

CHAPTER 2

NED THE POLITICIAN

Do you want to give our Nation to people who will kill us,
take our homes, try to destroy the Cherokee family?
NED CHRISTIE, c. 1885

Indian Territory featured timber, water, coal, game, rich soil for farming and cattle ranching, and as Osages later discovered, oil. The desire for these resources grew and hopeful non-Indians wanting tribal citizenship poured into all the tribal nations. By 1880 the Territory had developed into a political and economic hot spot. That year, 531 non-Indian families made claims to Cherokee citizenship and were rejected, but that did not deter the tide of interlopers who were intent on settling in the Cherokee Nation.[1] In addition to hundreds of squatters, at least 35,000 white traders, railroad workers, travelers, "pleasure seekers," and workers hired by Indians settled on tribal lands.[2]

Violence in the area administered by the forty Bureau of Indian Affairs agencies across the country continued unabated, and it became especially acute in Indian Territory. The commissioner of Indian Affairs wrote that problems escalated by the day, with "trespassing, harassing the Indians, provoking quarrels, thieving" commonplace.[3] Indian agent Robert L. Owen was more specific, expressing concern at the numbers of "cowmen, farming intruders, coal and timber thieves, tramps, vagrants, refugees from justice, professional thieves, and whisky-peddlers" who permeated the Territory.[4] Some of these individuals were violent "pale-faced cut-throats, the terrors of the country." Carrying weapons in the Cherokee Nation was prohibited, but it seemed that most residents carried arms.[5]

Generally, the Indian police were competent, determined, and zealous in their pursuit of whiskey peddlers, truant students, timber, cattle, and horse thieves, as well as more violent murderers, wife beaters, and rapists. They also served as messengers and guards. But they also were underpaid and overworked, stretched thin across the expansive landscape. Many officers from various tribes died each year.[6] Year after year, commissioners pleaded for more adequate compensation for the Indian police, but they did not receive any.

Cherokees, as well as members of other tribes, remained vigilant. During the time that Ned Christie appeared in the newspapers, railroads crossed the landscape and so many non-Indians intruded into tribal territory that it seemed a genuine possibility that those lands might be made available for white settlement seemed a genuine possibility and Oklahoma statehood appeared more like a reality. By the time Dan Maples died, the Cherokee Nation, and indeed, all the tribes, faced dissolution. The Christies were well aware of what could happen because they had witnessed firsthand how the federal government operated. After all, members of the Christie family watched as their loved ones perished during the removal ordeal. Watt's shop became an important gathering place for Keetoowah social and political strategizing. They debated how to deal with intruders, intermarriage with opportunistic whites, crime, and engaged in political intrigue.

Ned's father especially played a prominent role in Cherokee politics as a council member and as a juror in numerous Cherokee court trials. In the 1870s, he served on the Cherokee National Council along with Zeke Proctor and Nede Grease.[7] His brother Jackson had been nominated by the National Party for a Senate position in 1883.[8] The editor of the *Cherokee Advocate*, Elias C. Boudinot Jr., frequently praised these men, and in November 1885 he wrote about how pleased he was that national councillors Watt Christie, B. W. Foreman (Illinois), Nelson Foreman (Cooweescoowee), along with assistant chief Rabbit Bunch, Senator D. W. Lipe, W. P. Henderson, George Sanders, and Nede Grease, had visited the newspaper office.[9]

Because of Indian Territory's rapidly growing population, the rest of the country began learning more about it. Outsiders knew the Territory mainly as a place of vast resources and crime, but not much else. In 1958, Wild West writer Phillip Rand characterized the town of Tahlequah as a "dirty, sprawling frontier village" where residents lived in "wooden shacks and were in constant fear of the outlaws who hid in the caves during the day and came to Tahlequah at night to get drunk, kill each other or any unfortunate who might be outside."[10] This fabricated story is really about Christie, and Rand aimed to portray Tahlequah as unappealing and backward as possible because it was the capital of the Cherokee Nation. In reality, Tahlequah was hardly a community of hovel-dwelling miscreants. During

Nede Wade's Cherokee Nation Senate photograph, 1887. *Roy Hamilton Collection.*

the late 1880s, Tahlequah was home to the Cherokee Supreme Court Building, the National and Wolfe Hotels, McSpadden's Grist and Four Mill, Brown's Drug Store, J. W. Stapler and Sons store, National Livery Feed and Sale stable, Tahlequah Mills, the central telephone exchange, the post office, an ice factory, the electric plant, law and physician offices, and the *Cherokee Advocate* newspaper, as well as a variety of smaller businesses.[11]

The Christies came to Tahlequah to buy supplies, visit friends and for Watt to attend National Council meetings. Otherwise, like other full-bloods and traditionalists, the Christies preferred to stay in their communities away from whites and acculturated Cherokees. Traditionalists spoke Cherokee, practiced their religion, and observed other cultural traditions. Despite the disdain many of the traditionalists had for the "white Cherokees," some of them, including the

Christies, were well versed in how both the U.S. and the Cherokee Nation political machines operated and were willing to become a part of them when necessary for the betterment of the Cherokee Nation. Not one to sit back in silence, Ned spoke at every opportunity about Cherokee sovereignty "from the back of wagons, on tree stumps, once from the second story balcony of a hotel in the capital city of Tahlequah."[12]

Anyone who followed politics knew the Christie platform. On November 11, 1885, the Cherokee Nation Senate and Council elected three new members of the Executive Council: Ned Christie (often seen as "Edward" in documents), Daniel Red Bird, and David Muskrat. The *Cherokee Advocate* praised the men as "capable and safe advisors," assessing them as public men who "have proven and given satisfaction. They are in sympathy with the Administration and Chief Bushyhead will find them to be capable and safe advisors. The National Council has done well in the selection of these gentlemen to so important a trust."[13]

Considering two incidents that occurred less than a year earlier, some might have been curious as to why the Christies were held in high esteem. In November 1884, Ned's cousin George Christie twice shot Sicky Sanders, the son of Cherokee Senator Jesse Sanders, near Sanders's home on Caney Creek. The *Cherokee Advocate* stated that George, Sicky, and several others were drunk and were engaged in "friendly carousal" when the shooting started. Sicky was shot through the chest and the other bullet broke his femur. Sicky remained in "very critical condition," but his father reported him to be "cheerful and hopeful." George also had been hit; first reports stated that he too was in "dangerous condition," but a week later that changed to not seriously wounded. Sicky lingered for six months until he died May 1, 1885. George was subsequently charged with the murder and the last report stated that his trial would continue into June of that year.[14] There are no further newspaper reports about the outcome of the trial, but George had one child in 1883, and seven more between 1884 and 1897, so apparently he did not face conviction. George lived within four miles of his cousin Ned Christie, close enough to follow the last years of Ned's life. He named one of his sons after Ned and lived to be over one hundred years old.[15]

Then a month later, on Christmas Eve 1884, Ned and his younger brother Jack visited Leland Coleman Dick and his son Eli to shoot on Caney Creek "in the pigeon roost near the road leading from Gail Sixkiller's house to Step Preacher's." Wild pigeons came in droves in the fall of the year and residents killed thousands of them, sometimes for food but mainly for profit. White men bought pigeons from the Indians for five cents a dozen, then sold them for markup to Arkansas city markets for three dollars a dozen. George Christie (also known as George Dick, the husband of Jennie Grease who was the niece of Watt Christie) and his friend White Whitmire shot 1,000 pigeons in 1887 and lost a five-dollar bet to Cherokee sheriff Ben Knight (the man some writers falsely claim led the posse to kill Ned Christie in 1892) and his son, who shot 1,001. They were not out any money because they sold the birds to pigeon buyers at Siloam Springs, Arkansas, who shipped the birds to the Kansas City packing company.[16] It could be they were shooting the now extinct passenger pigeon. At one time, pigeon numbers were greatest in the Going Snake District, at the junction of Barren Fork and the Illinois River. A Cherokee near that roost recalled that in the 1880s pigeons were so great in number that they "swept across the sky in clouds, darkening the sun. As their number and weight increased, the branches would bend until finally they broke."[17]

Regardless of the species of pigeon, everyone became tipsy and after Ned said he had enough liquor, another pigeon shooter, William Palone, became angry that Ned refused to drink with him and called Ned a son of a bitch. Ned took this as an affront to his mother, Lydia. William died quickly after being shot three times by someone wielding a Winchester. Ned was arrested and charged with manslaughter, and he pleaded not guilty. The first witness to testify (the name is illegible on the handwritten transcript) stated that he did not see the killing, that he only saw Palone's body a few hours after he died. W. A. Downing also stated that he did not see the killing, but that he had seen Palone earlier that day. The next to testify, Coleman Dick, also was not much help. Although the shooting took place at his camp, he could only offer that those present included his cowhands, a man named Eli, and Ned and Jack Christie. He said he heard the gunshot and turned to see Palone fall, but did not see who shot him. Next, Palone's mother, Katy, testified that she did not see her son die, but that she saw the next day that he had been hit twice in the left side of his chest. The last two witnesses also saw Palone only after his death. Based on the testimonies of "witnesses" who had not actually seen the shooting, the jury returned a verdict of not guilty.[18]

Ned's brother Jack later admitted that he and Ned both shot Palone: "He insulted our mother. He had a gun and was pulling it out as he came toward Nede, pushing a whiskey bottle towards my brother the whole time. Nede shot before I did. That's it."[19] Although exonerated, Ned's association with this violent crime would stay with him. Not only did the future chief and Progressive Joel B. Mayes serve as chief justice of the Cherokee Supreme Court for that trial, Christie's name as associated with the murder of Palone would fuel later writers' imaginations.[20]

A year later, Ned's half-brother William Christie and a drunken Blue Duck were accused of killing a young man named Samuel Wyrick as he plowed a field on land that belonged to Martin Hopper, a relative of Blue Duck. This is the same Blue Duck who allegedly stabbed a man named Nofire at Ned's uncle Arch Christie's home in 1882. In his novels *Lonesome Dove* and *Comanche Moon*, Larry McMurtry creates a particularly loathsome character based on Blue Duck, reinventing him as the offspring of a Comanche and Mexican captive. This fictional murderer/rapist/slave trader is based on the real-life Cherokee named Shacongah Kawwannu, or in English Blueford "Blue" Duck. The real Blue Duck did not look like Frederic Forrest, with a prosthetic nose and wearing a vest with no shirt, in the television miniseries *Lonesome Dove*, nor did he look like Adam Beach's more handsome Southern Plains version in the miniseries *Comanche Moon*, but he did engage in bad drunken behavior.[21]

The grand jury failed to indict Blue Duck so the court released him, but afterward lawmen rearrested him and he found himself duly indicted. In February 1886, Judge Isaac Parker sentenced Blue Duck to hang.[22] A few months later William was acquitted of the murder of Wyrick.[23] Blue Duck's sentence of death was commuted to life in prison at Southern Illinois Penitentiary (now called Menard Correctional Center) in Chester, Illinois, but he contracted tuberculosis in 1895 and the warden allowed him to die at home in Catoosa, Oklahoma.[24] Throughout the latter part of the nineteenth century, several men named "Christie" engaged in illegal behavior. Writers intent on portraying Ned as a criminal persisted in connecting him to any lawbreaker with the Christie name, whether or not they were related to him.

Despite the mayhem, Bushyhead had pushed for Ned to sit on the National Council and Ned accepted. Before he could begin his duties, he was required to recite this oath:

> I, [Nede Wade Christie,] do solemnly swear that I have not obtained my election by bribery, treats, or any undue and unlawful means used by myself or others by my desire or approbation for that purpose; that I consider myself constitutionally qualified as a member of, and that on all questions and measures which may come before me I will so give my vote and so conduct myself as in my judgment shall appear most conducive to the interest and prosperity of this Nation, and that I will bear true faith and allegiance to the same, and to the utmost of my ability and power observe, conform to, support and defend the Constitution thereof.[25]

Cherokee chief Dennis Bushyhead. *Photography Collection, Oklahoma Historical Society.*

The Cherokees had created a constitution patterned after the United States Constitution, with three branches of tribal government: executive, judicial, and legislative. The latter had two sections: the National Council, comprised of three representatives elected from each district, and the National Committee, comprised of two elected representatives. The revised Cherokee Constitution of 1839 gave the National Council an array of significant powers, such as to make crucial Cherokee Nation laws and regulations, to create treaty stipulations, and to impeach the principal chief, assistant chief, or any civil officer.[26]

Ned assumed his new position as council member by attending his first session December 16, 1885, thereafter maintaining a regular schedule: early January 1886, late February, early to mid-May, thirteen hot days in July 1886, then reconvened in mid-October, again in late December, mid-February 1887,

and early April. Meetings lasted usually from 8 A.M. to noon, then from 1:00 to
5 P.M., and were sometimes held on Saturdays. Regular responsibilities of Ned
and his fellow National Council members included pardoning convicts, listening
to sheriffs' reports, amending and repealing acts and laws authorizing representatives to Washington, and approving high sheriff appointments, in addition to
appropriating money to furnish the capitol building, allowing the construction of
mission schools, defining the duties of the editor of the *Cherokee Advocate*, and
amending a law adjusting the number of names in a jury pool.[27] Residents of the
Cherokee Nation knew who sat on the council and they could easily keep track of
how members voted on social, political, and economic issues that impacted the
populace—and that included Progressives and intruders who wanted Cherokee
land and resources.

Several major issues took up many council meetings. One involved the number of white men desiring to marry Cherokee women. An 1839 law stated that
any white man who desired a Cherokee wife had to obtain a written license from
a circuit or district court clerk for five dollars and the couple had to be lawfully
married. If the man left his Cherokee wife, or if he already happened to be married and he left his previous wife "elsewhere," he would be treated as an intruder
and removed from the Cherokee Nation.[28] That law was amended in 1843 so that
licenses had to be authorized by the National Council and given by the National
Committee clerk. In addition, the prospective bridegroom had to take an oath to
support the Cherokee constitution and to abide by all laws.[29] Outsiders discovered
that Indian Territory was a land of vast assets and if they were clever enough,
they could marry into a tribe and further exploit the lands. After the Civil War,
opportunistic white men intermarried with women citizens of the tribal nations
and when they did, those men gained the access to their desired land.[30] By 1880,
82 percent of the men married to Cherokee women were white and only 14 percent were Cherokee.[31] Christie and the council therefore spent hours reviewing
the lists of men asking to marry Cherokee women as well as the even longer lists
of citizenship applications.

The expansion of railroads also dominated council meetings. By the early
1870s, the railroads had entered Indian Territory. One Indian Territory resident
commented that "they were building so fast that they did not take time to throw
up a grade for their rails, but laid them right on top of the ground, until they came
to grade, when a cut or fill would be made."[32] Commissioner of Indian Affairs H.
Price reported in 1881 that "it is gratifying to remark that the Indians have offered
no opposition to the passage of railroads over their reservations; on the contrary,

they hail their reservations; they hail their construction with every evidence of satisfaction."[33] While some Indians did support the railroad construction, the Keetoowahs and Nationalists of the Five Tribes stood vehemently against the expansion of railroads onto Indian lands.

As a council member, Ned had the opportunity to voice his stance about additional railroads and the council concurred, passing a law disallowing right of way to the Southern Kansas Railway through the Cherokee Nation, deeming that not only was the act of Congress allowing said right-of-way a violation of treaties "but of all law and equity."[34] Ned also helped define the rights of Cherokee citizenship as it applied to Freedmen and "friendly Indians." Because the Treaty of 1866 did not clarify the phrase "all the rights of Native Cherokees," the National Council determined that it meant "all the individual rights, privileges, and benefits enjoyed by white adopted citizens," and that it did not include rights to land or per capita payments.[35] This decision did not endear Christie or the other council members to enterprising whites.

Christie also took a stance on the Cherokee Outlet, the eighty-mile wide "strip" of land located west of the Cherokee Nation (not the same as the Cherokee Strip, a two-mile wide strip of land north of the Cherokee Outlet). The 1836 Treaty of New Echota gave the Outlet to the Cherokee Nation. After the Civil War, in which Cherokees sided with the Confederacy, the United States created a new treaty allowing other tribes, including Osages, Pawnees, and Poncas, to settle in the Outlet. As punishment for their support of the Confederacy the Cherokees were disallowed from using the Outlet and the United States had the option to sell the land. In the 1880s, cattle ranchers fenced off parcels and ran thousands of cattle, and Cherokees did not object. On March 7, 1883, cattlemen in the Outlet and Strip incorporated the Cherokee Strip Live Stock Association, and the tribe leased the land to that group for $100,000 per year. The association subleased to seventy-two outfits. Cherokees believed that by allowing the ranchers to stay, a few members of the tribe would receive "grass money," or rental money. The association intended to document brands, address the problem of stray cattle, and create a group to lobby against the desires of Kansas homesteaders desirous of settling on the lands. Cherokees, including Ned Christie, opposed these homesteaders. The association faltered in the harsh weather of 1886 and 1887 and after the government sold the Outlet in 1891, the association ended two years later.[36]

Also commanding Christie's close attention were the actions of the federal government. In 1887, Congress passed the infamous Allotment Act, written by Massachusetts Senator Henry Dawes with the intent of assimilating tribes into white society by dismantling their tribal governments and allotting parcels of lands to individuals. Initially, Cherokees, the other four of the Five Tribes, Osages, Miamis, Peorias, and a few other tribes were excluded.[37] Still, Cherokees, as well as members of the other Five Tribes, knew there was a real chance that they too would be included, so they began strategizing how to best deal with that possibility.

A seat on the National Council meant awesome responsibility for Ned Christie. Members of the council were expected to attend every meeting and to be punctual, understand the Cherokee laws and treaties signed with the United States, stay aware of the rapidly changing world around them, which included an unstoppable wave of trespassers onto tribal lands and the repercussions of their desire for Cherokee resources, and to make logical commentary and decisions affecting virtually every socio-economic aspect of the Cherokee Nation. Ned had only an eighth-grade education, but he learned quickly and purposefully acquainted himself about current events. These were no small duties and the *Cherokee Advocate* periodically published those tasks to remind readers what their Senate and Council were supposed to be doing.[38]

Council business took up a great deal of Ned's time, as did travel to and from the Council House. The trail that he took to Tahlequah from his home in Wauhillau was approximately twenty miles, a long stretch on horseback in the heat of summer and during the windy, cold days of winter. Fortunately, Ned did not travel to his home and back each day; rather, he stayed at the home of Nede Grease, his uncle and member of the National Party, who lived on Morgan Street, just a few short blocks from where the second Cherokee Female Seminary building (now called Seminary Hall) stands as part of modern Northeastern State University. Ned was compensated for his time, as was his father, Watt, who was named a councilman from the Goingsnake District.[39] In April of 1886, Ned was paid $84 for twenty-one days of service.[40] For November 1886, he received $153,[41] and another $68 for seventeen days in December.[42]

The meetings sometimes lasted for several days. While Ned was gone, his wife, Nancy, and her son Albert (with ex-husband William Adair) managed the animals and gardens, sewed clothes, and hauled water. Ned brought in some money for his work on the council, but they needed more. Nancy made some extra money by selling their homegrown produce to the high sheriff, John Hawkins, for the prisoners in the Cherokee prison, such as one order for two dozen eggs, one bushel of beans, two bushels of peas, one-half bushel of hominy, and one-half bushel of corn for a total of $4.70 profit.[43] The Christies were acquainted with Hawkins as well as other Cherokee lawmen and these associations make sense considering Ned's prominent position.

In March 1887, papers reported that a young man named Bub Trainor had been shot and wounded in Tahlequah. His name actually was Thomas Trainor, Jr., but literature knows him as "Bub," or often incorrectly as "Bud."[44] Bub drank some whiskey, attempted to kill Deputy U.S. Marshal Jackson W. Ellis, and got shot by Ellis instead. Papers gave a dramatic rendition of the event, stating that the wound was serious, caused by a .44-caliber bullet from a Smith and Wesson. According to the local *Cherokee Advocate*, the bullet entered through Trainor's front teeth and lodged in the base of his skull. "At least six local non-Indian physicians" did not want to try and remove it and stated that Trainor would die from his injury. Bub's mother requested that the full-blood medicine man "Hogsporter" (there was no one by that name, although there was a Hogshooter family) treat him. After an examination, "Hogsporter" declared that he could remove the bullet without operating. The paper described his machinations as "conjuring, talking to himself in unintelligible language and making mysterious signs." In three days, the bullet emerged a bit more elongated than it entered. Bub was able to ride his horse in ten days and made a full recovery. "This sort of treatment is quite common in the Territory among the Indians," stated the *Advocate*, "and this is only one example of the skill manifested by the medicine men."[45] The *Indian Journal* refers to the medicine man as a "conjuring Cherokee doctor."[46] One paper added a bit more drama to that story by adding that the bullet had been "mashed until it was an inch long and in the shape of a parenthesis" and that the bullet fired from a .40-caliber Smith & Wesson "entered just above his teeth just under his nose and lodged in the back part of the head near the base of the brain and very near the spinal column."[47] If he really did receive that gunshot to the face, Bub was a fast healer. Less than three weeks later he was in Tahlequah drinking again and Maples got shot.[48]

Liquor did indeed prove to be the scourge of the territory. Indian agent Owen estimated that 90 percent of crimes committed by tribal members were caused by whiskey.[49] The influx of booze never did slow down. In midsummer of 1889, Agent Bennett reported that 90 percent of the cases heard by Judge Parker at Fort Smith had whiskey connections. Bennett estimated that at least one person died per day from the results of liquor consumption, including murder, assault, and robberies, and he considered whiskey running the "most pernicious of all evils." By 1890 the percentage of cases stemming from liquor use rose to 95 percent.[50] Too much liquor in the Cherokee Nation was not a new problem. An enormous amount of whiskey found its way into the nation since the tribe reestablished itself in the late 1830s, either brought in by non-Indians or by Cherokees, and the tribe wrote laws in attempts to combat the flood. Numerous residents sold whiskey, from small bottles to entire wagonloads.[51] Whiskey arrived onto Indian lands via rail, horseback, and wagon to such profit to the peddlers that they were willing to take chances.[52] Papers reported that in 1881 at Fort Gibson, Cherokees and Creeks held a joint barbecue and during the ensuing drunken melee in which "whisky flowed as freely as milk and honey in the promised land," a man and his son were shot and decapitated.[53]

Bootleggers worked around the vicinity of Tahlequah. Nancy Scraper Shell (also seen as Schell) and her sister Louisa, lived outside of Tahlequah in Big Springs and ran a modest whisky-selling enterprise.[54] Their uncle Otter lived across the road from Ned Christie, and his daughter became Ned's third wife. Ned knew Shell and probably visited her sometimes when in Tahlequah. When Ned did not attend meetings, he visited with the Grease family, as well as other friends and family in the vicinity. Writers, however, have portrayed him as a heavy drinker who in his free time looked for booze. The first description of Christie as a drinker comes from the June 17, 1917, issue of the *Tulsa World*, a story about Christie that states he passed out from drinking whiskey in 1887.[55] It is true that Christie drank; his family confirms it. But he did not drink every day.

A sober Ned Christie attended the National Council meeting on the fifth of April. He remained in town without incident for five days, then, on Easter Sunday, April 10, 1887, the girls of the Cherokee Female Seminary were visited by an individual named Louis McLain, who attempted to lure some girls into the nearby woods with the dubious intention of "preaching the gospel" to them. At some point he dropped some pipe embers onto the wood-rail fence and the live embers traveled the rail until they jumped into a window and onto some curtains. The resulting fire quickly grew out of control and the building burned to the ground. Distraught over the loss of the building, former chief William Potter Ross stated this loss of the seminary was "a calamity hitherto unknown in the history of the country."[56]

Cherokees who advocated education considered the destruction of the seminary a true disaster. And for many, by this time the school stood as a symbol of Cherokee advancement, acculturation, and whiteness. Some students at the female and male seminaries possessed as little as 1/128 Cherokee blood and many looked phenotypically white.[57] Graduates of the Cherokee seminaries became lawyers, politicians, dentists, real estate agents, physicians, bankers, stenographers, and teachers.[58] Not all Cherokees, however, bought into what white-themed education had to offer. Many seminarians were traditionalists who did not stay long at the schools and for sure, not every Cherokee was distraught over the school's ruin. Ned could accept the seminaries, but his widow and Roy's grandmother Nancy told him that she hated the school because

> it was so "un-Cherokee," meaning it was more acculturated than she could tolerate. She told me all the girls going there, including Cherokee citizens, were white girls. She refused to go. Her father though, a very Cherokee man, encouraged her to go there. He thought the education would be good for her, even if it was not culturally Cherokee. She never went more than a few days to the seminary. She managed to be educated in what they called day schools. She could read, write and speak English; but, she could read, write and speak Cherokee first.[59]

Many other Cherokees refused to go. Despite its advanced curriculum and impressive architecture, the atmosphere of the school was not homogenous. The Cherokee Female Seminary student body could in many respects be considered a microcosm of the larger Cherokee Nation and of the territory, replete with a class system and internalized racism. Intermarriage with whites and other mixed-bloods continued and by the turn of the century many citizens with Native blood looked and acted like whites. In 1899, the preponderance of mixed-blood Cherokees in Tahlequah was illustrated by *Twin Territories* writer Ora Eddleman, who expressed dismay over the wealthy Cherokees and the "blond Cherokee women."[60]

Amidst the conflicting opinions over the school, as member of the National Council Ned had the duty of deciding what to do about the rebuilding. On April 11, Chief Bushyhead called a special session of the Executive Council for Thursday, April 14 and sent a personal message to Christie telling him to be there.[61] Christie, Daniel Redbird, David Muskrat, and William Eubanks met to consider the request from the chief and the board of education as to what the council believed the best course of action might be in dealing with the school's rebuilding. Colonel William Potter Ross made a presentation on behalf of the board and recommended that the students use the insane asylum building for their school. After hearing that possibility, the council decided to adjourn to examine the buildings that afternoon and to meet at nine the next morning. Bushyhead asked for another special session of the council, to which they agreed; then they adjourned to travel ten miles round-trip to the ruined female seminary in Park Hill in an effort to estimate the losses and see what might be salvaged.

After the council reconvened that afternoon, Bushyhead suggested that convicts be employed to "put the property in question in a condition to make it safe." The Council agreed to meet the next day.[62] On May 9, five days after Maples was shot, Chief Bushyhead recommended to the National Council that the seminary be rebuilt with "speedy resumption and permanent continuance," and the council, minus Ned Christie, concurred.[63]

As Ned concluded what would be his last session on the National Council on May 3, Deputy U.S. Marshal Daniel Maples approached Tahlequah from Muskogee to investigate the escalating whiskey problem in the area. The lawman Maples earlier had arrested several criminals, including Jesse C. Glover, who had shot rancher Humphrey Bunch in the head over a boundary fence dispute in April 1884.[64]

There are various versions of what happened to Maples on the evening of May 4, 1887, but the commonality in all stories is that Maples was alive that evening when he and his group stopped to camp next to the spring in north Tahlequah (today known as Seminary Spring on the southern edge of Northeastern State University). The next day Marshal John Carroll at Fort Smith received a telegram informing him that Maples was dead. Maples's wife, Maletha, and seven children buried him in Bentonville.

CHAPTER 3

BAD COMPANY

Owing to the prominence of the dead man's family connection it is feared that the crime will not pass unobserved but will recoil to the disadvantage of the nation.
INDIAN CHIEFTAIN, May 19, 1887

The popular J. W. Stapler and Sons store in Tahlequah sold everything from clothing to food staples to hardware. On August 6, 1886, one of the Stapler sons received a telephone call from Fort Gibson, the first long-distance call made in Indian Territory.[1] Ten months later, on Wednesday evening, May 5, 1887, Deputy Maples and fellow lawman George Jefferson walked the short distance from their camp to the Staplers' store to buy eggs and, some say, to use the telephone. As it grew dark, the men made their way back to camp and approached a log that spanned the creek running about ten yards from the spring. As Maples started across, a bullet struck him in the right breast, exiting his back under his shoulder blade. At this point, versions of the events diverge.

The *Dallas Morning News* published a story on May 6 that included most of these components, in addition to the theory that Maples had been killed by someone who lay in wait for him. The version that comes from one of the men with Maples is that the group stopped at the spring, set up camp, then decided to walk to town for food and "conversation with old friends." They started back to camp at 7:40 P.M., and about ten yards from the spring they began to cross an old log. Jefferson said, "Look out, Dan; don't you see that man standing at the other end of the log with his pistol pointing towards us?" Maples replied, "Oh, he is not going to shoot." Just then the mystery man shot Maples in the chest, piercing his right lung with the bullet exiting the backbone. Then, "notwithstanding the mortal wound," Maples stood, fired three shots, fell, then asked to be taken to his old acquaintance Dr. Blake. The unknown assailant shot eleven more times and

Jefferson fired six shots in return. The culprit ran one hundred yards up the creek, whooped, and disappeared. A man named Pelle (Peele) told the reporter he was in camp when he heard shots, then ran to investigate. He saw Maples "weltering in his own blood" and Jefferson standing over him.[2]

Pelle (Peele) continued:

> Jefferson and I just took a notion to rusticate a while, both being tired of town. Jefferson is a livery man and I am a lawyer, and we wanted rest and just thought that we would accompany Dan on this trip and fish and hunt while Mr. Maples attended to his official duties. We were going right on to Fort Gibson this morning had not this terrible calamity overtaken us. There will be sorrow at Bentonville and all over Arkansas when the news is flashed around that Dan Maples has been killed. No truer man lived. He was all through the war with my father, Congressman Peele, and made a brave soldier. Dan was at the battle of Corinth when my uncle, Senator Berry, was shot and lost his leg. He and Judge Pittman were the ones to pick up Senator Berry and carry him to a resting place.

The tears rolled down his cheeks as he spoke.[3]

A few days passed without news of who the killer might be. People speculated, but papers did not blame anyone. All that residents knew about the killer was what the *Fort Smith Elevator* published: that the "the assassin quietly disappeared into the darkness."[4] Chief Bushyhead offered a $300 reward for anyone with information, and private citizens compiled their own reward pool. The *Dallas Morning News* reported that there was a strong "clew" as to who did the shooting, but did not speculate further.[5] Because National Council member Ned Christie and his uncle Nede Grease were seen in the vicinity the night before, a constituency of Cherokees became concerned when they learned that Christie might be implicated.[6]

On May 11, Tahlequah residents held an "indignation meeting" chaired by Johnson Thompson and recorded by Secretary W. P. Boudinot in which they wrote resolutions demanding that Chief Bushyhead use all available resources to identify and capture the killer.[7] The Cherokees were indeed worried about such a crime having been committed against a white lawman in their nation, and in the capital city, no less. Some of the signers had survived the arduous removal and were cognizant of what the federal government was capable of doing to tribes. They realized that making a strong statement expressing outrage over the murder might be in their best interest. After the focus turned to Ned Christie as the killer,

Deputy U.S. Marshal Dan Maples. *Author's collection.*

however, there were no more statements from this committee, not even after Christie's death.

Despite claims that Maples had writs for Cherokee Keetoowah Bill Pigeon (also known among Cherokees as Wili Woyi) "to stand trial for many charges against him,"[8] Maples actually had no writs for anyone in the vicinity.[9] The first person to state that he did was the unreliable Eli Whitmire in 1937, and every writer since has copied that statement.[10] Regardless of what Maples may have been doing in Tahlequah, he died, and because the murdered man was white, Fort Smith had jurisdiction. That he also was a deputy U.S. marshal added urgency to the investigation.

Also seen that evening were John Parris, Charley Bobtail, Looney Coon, Steve Vann, John Hogshooter, and Bub Trainor. Of these six, only Vann had

Tahlequah Creek, looking south at the Branch restaurant in modern Tahlequah.
A plaque had been attached to the building around 1978 stating that this was the site
of Maples's death, but it was stolen around 1981. *Photo by author.*

not previously been charged with multiple counts of larceny, attempted murder, and whiskey peddling.[11] Bobtail had experience with the courts and prison system, having served eight months in prison at the Detroit House of Correction (DeHoCo) in Michigan for selling whiskey.[12] This is the same prison that housed Belle Starr a few years earlier. After Bobtail's term, he returned to Indian Territory, promptly stole a horse, and was imprisoned again until May 1886.[13]

John Parris had at least six indictments against him prior to 1887 for larceny, stealing property, assault, and selling liquor in Arkansas and Indian Territory. In March 1881, John Parris and James Parris allegedly stole hogs from M. W. Dial. John did not return to Fort Smith on August 1 as ordered and was again commanded to appear, on November 1. A jury found him guilty of larceny on August 10, 1882, and he received a one-year sentence at the Detroit House of Correction to begin August 28, 1882.[14] A second set of paperwork shows that George Parris also was accused of stealing the hogs, but only John received a sentence.[15]

On February 20, 1884, the court at Fort Smith charged John Parris with larceny, but did not convict him.[16] On July 4, 1885, Parris attempted to kill James Clevenger, a white man, with a pistol. He was supposed to appear in court in November 1885, did not show, and then was required to appear in February 1886. Another document required him to appear in May 1886. He was never sentenced.

On May 10, 1885, Parris was charged with "Introducing and selling Spirituous Liquors." In the file are other charges that he also sold liquor on January 10, 1886, and in July 1886, but the court dismissed the charges.[17] Parris again faced charges several years later for selling whiskey in May of 1889 and received a sentence of one year in jail at the Arkansas State Penitentiary in Little Rock, beginning February 11, 1890.[18] Other than his repetitive misadventures, not much is known about Parris. His name appears infrequently and only in regard to Christie.[19] John's parents, George W. Parris and Annie McLoughlin, produced thirteen children. John was half Cherokee and half white, born around 1855 making him thirty-two at the time of Maples's death.[20]

Bobtail was taken to Fort Smith the week after the shooting and several people were required to appear in court on May 16 and tell what they knew. Nede Grease, Little Stealer, and William Batt were called to testify, but they never traveled to Fort Smith. Those who did testify stated that they saw many things, but no one saw the killer. J. M. Peel, who had traveled with Maples, testified that he sat in camp while Maples and Jefferson went to town and had heard the shots:

> I was present when Deputy Marshal Dan Maples was killed near Tahlequah, C.N. He was shot just after dark (or hardly just dark) on Wednesday evening May 4, 1887 in the edge of Tahlequah C.N. I was in camp and Maples and George Jefferson had been up in the town and were returning to camp. My first information of trouble was shots fired near where I was (not over 60 or 70 yards away to the best of my judgment) at the shot I raised up and heard Jefferson's voice. I ran towards him and met him and he told me that Maples was shot. I soon after went to Maples and found him severely wounded. I remained with him until he died which event took place at Tahlequah, C. Nation 12 o'clock noon on May 5, 1887.
>
> The day before the killing we (that is Deputy Marshal Maples, George Jefferson, Maples, Sam, myself) were at Mitchell's Store at Oaks, C.N. I saw an Indian there that I believe to be this prisoner (and he has since admitted to me that he was there when we stopped) the next evening in camp near Tahlequah just a bit before dark and after Maples and Jefferson started over to town I saw an Indian that I am positive was this defendant coming around the bend of the road and where 60 or 70 feet of where I was at that point he turned into a dense thicket where he came out whittling a stick. He passed on back around the bend in the direction from which he came about immediately after he was out of sight. I saw two other Indians

come around the bend (one of whom I recognized from description I had of him as Bud Trainer) and sat down at the root of a large tree. They sat there but a minute or two where they put up and went back out of sight at that time dusk was just coming though in the open it was still light but was quite dark in the thicket within ten minutes of their disappearance I heard the shots fired which resulted in Maples death. I was with Deputy Marshal John Curtis where this defendant was arrested. We arrested him about 11 miles from Tahlequah near the head of Fourteen Mile Creek (his home however is at Oaks 22 miles north east of Tahlequah) in the afternoon the day of his arrest he admitted being in Tahlequah the day of the killing but denied being about our camp. He admitted being at Oaks when we were there the day before the killing but claimed that he did not go to Tahlequah until the day of the killing. The day after his arrest he told me that he was in Mitchell's Store at Oaks the day before the killing and learned that we were at marshal's party (we were in Oaks, just before dark) that he got on his horse and rode through to Tahlequah that night that he went to Ned Christie and told him that the marshals were coming and then he went and told John Parris and John Hogshooter. I asked defendant if they (these men) got together and all did get together he told me that Loony Coon, Ned Christie, John Parris, Ned Greece, Steve Vann and John Hogshooter got together and agreed to kill the marshals and that he was present and heard the agreement. He also told me that John Parris shot at me with a Winchester (three bullets hit the tent against which I was sitting where Maples was shot) or else he told me that John Parris told him that he shot at me. I am not certain which way he put it. I then asked him who stood at the end of the foot log and shot Maples (Maples was shot by a man who stood by a bog tree at the end of a foot log over which Maples was starting to pass when he was shot) and he answered me that he would tell me when he got to Ft. Smith.

Another deputy marshal, J. F. Stokes, also from Bentonville, rode with Deputy Marshal Curtis to arrest Bobtail. His testimony was similar to Peel's:

On the day after his arrest I got into a conversation with defendant as we rode along and he told that he was at Mitchell's Store the evening before the killing and saw the marshals there, that he rode through to Tahlequah that night and told John Parris and some women who were selling whiskey that the marshals were coming and that John Parris sayed [sic] he would kill them. He told me that he and another feller (he refused to tell me the fella's name) were lying down in the left hand side of the road. When the marshal was shot that he immediately went up to the house where the women were and that he saw John Parris come up bareheaded with his pistol in his hand and he sayed [sic] John Parris said that he had shot the Marshal, he then asked me if I was going to Ft. Smith. I told him I did not know. He told me that when he got to Ft. Smith he would get with a Cherokee who could talk just English and interpret for him and then he would tell me a heap more. But that it bothered him to talk English.

On May 16, 1887, George York, yet another Bentonville, Benton County, Arkansas, resident also shared his view of events:

I know the defendant. I was with Deputy Marshal Curtis when he arrested their defendant. I had considerable talk with defendant the day after his arrest. He admitted riding from Mitchell's Store and Tahlequah and notifying John Parris and others that the marshals were coming and that those parties made up a plan to kill the marshals. He also admitted being in the brush nearby when the shooting took place. He also told me that he saw John Parris going away from the locality with his pistol in his hand and that Parris told him that he had killed somebody. He told me that just before the killing he was close to the camp and remained in the brush in the immediate vicinity until after the killing.[21]

Amid the speculation about Maples, on May 30, 1887, Trainor was indicted for assault with intent to kill J. W. Ellis. Attached to his indictment is a handwritten note that reads, "He is the same one wanted for murder of Maples but may not be held on that charge—Kell and Ellis thinks he can get him." Bud T. Kell was a Cherokee and first marshal of Muskogee. The Maples killing must have overshadowed the Trainor-Ellis encounter because Bub never faced an assault conviction.[22]

Residents continued to speculate on what happened that night. Christie remained fearful, and did not appear for the June 27, 1887, National Council meeting.[23] Two months after the death of Maples, more witnesses were required to convene in July 1887 at Fort Smith to tell their stories, this time in regard to John Hogshooter.[24] On July 6 Nancy Shell (spelled Schell on the file folder, and cousin of Ned's third wife, Jennie Scraper), a woman indicted previously for selling liquor,[25] testified:

I saw defendant on the evening that Deputy Marshal Maples was killed. He was at my house (about ¼ mile from where Maples was shot). He was alone and not around so far as I know. He stayed but a few minutes when he left going in the direction of where Maples was shot. In a few minutes after he left Ned Grease and Ned Christie came to my house and stayed only a few minutes when they left (I did not notice which way they went) and in about half an hour (around just after dark) I heard shots and in perhaps half an hour I heard from Kate Terrel that a deputy Marshal had been killed. I did not see Hogshooter until the next day. Defendant was sober when at my house the evening of the killing.

Next to testify, sheriff's guardsman Sam Manus, who married Ned's sister Mary:

I live in Tahlequah, Cherokee Nation. I know defendant. I am in the sheriff's force (guard) and was at Tahlequah when Deputy Marshal Dan maples was shot. I met Maples and had short talk with him just after dark. I left him at the telephone office and went into a house. In about fifteen minutes I heard shots and ran up there. I found Maples laying on the ground. Wounded. He told me that he had been shot by a man who spoke in Cherokee then the crowd cumround [sic] to gather and I sent for a doctor. I helped carry him to Dr. Blake's. Maples died the next day. I don't remember whether or not I saw Hogshooter the day of the shooting but ten or fifteen minutes after the shooting I saw him at Turk Vann's house (when we took Maples after he was shot and before we took him to Blake's.) Defendant came [illegible] in a few minutes after we got there with Maples. I saw him at Vann's in company with Charley Bobtail, Ned Grease, John Parris. They left Vann's together. Around [illegible] the same evening I went to Ned Grease's house and there I saw Hogshooter, Charley Bobtail, Ned Grease, Ned Christie, Steve Vann and one [illegible]. I have never had any conversation with defendant about the killing. Ned Christie was the only one that I noticed with arms. Charley Bobtail told me that he knew who did the killing but he did not tell me who it was.

The third person to testify, Tahlequah resident R. S. Gragan, stated:

I know defendant. I live in Tahlequah and was there the day Deputy Marshall Maples was killed. I saw Hogshooter about half hour before sundown the evening Maples as killed. He and Looney Coon were in front of the post office when I first saw him. They were talking and Looney Coon asked me if there were marshals in town. I answered that I did not know. He sayed [*sic*] Hogshooter says there are. Just then two men came along and Looney Coon pointed to them and says, "Yes there they are." Defendant and Looney Coon went in the direction of where Maples was killed. About an hour after that I heard several shots but did not learn until the next morning that any one was killed. I saw defendant about Tahlequah the day after the killing. I never had any talk with him. He doesn't speak English. I don't speak Cherokee.

The final witness, Cull Thorne, had more to say:

I live in Tahlequah, Cherokee Nation. I know defendant. I was in Tahlequah when Deputy Marshal Maples was killed. I heard the shots and within half an hour I went to where he was (right at the creek in the edge of town) and helped carry him to Vann and then to Dr. Blake's. The day of the killing I saw defendant Ned Grease, Ned Christie, Charley Bobtail, [illegible], and Looney Coon together. Looney Coon was around. I did not notice that the others were around. This was about half an hour before the shooting. I left them and went home and very soon I heard shooting an in a very short time I went to where the shooting took place. I did not see anything of defendant that night nor the next day that I remember of. I have never had any talk with him about the killing that I remember of.

E. B. Harris was quick to distance himself from the entire affair, stating that he did not know the defendant, nor did he see him the day of the killing.[26]

No one stated Ned Christie was with John Parris, nor did anyone say that anyone left Shell's home drunk. Because Christie and Parris were in the same vicinity, some writers create the scenario of them as good friends drinking together. Speer even entitles the chapter outlining Maples's death "The Drinking Party." She claims that "Ned likely felt relaxed as he visited with friends on the street. Among them was a man named John Parris." She also writes, "Parris always knew where a drink could be found," and then creates the story that the two men "could be seen heading towards Dog Town."[27] She copied this scenario directly from Steele, who wrote, "That evening Ned and a friend, John Parris, went to the home of Jennie Schell for whiskey. . . . Cherokee Light Horse police questioned her about the crime. She told them that Ned Christie and John Parris, both very drunk, had left her house shortly before the shooting."[28] The woman's name was Nancy, not

Jennie, there is no other source or witness who states that the men were headed toward Dog Town together, and no lighthorseman came forward as a witness. Christie and Parris have not been placed together in any other scenario other than in Steele's and Speer's books.

On the day of that testimony, Bub Trainor's father, Thomas, attempted to kill Sheriff Hawkins in Tahlequah. Thomas hailed from Boston, Massachusetts, and worked as a buggy builder. He sold a variety of wagon components, as well as prisoner shackles, and tools such as crowbars.[29] After drinking heavily for a few days, he ventured into Tahlequah. Witness William Harnage, a local resident, told the *Cherokee Advocate* that around sundown High Sheriff Hawkins shot Trainor dead after Trainor came up behind prison guard Than Wofford and took his pistol from its holster. Trainor then fired at Hawkins, who shot back, perforating Trainor's bowels and a kidney. Trainor lingered in severe pain until the next morning. Prior to his death, he said, "I am sorry, sorry, for all the wrong I have done. Jesus forgive me." The *Indian Journal* frankly stated, "Tom Trainor, a well-known character of Tahlequah, while drunk on Thursday last, attempted to shoot Sheriff Hawkins, and in return received a free pass from the sheriff ta [*sic*] the other world. The pass being a leaden pill from a six shooter." Because Trainor was a white man, Hawkins was arrested, indicted for murder along with Ned Christie's brother-in-law Sam Manus, even though Manus was not present at the killing. After interrogation by Commissioner Tufts at Muskogee, his friends bailed him out with eight thousand dollars, his trial set for December.[30]

The *Advocate* concluded the story by writing, "We had known Tom since we were a boy—and we knew him to be a man of many good qualities and fine sensibilities, and one who, had he never indulged in strong drinking would have been foremost anywhere as an enterprising and public spirited man. We extend our heartfelt sympathy to his bereaved family and deeply regret the deplorable circumstances that led to his taking away."[31] The dismissal of the White man Thomas Trainor as an attempted murderer is important to Ned Christie's story. After Maples's demise, no paper makes the same statement about the Cherokee Christie, a man who exhibited many of the same "good qualities" before his character assassination by newspapers.[32]

Business continued when High Sheriff Hawkins wrote to Chief Bushyhead on July 19 saying he had a warrant for Bub Trainor's arrest, but he wanted to know if he had permission to seize him if he came within five miles of Tahlequah. His deputy George Roach had the warrant but went home without attempting an arrest." Hawkins heard that Bub had left town and, being a cautious man, asked again if he or any of his guard could arrest him.[33] That became a moot point because after hearing the witness testimonies, the grand jury indicted Christie, Bobtail, Parris, and Trainor on July 23, 1887.[34]

Christie continued to stay out of sight. He did not attend the August 22, 1887, National Council meeting; but, the council was amenable to waiting for him and hoped he would arrive the next day by 9:00 A.M. None of the council members, nor Chief Bushyhead, believed him guilty and they were willing to suspend the meeting for him. Christie did not appear that hot Tuesday morning, so the council patiently delayed the meeting for another twenty-four hours. At that time, Chief Bushyhead received a message from Christie stating his intent to resign from his position as councillor. His disappointed colleagues stated that for the sake of "public interest" they would specially appoint a reputable replacement for him, either temporarily or permanently.[35] According to the Cherokee Constitution, no one convicted of a felony "shall be eligible to any office or appointment of honor, profit, or trust within this Nation."[36] Christie had not been convicted of anything and his colleagues, including the chief, did not jump to conclusions. That Christie would blindside a man—and murder him—would be wholly out of character for him and the council members hoped he would emerge from hiding and be exonerated. But, for the sake of the Cherokee Nation, Christie's spot had to be filled.

With Christie in absentia, the council replaced him with William Eubanks, a translator for the tribe and for the *Cherokee Advocate*. He later served as translator with the Dawes Commission, created a shorthand version of Sequoyah's syllabary, studied astronomy, and became a prolific writer on topics such as magnetism, the burning bush, karma, the similarities of Cherokee and Hebrew words, sunspots, and the destructive aspects of allotment, railroads, and missionaries.[37]

Eubanks stepped into a volatile political state within the Cherokee Nation. Amid the furor after Maples's death, crime continued in the tribal nations. The rift between the Nationalists and Progressives escalated and elections for principal chief were set to occur in August. Intratribal factionalism pushed the Maples case to the back burner for a while. Chief Bushyhead and the council were also preoccupied with issues of the Cherokee Strip, whites who tried to gain Cherokee citizenship, land sales, intruder encroachments, and adverse opinions from whites in neighboring areas. Mary Cobb Agnew, who grew up in the Flint District, recalled that "the white people called us barbarians, half-wits, and we couldn't run our own business."[38] For several years, there were too many serious threats to Cherokee sovereignty to worry about, so Christie's name only occasionally appeared in the papers. Christie took advantage of the lack of attention and stayed out of sight with his family at their homeplace.

John Parris confidently appeared in Parker's court October 5, 1887, to proclaim his innocence. He argued that several specific witnesses would corroborate his plea, including Mary Guinn, Josie Schell, and Looney Coon, who would testify that at the time of the shooting Parris stood talking to "some other people" near Guinn's house, which is a quarter of a mile from the shooting site, and after the shooting, he "went on down the road." On February 23, 1888, and again on May 1, 1888, the witnesses were ordered to come to Fort Smith to tell what they knew of John Parris's actions the night of Maples's shooting; but none ever came to Fort Smith on his behalf.[39]

Bobtail, however, stated that Parris killed Maples. There is no document that says Parris pointed the finger at Christie, but later writers insist that he did. In 1937 a Cherokee, Robin Stann, claimed that Parris "turned state's evidence" and swore that Ned killed Maples after the two argued by the spring. This informant claimed that Parris's testimony convinced the courts to focus on Ned.[40] This alleged sworn statement by Parris cannot be located in any court document, but writers continue to use the 1937 interview as fact. Speer fabricates the scenario of Parris appearing at trial on October 5 where he swore that Christie shot Maples. There was, however, no trial on that day, Parris never did go to trial, and there is no record of Parris accusing Christie of the crime. The only event occurring on October 5 is Parris asking for more witnesses.[41]

Papers still needed to publish something about Maples and writers relied on random speculations. The *Indian Chieftain*, for example, published this story in December 1887 about Jackson Christie, a man who was not even in Tahlequah at the time of the shooting:

> Bud [Bub] Trainor is in the United States jail under a series of charges, as follows: Introducing and selling whisky, burning the Oaks post office and being implicated in the killing of Deputy Marshal Maples. It is now positively asserted that Jackson Christie is the man who killed Maples. As reported, Christie was going home drunk and on reaching the creek observed two men on the other side. He drew his pistol but it would not stand cocked and so he fired by holding the hammer and allowing it to slip from under his thumb. The presumption is that he thought he was shooting Jack Manus for whom he held a grudge. Christie is said to be on a scout with Stand Rowe, in Saline District.[42]

Bub Trainor also had witnesses. He claimed on May 11, 1888, that he could not go to trial without the testimony of Nancy Shell, Will Densmore, and Lucy Hicks, all of whom would testify that at the time of the killing he was at Nancy Shell's, one-half mile away, eating supper. As with Parris, there is no paperwork showing that anyone testified for Trainor.[43]

According to numerous sources, Ned wrote a letter sometime in 1887 proclaiming his innocence to Judge Parker at Fort Smith.[44] There is, however, no evidence that Christie wrote anything. Roy Hamilton attempted to locate the elusive letter and when he visited the Fort Smith archives in the 1980s, he was told that the archives possibly had once possessed a copy of said letter, but if they had, the document had since been stolen.[45] Some writers proclaim that Christie's father, Watt, and "several members of the National Council brought pressure on him to surrender and stand trial," but there is no confirmation of that, either.[46] It is unlikely that Ned's Keetoowah family and friends would encourage him to stand trial, especially given how they felt about the federal government.

If Ned did write a letter of denial and spoke to various prominent people about it, those protests were to no avail. The court ordered U.S. marshals Fields and Isabel to find and accost him. Parker would have refused him, as per the March 3, 1885, act that required the court at Fort Smith to have jurisdiction over the crime of murder. The Telephone's assessment of Christie's feelings are a bit theatrical, but close to the truth: "The charge, whether false or true, made Ned Christie an outlaw, for he, like many of his race, looked upon the U.S. Court and 'Aunt Delilah' with a sense of awe, and thought it almost certain death to be arraigned before the Ft. Smith tribunal under such a charge."[47] Fear of being caught and receiving a death sentence is why Ned did not appear at the summer National Council sessions and why he resigned in August.

Ned knew the Cherokee Nation laws and he had learned how criminal cases involving Indians against Indians and Indians against non-Indians were handled. He did not want to face the court of Isaac Parker, the no-nonsense judge who had listened to some of the vilest cases to emerge from Indian Territory. In 1885, Parker stated that seven-eighth of his cases emanated from the territory, including murder, rape, horse theft, whiskey running, and timber rustling.[48] From September 3, 1875, to April 8, 1887, forty-six men had been hanged at Fort Smith under Parker's tenure as judge. These hangings were mentioned in a variety of Indian Territory newspapers and Ned had to be aware of them. If Ned did not read the papers, then someone in his politically active family would have told him.[49]

Isaac C. Parker, judge at Fort Smith. *Noah H. Rose Photo Collection,*
Western History Collections, University of Oklahoma.

Further, Ned knew that even if he eventually was found innocent at Fort
Smith, the ordeal would be almost unbearable. Once a prisoner arrived at
Fort Smith, he faced squalid prison conditions until his trial began. Anna L.
Dawes, the daughter of allotment proponent Henry Dawes, visited Fort Smith
and assessed the stinky and crowded underground cells as "horrible with all
horrors—a veritable hell on earth" and an example of "mediaeval barbarity."
Each cell featured four small windows and a ceiling seven feet high. A veranda
stretching the length of the building prevented sunlight from reaching into the
cells. After the flagstone floors were cleaned in the hot summer, "rising steam
and dampness" compounded the unpleasant stench that arose from the open
urinal tub that was kept in old fireplaces. These were not completely emptied;
rather, the men "honey-dipped" waste from the urinal and deposited that into

an outside pit. Prisoners slept on cots, washed their faces in "slop pots," and only occasionally bathed in a larger barrel.[50] Arkansas attorney William M. Cravens had served in Judge Parker's courtroom and agreed with Dawes's assessment of the prison conditions. He testified to the Committee on Indian Affairs in 1885 that the prisoners were kept directly below the courtroom and during afternoon sessions because "there is a very bad odor there," bad enough to render the Fort Smith courtroom an "abominable place." Cravens asserted that Judge Parker found it "an amusement" to hold court in such a smelly place. Parker sat in attendance and shot back: "The Chairman forgets that I served in the House of Representatives, and it is much better here than there."[51] Anna Dawes accuses the U.S. government of negligence because a U.S. marshal had sent his report detailing the transgressions to Department of Justice in 1884 and nothing had been done to improve the situation. Ned could take care of himself, but the possibility of conflict arose among prisoners. A spectrum of personality disorders, races, and cultures mingled in the cellar. Innocent men, or those accused of minor crimes, were forced to deal with the "wild and ungovernable men around them." Even Judge Parker expressed his concern about young prisoners interacting with aggressive criminals who might influence them.[52]

Many tribal members believed tribal courts to be unbiased and fair and, indeed, many tribal judges and juries were impartial. But, because of the escalating crime rate in Indian Territory after the Civil War, tribal courts became overloaded with cases and some Natives who committed crimes against other Natives were sent to Fort Smith. That, of course, was not ideal because tribes preferred that the United States stay out of their tribal cases. Ned understandably wanted to be tried by his peers, but that may not have worked out the way he wanted because tribal courtrooms were not always impartial. In the Choctaw Nation, for example, political factionalism between Nationalists and Progressives resulted in dozens of decisions going in favor of truly guilty parties because the defendants knew or were related to the jurors and judge.[53]

According to family stories, Ned consulted with his family and fellow Keetoowahs. He especially took to heart the counsel of his brother-in-law Seed Wilson, the husband of his older sister, Rachel. Wilson, a medicine man, performed a three-week ceremony for Christie in the forests of the Illinois District, south of Wauhillau. Fortified by Seed's protection, Ned found new emotional strength. He returned home feeling determined to remain in the Cherokee Nation until his death. "I would rather die at home, in my own Nation, with my people," Ned told Wilson. "I won't die in the white man's country."[54]

Bub Trainor stayed in the news. On October 6, 1887, Trainor, along with John Leach, William Chue, and Joe Miller, were accused of burning the store and house belonging to William Israel, but reports also falsely stated the second owner was L. L. Duckworth. The gang allegedly took keys from a clerk and ran him off, loitered three days in the store, used the horse feed, sold goods, and pocketed the proceeds. Bored, they burned the building, which included an adjoining family dwelling, and shot at the fleeing women and children before setting fire to the stable, crib, and other outbuildings. After that, the men robbed a few passing wagons.[55]

Several papers outside of Indian Territory featured a rousing story about the incident on October 22, 1887. News first emanated from Muskogee, traveled to Little Rock, Arkansas, then to Wewake, Indian Territory, and from there around the country. To say that details became jumbled is an understatement. The *Daily Commonwealth* has the most creative headline: "BATTLE WITH OUTLAWS. Bud Trainer's Gang Attacked by the Vigilantes. The Notorious Outlaw Said to Have Been Slain—Fifteen Killed, Eight of Whom Were Members of the Vigilantes—Full Details of the Desperate Encounter."

According to papers, Trainor's "gang" fought a vigilance committee led by "a Scotch half-breed" named Robert Thompson who followed Trainor from Duckworth's Store to the north fork of the Arkansas River. In rambling descriptions that varied from paper to paper, the "gang" took cover and engaged in much scrambling up and down the riverbanks, hiding behind trees, opening fire, and so forth—"No sooner was a head, arm or any part of a body visible on either side, than a leaden bullet was seeking to find a lodgement therein . . ."—Bill "Chuel" was shot dead, John Leech shot off his horse, and again, depending on the fancy of the writer, between fifteen and thirty men were killed. A "well-to-do stockman" Henry Ayers stated that he believed Trainor was killed. He was not killed, of course, and neither were the other two men. Finishing with a flourish, the paper declared, "Henderson says he will collect 100 men and follow the robbers to Hades if necessary but what he will wipe them out." The jury, however, found Trainor and Miller not guilty. Leach followed in the footsteps of his criminal father, William, whom he watched hang in 1875 for murdering a man and burning his body.[56]

Newspapermen also often disagreed with one another. Elias Cornelius Boudinot, editor of the *Cherokee Advocate*, and supporter of the Christies and other Nationalists, had strong feelings about the 1887 election and took issue with a variety of newsmen who held a pro-Downing, Progressive stance. He became increasingly angry at the editor of the *Tahlequah Telephone*, B. H. Stone, a white man who had worked as a photographer in Tahlequah. Stone started the *Telephone* in June and housed the paper in his photography studio.[57] The stories put forth by Stone were described as "independent and spicy" (that is, gossipy) and Stone made numerous speeches promoting Mayes for chief.[58] On October 21, 1887, Boudinot entered Stone's office, found him reading in his chair, and shot him through the neck. The *Indian Chieftain* claimed that he was found, dead, still holding the papers, but other reports stated that he lived for seven hours and before expiring he told the physicians that Boudinot had shot him.[59] Stone's widow, Emma, despite being "crushed with grief" took over as editor for a few months, then sold the paper to the Telephone Publishing Company. A jury at Fort Smith acquitted Boudinot of murder.[60]

Plenty of other stories about violent activity appeared in Indian Territory papers, including Christie's imagined activities concocted by newsmen. Other than Bushyhead's involvement in the "Letter of Indignation," the Cherokee leadership did not make any statements about Christie's guilt or innocence. The subsequent chief, Joel B. Mayes, did not comment, either.[61] There were reasons for their silence and the commonality is political strategy.

In 1887, the Dawes General Allotment Act was passed by Congress. The Five Tribes, among others, were not included initially and they wanted to keep it that way. Since August 1886, six deputy marshals had been killed in Indian Territory and the federal government took notice.[62] The tribe had no jurisdiction over the Maples case, but all the men who were seen before Judge Parker about Maples's death were Cherokees. Tensions ran high and Cherokees knew it would not be wise for them to publicly discuss a volatile case involving a dead white deputy U.S. marshal at the hands of a resident of the Cherokee Nation. That would lend more credence to arguments posed by those who believed the tribes should be abolished. In addition, that Boudinot, a Cherokee, allegedly shot Stone, a white man, may have provided further impetus to stay quiet. The *St. Louis Post-Dispatch* even predicted how the murder could impact the tribe: "There are those who say the killing of this genial, inoffensive editor will have results which cannot not be estimated. The question of severing tribal relations and opening up the Indian Territory to white settlement will be sharply emphasized by the tragedy. In fact, before the case is finally settled it may become an entering wedge leading to that end."[63]

U.S. Marshal John Carroll wrote to Dennis Bushyhead from Fort Smith on May 11, 1887, less than a week after Maples died, making it clear his concern about law enforcement in the territory. Bushyhead was concerned too, but he also was loath to draw attention to the Cherokee Nation by stating that he supported Christie's innocence. After all, Bushyhead might be mistaken.[64]

Opinions about the looming Cherokee election of 1887 dominated the Letters to the Editor sections of all the newspapers. Bold editors began endorsing political parties and criticizing those they did not agree with. The *Tahlequah Telephone* published its first issue on June 10, 1887, and subsequent issues made clear its bias for the Progressive Party.[65] The Nationalist and Progressive Parties continued their struggle and the *Indian Citizen* referred to the Nationalists as "primitive Cherokees," whereas they found Progressives supported and instigated "advancement in learning and civilization" and the "advent of missionaries and the introduction of schools." It encouraged the passing of the old ways and "the new in all its vigor and imperativeness must be met." Despite the numbers of traditionalists in the Cherokee Nation, notably the Keetoowahs, the *Citizen* asserted that "the primitive Indian is almost gone, and what is left of him is being force-marched into the ranks of a higher civilization, or perish. Best 'let the dead bury the dead,' because the concerns of each generation are not of the past. The way is where progress leads."[66]

The Keetoowahs, including the Christies, did not agree and continued to make their concerns known about tribal affairs. The *Indian Chieftain* published a short article about the "laws" passed by the Keetoowahs, supporters of the National ticket, in the 1887 election. The paper claimed that the National Party was making "a strong effort to place under foot the different parties, the first of which is the Downing Party, and second the adopted white citizens and third who in the late war went south and north, [fourth] the negro, and fifth the Delawares and Shawnees." The Keetoowahs wanted "nothing to do with them whatever" and if any Keetoowah was charged with a crime they said they would do "everything in [their] power to have him cleared," and conversely, they would "do everything in [their] power" to have anyone outside the party convicted.[67] This certainly meant Ned Christie. Once again, Bushyhead had no desire to bring that combative rhetoric to a wider audience. Tribes in the Indian Territory were not in a position to interfere with the federal court at Fort Smith. If Nede Wade Christie had been accused of murder, the tribal leadership had best stay silent lest federal officials believe that Cherokees could not live together peacefully.

Finally, the tribal leadership could not offer opinions on the shooting, mainly because they simply did not have enough information to make informed commentary. They listened to myriad voices about who could have killed Maples, but nothing seemed to be clear-cut after his death and it took months before witnesses testified at Fort Smith. Instead, residents gossiped, speculated, and imagined scenarios. Because Christie refused to show up to face Parker and tell his side of the story, countless newspapers and residents of Indian Territory and the surrounding areas began to suspect that, if he would not go to Fort Smith to defend himself, he might be guilty. Unfortunately for Christie, the most colorful of the tabloid stories made their way across the country via newspapers and were interpreted as fact.

Bobtail, Parris, and Trainor soon faded as suspects and Christie, the only man not to show his face in court, became a target. However, there were other reasons why those two men were allowed to go on their way. Bub Trainor was one-sixteenth Cherokee blood. His father, Thomas, was white and his mother, Lucy, served as a courier for the Confederate Cherokees during the Civil War. Even though Thomas attempted to kill a sheriff, people liked him so much that they were not only willing to forgive that transgression, they also decided to ignore the possibility that his errant son Bub may have killed Deputy Marshal Maples. In October 1887, the *Arkansas Gazette* quotes the Fort Smith correspondence by attempting to defend Trainor. "Bud Trainer has never been the leader of any gang, and has probably never had any associates since he became a fugitive from justice . . . [His] career as an outlaw dates back only to March last." The story recounts how Marshal Ellis attempted to arrest Trainor for selling whiskey, but then he got shot instead. Thinking the wound fatal, Ellis left the area, but then the young Trainor escaped, a "fugitive from justice . . . associating, however, with men of bad morals." Despite the paper acknowledging that Trainor and two friends burned Duckworth's Store, they "have never been pursued by anybody" yet "ought to be in jail." Ultimately, the only charge against him "since the killing of Maples is the Duckworth Store burning" and the paper reiterated that Trainor was a mere boy. The paper also brings up his father, Thomas Trainor, again, pointing out that he served in the regular army, mustering at Fort Gibson, then married a Cherokee and became a Cherokee Nation citizen.[68] Contrast this analysis with the beating Christie's reputation would undergo from newspapers. Ned had fewer charges against him; but he was an outspoken Keetoowah and Nationalist. There is no record of the Trainor family criticizing the government or Cherokee entities with political power.

John Parris did not offer political opinions, either. As time went by, it appears that Parris simply faded away because there is no more mention of him in the papers. He left Indian Territory at least by the time of Christie's death and he disappeared from the record.

The *Fort Worth Daily Gazette*, supposedly quoting a news story from Fort Smith (that cannot be located) stated in late November 1887 that Trainor accused Christie of killing Maples and that "Christie does not deny the charge but on the contrary admits it to his friends and says he does not propose to surrender."[69] There is no other evidence that Christie said that to anyone except for claims made of imaginative elderly Oklahoma residents in 1937. Ultimately, it did not matter if Christie said it or not. The papers said he did and that made it so.

Christie would not willingly go with marshals and he would have to live with that choice. Until his death, Christie and his family felt constant disquiet, wondering when lawmen might emerge from the thick tree line that bordered their land. Their anxiety increased on Christmas day 1887 when a traveler found sixteen-year-old George Grease, the son of Ned's uncle Nede Grease and a first cousin once removed from his wife, Nancy, frozen to death four miles from Tahlequah. The paper described George as "good and industrious." It postulated that Greece [Grease] had been murdered by someone who "has that poisonous stuff which is sold for whiskey. That person is as much responsible for this death as if he had shot him."[70] George's death was a portent of things to come for the Christie family.

Dramatic newspaper stories about Christie continued to appear. In mid-January 1889, after an unknown person was shot dead on Jesse Pigeon's place on Caney Creek, newspapers stated that Christie did the killing.[71] In March 1889, papers reported that Zeke Proctor and a man named England killed Christie, but also admitted "we can give no particulars—nobody seems to know anything about it."[72] The *Fort Smith Elevator* followed up the report nine days later by opining that "if Ned has been monkeying around Zeke Proctor it would not surprise us if the rumor was correct."[73] Often, papers took stories from other papers but delayed in reporting them. A Chicago paper referred to Proctor as "a notorious Cherokee desperado" who was taken to Saint Louis in September 1887 and charged with murder. The paper described him as "a ring leader among a band of murderers living in Goingsnake District and was at the head of the Indians in their bloody battle with deputy marshals 15 years ago."[74] Just a year earlier, however, the *Cherokee Advocate* once again mentioned that Proctor had come to town to visit in January, and received "warm greetings from his numerous friends."[75] In the early summer of 1889, the *Fort Smith Elevator* for a second time reported that Christie and Jesse Pigeon were involved in a murder, although the paper did not report who had died.[76]

Ned was not the only Christie in a bind. His half-brother William, who had been arrested a few years prior for whiskey peddling, sentenced to jail at Fort

Smith in 1885, and acquitted of the murder of Wyrick, now faced yet another trial in a Cherokee court for murdering Robert Walker near Tanksley's Store. William also allegedly shot off the crown of John Blair's hat.[77] William had a preliminary examination before the district clerk, Allen Ross, and then stood trial with associate justice Roach Young trying the case.[78] Interestingly, Roach Young's mother was Betsy Christie. She was William's cousin and the daughter of Arch Christie (Watt's brother), making the judge the cousin of the accused.[79] Arguments of both the defense and prosecution were so convoluted that the *Cherokee Advocate* described the attorneys as "tearing into each other's testimony, rendering them into pieces," with the result being a "Scotch." The jurors could not make their way through the "tangle" of closing remarks. After spending a night and half a day "trying to unravel it," William was acquitted. The *Advocate* also bemoaned the state of the territory: "The case grew out of the soil so fertile everywhere of 'sorrow and wounds we cause'—whiskey." Indeed, even though the Cherokee Nation passed laws against selling whiskey, numerous whites and Indians profited from selling liquor across the Indian Territory line.[80]

Stories such as these persisted, the disagreements between the Nationals and Progressives continued, and more intruders poured into the tribal nations. All these happenings were not stirring enough for the *Indian Chieftain* whose editor proclaimed, "Times are awfully dull just now—no weddings and no fights."[81]

The *Indian Chieftain* could not have been more wrong.

. . . .

CHAPTER 4

ON THE RUN

Several deputies have bit the dust on account of a
too great desire to effect his capture.

ARKANSAS GAZETTE, November 5, 1892

The *Indian Chieftain* may have assessed the Cherokee Nation as "dull" in September 1889 because it could find nothing to dish about, but Ned lived anything but a mundane life. He lived at his home with his family and went about his many daily chores, but unease continued to build. Nancy, Albert, and Ned kept constant watch for lawmen as they gardened, made home repairs, and cared for the horses, cows, and chickens. He still had no intention of traveling to Fort Smith. Because he dodged Judge Parker, a third indictment was written in May 1889 with an order for his appearance on September 26, 1889.[1] A $500 reward had been raised for his "capture," a term that often meant "kill."[2]

Newsmen were aware of the growing interest in the Maples case, so they revved up their stories, and theories about who killed Maples appeared with more frequency. The *Indian Chieftain* speculated with no details that "Christie is the man who is supposed to have killed Marshal Maples, a couple of years ago, though there is hardly a doubt but he mistook him for High Sheriff Hawkins, who he was lying in wait for."[3] The paper gave no rationale as to why Ned would have tried to kill the man he knew and who bought his garden produce.

Crime continued to escalate. Many were preoccupied with the Maples murder in Tahlequah while other disturbing events took place in the Cherokee Nation. Unfortunately for Ned, it involved the Christie family. In the Flint District, a group of men became drunk on buckeye whiskey, what the *Cherokee Advocate* called "a kind of patent stuff expressly prepared, in the State of Arkansas, for the trade of the Indian Territory and for the sure destruction of its people." Ned's

Ned Christie, c. 1889. *Northeastern State University, Tahlequah, Oklahoma.*

second cousins, Jim and French Christie, and cousin John Blair got into a "shooting affray." According to the paper, Jim Christie shot his first cousin Blair in the leg and Blair retaliated by shooting Jim in the head, killing him. French Christie was also shot in the arm.[4] Blair escaped from jail in late June.[5] In January, Bill Christie shot and killed a man named Bob Walker "near Tank[s]ley's store on the Caney" and Blair who accompanied Walker, had his hat shot off."[6] A week later, the *Indian Chieftain* reported that Blair had been ambushed, probably by Bill Christie. The paper offered that "in all probability he won't need any more shooting for this is said to be fatal." Like many news stories, these items were merely snippets, with no details. That paper then tells us on May 10 that Blair "yet lingers along, and may get well, for he is now under the medical (or rather conjuration) treatment of a noted Cherokee conjurer."[7]

Ned's gun display at Fort Smith. *Photo by author.*

Ned decided to have his picture taken in 1889. Some claim that the rifle he props up on the chair was his and is the same weapon on display at the Fort Smith National Historic Site museum. The rifle he holds, however, is a 24-inch barreled rifle. The rifle on display at Fort Smith is a carbine, four inches shorter, and may not be Christie's, despite the engraving in Cherokee that spells his name on the stock.[8]

Regardless of whose weapons these are in the photos, no one really knows for sure what Christie had in mind while posing. Christie may have thought it important to deliver the message that he planned to defend himself from lawmen's advances. The photograph was not published in newspapers and McKennon states it appeared for the first time in his *Iron Men.* The original picture was last in possession of Aubie Camp Ellis, widow of William "Bill" Ellis, one of the possemen who killed Christie in 1892. Nancy, Ned's widow who later married Ned's brother Jack, had two sons, John and Charley, who told other family members that after the home was dynamited, Ellis took Christie's original picture from the ruined house and Ellis's wife, Aubie, kept it. She lived in Wetumpka, a town in the Creek Nation, until her death in 1965. The city paid for her burial in Antlers, Oklahoma, and auctioned her possessions. Roy Hamilton attempted to track down the original photograph in the 1980s, but discovered while visiting the funeral home that Aubie Ellis had no living family. A woman at the county clerk's office told Roy that housecleaners threw away all of her pictures.[9] Regardless of what Christie intended, the picture has been interpreted by fans of outlaw history as aggressive and challenging.

Even with unknown people intent on catching or killing Ned, he remained alert and thoughtful. True to their word about doing "everything in our power to have him [a fellow Keetoowah] cleared," members of the Keetoowah Society helped Ned watch for posses, although they could not do so every day and night. Ned continued to spend his time hunting, drying meats, and keeping his land clear of unwanted brush, while at the same time keeping one eye out for intruders. Nancy managed their garden and sewed clothes and quilts, so many that her fingers often bled. They had several milk cows, a few riding horses, and two oxen for plowing. Nancy continued to make money by selling their vegetables and eggs.[10] The Christie family remained basically self-sufficient except for purchasing items from Levi Keys's nearby store, especially in winter months when food was scarce. They had four black and tan watchdogs that looked like hounds. Roy Hamilton received one of the canine descendants. He christened the tailless dog "Bob" and Bob lived to be twenty-three years old.[11]

In 1969, Jack Kilpatrick quoted from a ledger written by a resident of the Cookson Hills who might have known someone who spent time with Ned and Nancy:

> They say that he used to cook cornbread in his fireplace all the time. In cooking cornbread, he put it into a big pot which had a lid; and to cook it put fire on top of the lid. He also had dried squirrels, and he pounded up these dried squirrels in a wooden mortar. He put the big pot upon the fire and put cornmeal and water into it. Then he added the squirrels to this, and when all was well done, it became delicious to eat. And he also put sweet potatoes into the fireplace and covered them over with fire, and he also cooked peas. He himself, the late Ned Christie, was the cook.[12]

Pounding dried squirrels is a common way to prepare them. Apaches and Chippewas often caught rabbits and squirrels, singed off their hair, dried and pounded them, bones and all, for a nutritious dish.[13]

Other Christies also went on with their lives, although they worried about Ned. His father, Watt, stayed politically active and had been nominated for the Grand Council of the National Party, and brothers Goback and Jack continued with their metal and gunsmithing.[14] While Ned spent precious time with his family at home, papers claimed that Christie had embarked on a bootleg whiskey business. Although Ned and Nancy worked hard to maintain their home and to find enough resources, in winter he found it necessary to find another way to ensure that his family would have enough food and supplies, just like his relation Nancy Shell did.[15] Hundreds of other Indian Territory residents tried selling whiskey, from just a few bottles here and there to dealing in entire wagonloads of liquor. Other than Wild West writers' claims that selling booze was a mainstay of Christie's livelihood, there is no other documentation that proves the former Cherokee councilman embarked on anything besides a small-scale side business.

That did not stop papers from rationalizing why Christie had an encounter with Bear Grimmett. The *Dallas Morning News* reported that in February 1888, Ned planned to pick up a shipment of whiskey that arrived by train, but a Cherokee named Bear Grimmett got there first. Grimmett took Christie's delivery and Ned found out about it. So he, along with his cousin's husband, Joe Eagle, set out to find Grimmett and reclaim Christie's cargo. Ned did just that, but Grimmett somehow ended up dead. The paper claimed that Bear Grimmett had threatened Christie, whom the paper described as the "noted desperado" and "head of a gang of ruffianly outlaws." The paper stated that Christie "hunted down" Grimmett to Sallisaw River in the Flint District and "tore his head off" with a load of buckshot.[16] Other papers added more spin, that Christie, "the leader of a gang of desperadoes," and an "outlaw chief," shot and killed Bear Grimmett because Grimmett "was in possession of information which would criminate the gang and they went gunning for him."[17] A few days later, however, an account read that Joe Eagle killed Grimmett.[18]

Because the parties were Cherokees, a preliminary hearing convened in a Cherokee court in an attempt to ascertain who killed Grimmett. Men who rode with Grimmett were Saddle Blanket and Rat Panther, while Ned was accompanied by Joe Eagle, Jess Pigeon, Taylor Christie (Ned's second cousin), Bill Blair, George Lanahheate, and Jess Pigeon, one of the signers of the letter drafted at the indignation meeting in May 1887 and a sometime guard at the national prison.[19]

Saddle Blanket testified first, stating that Pigeon and Lanahheate had ridden in on the same horse and stayed about twenty steps away from the fray. "Joe Eagle shot Grimmett twice and Ned Christie helped." He watched as Grimmett fell after "he got down to fix his stirrup leather and they shot him in the back," then he turned and ran, but as he ran he heard one of them say, "Go kill Saddle Blanket too." From his perspective, Pigeon and Lanahheate did not "do anything at all." Rat Panther stated that he only knew Taylor Christie and Bill Blair and that he did not see either of them do anything, either. He saw the weapon ("about three feet long") yet inexplicably could not say who was holding it. Ellen Scott, who lived close to the site of the shooting, testified that she heard the shots, then saw Taylor Christie, Pigeon, and Blair "leaving there" and then she heard more shots. Her children were making "such as fuss" that she could not hear what was being said at the shooting site.

Next up, Jess Pigeon stated that Bear and Eagle "shot about the same time," then he watched as Blair and Taylor Christie ran from the shooting site, followed by Saddle Blanket and another man he did not know. Pigeon twirled his horse to run and George Lanahheate fell off the back. When asked where Christie stood, he answered that Christie stayed where Bear was shot, next to the man "that I did not know that run off that Ned was standing by."

Taylor Christie said that he and Blair approached from Sallisaw Road and encountered Saddle Blanket "and his crowd," and then Christie and Joe Eagle rode up. Christie passed by to meet with Rat Panther and Grimmett. Eagle said, "Good morning friends." Grimmett got off his horse and Eagle "rode sorter around across the road and stayed." Taylor stated he looked away, shots were fired, and then he looked back and saw Grimmett on the ground on his left elbow with his pistol in his right hand. At that point Taylor and Blair ran off. Taylor also stated that he did not see Christie shoot. Bill Blair stated that he watched Joe Eagle shoot Grimmett and that Christie was standing there at the time, but he did not see Christie shoot, either.

The last person to testify, Peter Bird, stated that he heard of the killing while at the local home of Lucy Pritchets. Prior to his arrival, the women at the house saw Ned Christie, Joe Eagle, Jess Pigeon, and George Dananheate. As Taylor Christie and Bill Blair passed, Taylor said, "Them fellows going on there have done very bad they have killed Bare Grimmet [Bear Grimmett]." He then said that Jess Pigeon told him he saw Joe Eagle shoot Grimmett twice. On March 30, 1888, the preliminary court convened and sought an indictment for Ned Christie, Joe Eagle, and George Dick in the murder of Grimmett and on March 30 sought an indictment against Taylor Christie, Blair, and Pigeon.[20] There is no more mention of this incident, so presumably Christie escaped conviction.

Speer and other writers assert that around this time, Bub Trainor became a deputy U.S. marshal. She writes, "Shortly after his release from jail, a seemingly strange thing occurred: Trainor was hired as a deputy U.S. marshal by the Fort Smith Court." There is, however, no proof that Trainor became a lawman. Her claim comes from Shirley's book, *Law West of Fort Smith*, which cites newspaper sources that read Jim July (Jim Starr) had been indicted for horse theft, not that Trainor became a deputy marshal.[21] Renegade Jim Starr, also known as Jim July in the Creek Nation, had committed a string of misdeeds, from horse theft in 1887 to an 1889 train robbery at Berwyn. Starr may be best known as a lover of Belle Starr. The *Fort Smith Elevator* stated that he could speak "nearly all the different Indian languages," a rather dubious accomplishment.[22] Starr's bondsman Mershon offered a reward for his capture because Starr did not appear in court and his bond therefore was forfeited. Starr found his way back to Ardmore, however, and Mershon withdrew the reward, but the ever-eager Bub Trainor, with accomplice Bob Hutchins, shot Starr. Trainor and Hutchins were subsequently arrested. After being shot, Starr sent Mershon a telegram: "I filled the bond and sent it to you and was fixing to come. Can prove name. If I die have Trainor and Hutchins tried for murder. They shot me foul." Starr lay suffering until he finally died then was buried in the local potter's field.[23]

Anderson and Yadon write in their *100 Oklahoma Gangsters, Outlaws, and Lawmen* that "Bud found himself fully qualified to become a deputy U.S. marshal on December 31, 1888, with Clem Rogers, father of entertainer Will Rogers, serving as bondsman for the position."[24] Not surprisingly, they used Bonnie Speer's book, *The Killing of Ned Christie*, which cited Shirley's *Law West of Fort Smith*. The cyclical problem here is that Anderson and Yadon misrepresent Speer, who also misrepresents her sources.[25] There is no other mention of Trainor tracking down Christie. Judge Parker was no fool. Bub Trainor had proven himself repeatedly to be violent and impulsive. Trainor did not participate in any attack on Christie's home, nor did he assist the lawmen who did.[26]

There are many stories that portray Christie as a thief. Catherine Wilhite's uncle, Levi Keys, owned the Wauhillau trading post, the same store frequented by Christie and his wife, Nancy. Forty-five years after Christie's death, Lucinda Sanders Wilhite, a niece of Keys, makes the doubtful statement in an interview titled, "The Cherokee Outlaw," that Christie "used to come here and rob the store." Lucida claimed that Christie even asked Levi Keys if he could hide in the loft but Keys turned him down. Another niece, Catherine Wilhite, related that Christie and his unnamed partners used an axe to destroy the store door. But not just any door: her uncle had created a heavy door, "made cross ways" because Christie had a habit of robbing this particular establishment. Once when her father heard Christie chopping at the door, he came running with his Winchester. "Old man" Duckworth came with him, holding his "long old rifle." Presumably they were outside when they heard the noise because her next statement is "they hid in a thicket." Meanwhile, her Aunt Lucinda arrived and they all went into the store after they managed to push aside the damaged door. Standing inside of the store was "the Christie bunch." She does not say what happened afterward and there is no explanation as to why she and the others entered the building if they knew Christie was inside. Regardless, there is no more to that story other than her claims that her father could have shot them and did not and, whenever Christie and his "bunch" heard that a marshal was headed toward his "fort," they would "ride into town" to avoid them.[27]

It is unlikely that Christie would rob a store a mile from his home, return to his house where everyone in the vicinity knew was located with his booty, then not expect someone to come and accuse him of thievery. In contrast to the assertions made by Keys's niece, Ned's descendants say he regularly traded at Levi Keys's place and had no reason to rob it.[28] Keys was acquainted with Duckworth, owner of the property destroyed by Miller. It is more likely the women heard stories about that store burned by Miller and in their later years confused the two.

On Tuesday, May 28, 1889, after campaigning for support for his appointment as U.S. marshal, the Honorable Jacob Yoes was named just that: U.S. marshal for the Western District of Arkansas under Judge Isaac Parker. He preferred to retain the deputies of the Honorable John Carroll, his predecessor: Tyner Hughes, Jim Lee, and Charles Barnhill. R. B. Creekmore of Van Buren took the position of second chief deputy, along with Heck Thomas. Both men, prominent in western outlaw lore, would meet Ned Christie several times.[29] Barnhill played a prominent role in capturing Jackson Crow, the Choctaw freedman who was hanged in 1889 for the murder of Choctaw Nationalist and former lighthorseman Charles Wilson. Another appointed officer who met Christie was R. B. Creekmore of Van Buren, who took over the position of second chief deputy from James Pettigrew.[30]

Yoes was a native Arkansan, the eldest of six children. His family lived on a farm close to the West Fork of the White River in Washington County. He and his wife, Mary A. Reed, produced eleven children. Prior to his career in law enforcement Yoes worked as a farmer, then enlisted in the Company D, First Arkansas

Deputy U.S. Marshal Henry "Heck" Thomas. *Frederick S. Barde Collection, Oklahoma Historical Society.*

Union Cavalry. He was shot in both hips during the 1863 Battle of Prairie Grove and imprisoned at Van Buren. He was commissioned as a first lieutenant but refused the appointment. The well-liked Republican Yoes was elected Washington County sheriff, a representative in the state legislature, and served as a census taker. Yoes also brought in income from his various stores in Graphic, Mountainburg, Walker Switch, West Fork, and Woolsey Switch.[31]

Another player in the Christie story is Heck Thomas, the subject of numerous Wild West books, essays, and far-fetched stories. It is true that Thomas served in the Civil War as the courier of his uncle General Lloyd Thomas. In 1867 he served as the youngest in the Atlanta police force and during the Brush Arbor Riot suffered his first bullet wound. Thomas then moved to Texas as an express messenger and was involved in capturing gangs led by Sam Bass and Jim and Pink Lee. In

Glenn Shirley's fanciful expose on Thomas, *Heck Thomas, Frontier Marshal: The Story of a Real Gunfighter*, the imaginative Shirley describes Thomas as so perceptive that he could size up a captive in a couple of days and decide if that person should be kept in chains or be trusted to wander freely in camp. Along with his almost Superman-like ability to capture and retain outlaws, Thomas always has with him a "daredevil crew." Shirley describes how in one sojourn through the San Bois Creek area of the northern Choctaw Nation to find a gang of outlaws, Thomas trekked through what is in reality a heavily forested landscape crossed with waterways. Shirley instead changes the environment, stating that the area teemed with "prairie dogs and rattlesnakes," which served as his closest neighbors, and that any Indian he encountered "made signs and grunted."[32]

Thomas no doubt experienced an active and dangerous career. The *Daily Oklahoman* described him as "one of the most fearless and successful deputy marshals and one of the "best dressed, 'dudish' men in the country," as well as "genial, harmless and likeable" in his older age.[33] Helen Churchill Candee wrote about Thomas in 1900, describing him thus: "Equipped for the pursuit, he was a thrilling sight, two yards of supple strength furnished like an armory, and swaying easily on a swift-footed mount."[34]

In mid-September an attempt was made to capture Christie, but when the posse approached his home they reconsidered and retreated to wait for reinforcements.[35] Then on Thursday, September 26, 1889, before dawn, Heck Thomas and L. P. Isbell, along with three men approached Ned's house and drew closer until Christie's dogs raised the alarm. One of the posse members yelled at Christie to surrender. The posse heard him climb to his attic where he removed a plank from his loft and fired. They asked again and got the same response. Thomas then set an outbuilding afire while the others hid behind trees. Each posse member took cover behind large oak trees, although Marshal Isbell moved enough for Christie to hit his shoulder, resulting in a "crippling injury."[36] A figure bolted from the house. Thomas thought it was Christie and commenced firing, hitting the individual at least once. That person was "Little Arch" Wolfe, the son of Ned's cousin Betsy, and who often is referred to as Ned's son (and also known as "Walkabout"). Meanwhile Isbell's condition deteriorated and it took almost seven hours to get him back to Tahlequah. After weeks of recuperation, he was transported by his family by train to recover in their home in Vinita.[37] Little Arch had been shot "cat-a-cornedly from back to front through his right lung."[38] The lawmen did not immediately realize that Christie had been hit in the face.

In the aftermath of the September attack, papers picked up on the story, but not all of them got their facts straight. Some, like the *Indian Journal*, stated, "Ned Christie, a desperate outlaw and slayer of Deputy United States Marshal Maple [Maples] over a year ago, was killed early this morning."[39] On September 27, 1889, reporters in Tahlequah sent out a news release that Ned, "a desperate outlaw," has been shot and killed by deputy U.S. marshals.[40] Another report stated that Ned was found in the burning house with a "bullet hole between the two eyes, though not dead. . . . He was removed from the house and the supposition is that he died."[41] And one even reported that "Mrs. Christie, wife of Ned Christie, whose house and contents were recently destroyed by fire in an attempt to arrest Christie, died one day last week at her father's house in Wauhilla."[42] This was, of course, untrue since Nancy died in 1921.

The *Cherokee Advocate* voiced incredulity that the officers purposefully shot Arch. The paper admonished readers who believed the posse did have warrant to shoot that, "after warning women and children from the house, the officers could not have purposely shot at a child, knowing him to be a child, when he was leaping through smoke and brush at a considerable distance from the firing party." The paper stated that the officers did not know about the boy's or Christie's injuries until they were told by the mail carrier, who had delivered mail to Ned's father's home where Christie lay recovering.[43] Given the possemen's enthusiasm at getting Arch convicted after Ned's death in 1892, it actually is easy to believe they willfully shot at him in 1889.

Reports varied about the extent of Christie's injury. Residents also chimed in. One recalled years later that "as Ned was shooting from his attic window a bullet entered his mouth and came out through the back of his neck. A few days later I asked Ned if that shot wasn't very painful. He replied, 'No, like a bee sting.'"[44] Saugee Grigsby's version is that Ned was so anxious to kill as many men as he could that he tried to run away and was shot "through his nose."[45] Eli Wilson, who claims he knew Christie well, stated forty-eight years after Christie was wounded, that Christie had been shot "right at the upper end of his nose . . . and the bullet stopped at the back of his head just inside the outer skin. You could feel the bullet rolling around loose inside of the skin."[46] Yet another sensational story asserts that the bullet hit the bridge of his nose, "then angled in such a crazy manner that it destroyed the right eyeball and smashed through the thick brow bone, finally lodging above his temple." This article states that the bullet not only caused "grotesque facial features," it also caused him to never again speak English. It further asserted that the attack and injury caused a dramatic personality alteration: he became vicious and driven by hatred of all white men.[47] McKennon, in his never-ending collection of vignettes, asserts that "Ned Christie had been a man extremely proud of his dark and fierce good looks. The disfigurement affected him deeply, and he swore a mighty oath to never again speak the English language."[48] There were at least five men who arrived to try and accost Christie and any of them might have been the ones who shot him, yet because of Heck Thomas's stature in the annals of outlaw lore, he is the one given credit for the facial injury: "Then, as Christie tried to run for it in the dark, Thomas nailed him with a rifle shot that tore out the handsome Indian's right eye and ripped his face."[49]

Ned was not blinded; in fact, he could see out of the eye although the shooting left his vision a bit blurry and for the next few years the vision improved. Nor did he look deformed and certainly not "grotesque." He received treatment from his brother Goback (who the *Fort Smith Elevator* called an "Ingin doctor") as well as the white physician Nicolas Bitting, who owned the local mill.[50]

Indian Territory resident Eli Wilson claimed in 1937 that he knew Christie's strategy, which was to stop firing so the posse members would assume he was dead. After they came close to investigate, he would "open up with the best sharp shooting and mow down a bunch." There have, however, been no other reports of Ned shooting horses nor of him having mowed down anyone. Wilson said that Christie just had to kill one or two men, or to seriously wound one or two, and the rest always made an excuse to leave. Wilson said Christie told him that he would peep through some hole in his log house and watch them loading the men into wagons to haul them away. Christie allegedly told Wilson that nearly every time they were loading the dead people in their wagons they got rather careless about staying behind trees and he could have killed two or three more of them easily.[51] This is a gross exaggeration because in the five years after Maples's death, only four men were injured during the sieges on Ned's properties. No "dead people" were loaded into wagons.

The *Weekly Elevator* published an article after the attack on Ned's home about the difficulties deputy marshals faced. The article discussed the lengthy trips the marshals made, the "long rides, hard living and much expense," and the extravagant expenses the marshals were forced to pay. According to the paper, some citizens wondered why they expended so much energy on "light cases." Chasing "big game" took much time and money they did not have. The paper urged Congress to adequately pay the underpaid and overworked deputy marshals for their work and when wounded or sick, and to deliver pensions to their widows and orphans. After this failed effort to capture Christie, Fort Smith issued a third indictment. By that time a $500 reward had been raised.[52]

"Ned's Mountain." Looking north, his lookout was situated at the top of
North 4630 Road off to the left in the trees. There are no "steep walls" for the "fort"
to have leaned against, as reported in Wild West literature. *Photo by author.*

Christie did not want to leave the vicinity where he grew up, so he constructed
a new house of double logs on the west side of Bitting Creek next to Thornton
Spring, about eleven miles east of Tahlequah; specifically, "100 yards north of
Luther Worley's barn."[53] Ned used a steam engine and boiler that was mounted
on cast-iron wheels to construct the fortified home of double logs, which had
with portholes on every side. Today, the home is gone, and there are no pictures
of it, but there are several accounts about its structure. One man asserts it mea-
sured 20 x 20 feet, featuring a trapdoor that led to his underground access out
of the home, along with a 10x10-inch window that he used as lookout. A mile to
the east he constructed a rock lookout that some referred to as "Ned's Fort" with
the hill it stood on, "Ned's Mountain."[54] If one goes to that site, it is obvious that
the view does not afford complete panoramic views of the surrounding countryside. At that time, trees would have obscured a 360-degree view and, at only
around eight hundred feet above sea level, it is not a "mountain." Nor is there a
"canyon" in the vicinity, as suggested by Pride in his sensational recounting of
Christie's demise in "The Battle of Tahlequah Canyon."[55] The structure was not
really a "fort" nor was it a "stronghold." It was a small stone structure measuring
approximately 10 x 10 feet with six-foot-high walls with portholes.[56] The *Omaha
Daily Bee* incorrectly asserted that Christie built not just one but two forts, each

with panoramic views and situated in a manner as to "create a cross-fire effect in the only approachable route."[57]

McKennon writes in his sensationalistic *Iron Men* (1967) that after the siege on his home in 1889, Christie sent "an Indian boy" to the *Cherokee Advocate* office with a gloating message: "I thought I saw a big, black potato bug in my garden but it turned out to be the hat of that 'little marshal'-Dave Rusk!"[58] This is a fabrication because Marshal Rusk did not participate in any attack on Christie until the final siege in November 1892. On June 2, however, deputies Joe Bowden and Milo Creekmore did attempt a sortie against Ned, but realized they were outmatched and quickly retreated.[59]

The Christie name had already appeared in stories about robberies and murders and writers linked them to Ned without checking relationships. In 1891, Sam Hickory and Tom Shade murdered deputy marshal Joseph Wilson. Shade got caught but Hickory remained at large. Newspapers reported that Hickory probably "joined the famous outlaw, Ned Christie, and others."[60] After the murders of Josiah Poorboy and Thomas Whitehead, that paper's assertion was perpetuated by John Brown, "who has for a number of years scouted with the noted outlaw, Ned Christie."[61]

McKennon also wrote that Dave Rusk moved his family to Joplin, Missouri, for safekeeping, "with the enmity of Christie at a high point." While Rusk was away, he left his store in the small community of Oaks in the charge of William Israel. As Israel went about his daily routine, "a number of horsemen galloped up" and dismounted, except for Christie who brazenly "rode his horse right through the front door and into the store building." Christie held Israel at gunpoint while the other men ransacked the store. Then, using tar from a barrel used for roof repairs, the gang proceeded to "tar and feather the unfortunate clerk, forcing huge quantities of raw, frontier whiskey down his throat during the process." Then the outlaws chased Israel into the woods, firing after him, and set Rusk's store afire.[62] According to Kirchner, who obviously uses McKennon's story for his book *The Deadliest Men*, "The raid made Christie one of the Old West's most wanted outlaws." Kirchner, however, adds in his version that the wayward gang included Arch Wolfe and the motivation for this behavior was their anger that Israel would work for Deputy Marshal Rusk.[63] There is no other report about Christie traveling to Rusk's store. Oaks is approximately thirty-five miles from Wauhillau and considering Christie's concern about his home and family, it is unlikely that he would expend the effort to ride seventy miles round-trip, much less to haul "huge quantities" of liquor, just to torture Dave Rusk.

Apparently, the inspiration for this yarn is the aforementioned court case involving Bub Trainor, Joe Miller, and John Leach, who in October 1887 were accused of setting fire to the Duckworth Store.[64] The charge made against the three men was dramatic: "feloniously, willfully and maliciously set fire to, and the same house then and there, by such firing as aforesaid feloniously willfully and maliciously did burn."[65] Like many other writers, McKennon had no qualms about purposely changing the names and context of exciting yet unrelated events in order to portray Christie in a negative light.

Phillip Rand had a different story to tell about Christie's months prior to his death. He stated that on September 5, 1892, Christie and "his band of cutthroats" rode into the town of "Prairie Groce, Arkansas." They shot and killed fourteen men, women, and children and robbed the bank of $22,000. "Irate citizens" formed a posse, but Christie fled into the "box canyons north of Tahlequah, where it was almost impossible to find him."[66] There is no "Prairie Groce," but there is Prairie Grove. Still, there are no records of Christie visiting Arkansas during this time and at no point did any "posse of irate citizens" attempt to find Christie.

Christie's name appeared in seemingly unconnected cases. In June 1888, Calvin and Albert Scraper were tried for assault with intent to kill John Stover, a man who was serving a sentence for killing another member of the Scraper family, but they were acquitted.[67] The unreliable *Muskogee Phoenix* stated on December 31, 1891, that the son of Honorable Arch Scraper, Albert Scraper, had been murdered Saturday, December 26.[68] In April 1891, Goingsnake sheriff Thomas J. Welch wrote to Chief Harris expressing his frustration over the complaints that Welch had not looked hard enough for the killer of Arch Scraper, son of Judge Scraper. He concluded his letter by adding, "Ned Christy lives in this Dist but I havt no Writ for him and nothing in the Clerks office against him."[69]

Even though Ned Christie stayed at home, newspapers continued to give readers imaginative tales of his activities. In November 1890, the *Fort Smith Elevator* reported that he engaged in an argument with the Squirrel brothers over a game of "draw." One of the brothers cut Christie in the shoulder and twice in the head and Christie retaliated by shooting him.[70] Numerous publications rely on one source, the *Indian Chieftain*, quoting the *Muldrow Registrar,* which asserted that the famed black lawman Bass Reeves led an attack on Christie's home in late November 1890 and burned it to the ground. The story also claims that Christie "is perhaps the most notorious outlaw and desperado in the Indian Territory" and "is said to be on the path fiercer than ever and vows revenge on the marshal and his posse."[71] There is no other source that discusses this event besides those that parrot this one.[72]

Bass Reeves never encountered Ned Christie, but that did not stop the flurry of news articles, such as the one in the *Boston Herald* from misstating on January 27, 1891, that "a terror in the community," Ned Christie, shot and killed famed Deputy Marshal Bass Reeves.[73] Not every paper could even properly copy the incorrect story. For example, the *News-Journal* in Mansfield, Ohio, and the *Waukesha Journal* in Wisconsin, reported, "Deputy United States Marshal Bassey [Bass Reeves] was shot and killed at Fort Smith, Ark., last night by a negro outlaw named Ned Christie."[74] The local paper with a penchant for publishing propaganda, the *Muskogee Phoenix*, included its version, that Christie killed Reeves near Tahlequah. "Reeves was a negro and well known in this city. Christie was being arrested for the murder of Ban Moffets some months ago." Another story in the same paper states that Christie "had two cabins burnt by officers within a few months in a fruitless effort to capture him."[75] On February 5, 1892, the *Muskogee Phoenix* retracted the story and stated, "The report that Bass Reeves had been killed by Ned Christie in Flint District, Cherokee Nation last week, was without foundation. Reeves was 150 miles away from the reparted place of killing at the time of the alleged killing."[76] There was no further word on Moffets.

The *Muskogee Phoenix* again repeated news without fact-checking in June 1891 when it published this snippet: "News reached here yesterday of the murder in cold blood on last Thursday of a farmer near Mays, I.T., by Ned Christie. Christie fired two shots, one entering the man's arm, another going through his body. The farmer informed the marshals of his whereabouts. Christie is at large. He told his friends he had been guilty of 'child's play,' in having to shoot at a man twice to kill him."[77]

Tribes had their hands full with serious problems impacting their nations. If Christie was indeed the scourge of Indian Territory, one might expect his activities to be a priority for tribal leaders, but even Chief Joel B. Mayes never mentioned him.[78] Instead, the Cherokees—as well as other tribes—continued to be preoccupied with the growing number of intruders onto their lands, railroad expansion, criminal activity, and the potential loss of their lands and sovereignty. On April 22, 1889, almost two years after Maples died, the gun sounded and thousands of land-hungry, non-Indian "Sooners" swarmed across the Unassigned Lands, which had been taken from tribes, in a mad dash to stake their claims. Tribal lands had diminished and violence persisted.[79] Lawmen, however, did not forget about Christie. They did not care about his political adherences. They were more concerned that the murderer of Maples be punished. On October 15, 1890, Judge Isaac C. Parker authorized Marshal Jacob Yoes to pay a reward of one thousand dollars for the arrest and delivery of Christie to Fort Smith.[80]

In 1890 the *Fort Worth Gazette* reported that a Cherokee named Bill Pigeon was spotted around Ned's home. Papers reported that Pigeon had killed a deputy marshal, Jack Richardson, and was considered by many to be "as desperate an Indian as Christie."[81] Others connected with the Maples killing also stayed active. In November 1890, John Hogshooter, along with Charles Duck, was arrested and charged with "introducing and selling whiskey" to several Tahlequah citizens. He carried the liquor in jugs, covered in sacks. One man, John T. Brown, testified that he bought a gallon from Duck and paid him with a six-shooter.[82] Charley Bobtail also continued to sell whiskey and was indicted in July 1891 and on January 7, 1892, for selling more whiskey in May and September.[83] John Parris again faced charges several years later for selling whiskey in May of 1889 and received a sentence of one year in jail at the Arkansas state penitentiary in Little Rock, beginning February 11, 1890.[84] Upon his release, Parris stayed away from further incidents, or even left Indian Territory, because it is here that we lose track of him. George Parris, brother of John, was indicted for horse theft on May 5, 1892.[85]

Local papers, notably the *Muskogee Phoenix*, persisted in describing Christie in inflammatory terms: "Christie is wanted for the murder of United States Deputy Marshal Maples, and various other crimes of great number and enormity."[86] Individuals not related to Ned found themselves associated with him by their deviant behavior. James Craig, for example, was arrested and charged with adultery "in the Christie neighborhood."[87] One paper suggested that Christie had always been an outlaw because at the time of Maples's demise, Christie was already "a member of the Cabin Gang," an interesting deduction considering he was not known as a member of said gang until after he built what many referred to as a cabin in 1889.[88]

After Christie's demise, Yoes exaggerated several points about Christie that would be used by later writers. First, he tried to give the impression that in the two years prior, he had been focused on Christie and had observed that after Christie had recovered from his eye injury, "he commenced his career of crime introducing whiskey by the wagon load and robbing stores with impunity. He killed and wounded a number of Cherokee people." This is a dubious claim; there are no newspaper reports of Ned robbing anyone, selling whiskey, and certainly not wounding anybody besides the men who tried to kill him on his own property.

None of those wounded people were Cherokees; they were two white men. Yoes also stated that if "a force" came after Christie, he "managed in some way to be informed of it, and get out of the way." If it was a small group, Christie would "fight," but a large group would result in Christie leaving. Yoes stated that "every effort has resulted in wounding of some of the men of my force."[89] There were, however, only two efforts put forth by Yoes. And only once did Yoes's men discover Christie not at home.

Aged Wes Bowman, who saw Christie die in 1892, inferred the same thing in 1952, stating that "Christie had ridden a crimson trail through the area, leaving in his wake the bodies of murdered men."[90] There are not, however, any reports of Ned robbing stores or killing anyone other than in Yoes's letter, Bowman's interview, and the convoluted testimonies of the elderly nieces of Levi Keys (Lucinda Sanders Wilhite and Catherine Wilhite).

Another Christie found himself in hot water. Ned's half-brother Ball sometimes called "Red Ball" (often incorrectly referred to as Bill or "Bald") was indicted for murder and whiskey peddling. He and two other men were accused of killing George Daugherty in July 1891, but only one man was executed. Ball was released by a hung jury on January 18, 1892.[91]

In the *Indian Citizen* article, the paper alleges that Christie had committed "crimes of various degrees of enormity" and refers to Ned and his friends as "a gang of desperadoes."[92] Later that month, the persistent *Indian Citizen* reported that the bullet-ridden body of Bowden had been found in the woods between Tahlequah and Braggs and claimed "Ned Christie, the Cherokee outlaw" did the deed.[93] Bowden's death was only a rumor. In July 1891, the *Advocate* sarcastically criticized papers that mistakenly reported Marshal Bowden's death: "As this is the age of wonders and of wonderful occurrences, however, it may be after all, Bowden was killed and that the Bowden we see perambulating the streets of Tahlequah, is the ghost of Bowden materialized. As we have never been a very stout believer in a fellow coming back after he has passed over the River, we are of the opinion Bowden was not killed, and that the Marshal Bowden we see russling round is not a materialized spirit. If he is he has certainly broke the record in the materializing business."[94]

Perhaps thinking that he could capitalize on the recent attack on Christie's home, on June 8, 1891, William Adair wrote a letter to Captain Gideon S. "Cap" White, a man who would later take part in the destruction of Ned's home, claiming that Arch Wolfe and Tom Wolf shot him three times on June 4, four days before he wrote this letter:

Flint PO I Terr
June 8/91
Mr. White

Dear Sir,

Have you had me registered as a false you no doubt recollect when you was up here last fall you told me you would register me if you have not please do so

Ned Christie's mob shot me in 3 places on the 4 of this month and know 3 of them saw them namely Ned C. Tom Wolf and Arch Wolf

I want writs for Tom W and Arch W for assault with intent to kill

I ask the protection of the government

Please attend to the matter at once and write me soon and oblige

Your friend
WILLIAM ADAIR
Flint P.O. C.N.

N.B. [nota bene] I am getting along very well there is a great deal of excitement here now Ned C and his men numbering 13 or 15 are at his home & intend to fight it out.[95]

The accusation is intriguing. This is the same William Adair who had been married to Ned's wife, Nancy, but she was unhappy with him and left him after the death of their daughter. And "Ned C" never had that many men with him. No warrant was issued and the matter was to be taken up again at the November 1892 term. Also, Adair managed to be up and around very quickly after being shot three times. There was no mention of how badly he was wounded or even where the incident took place.

Lawmen were not just concerned about Ned Christie. Arch Wolfe, Ned's teenaged cousin, often found himself accused of crimes. George Crittenden, Dave Hitcher, Jack Soap, R. B. Stand, Big Turn, Charles Tarpin searched for Arch Wolfe, who had been charged with larceny, but what he supposedly stole is not mentioned. Each man received three dollars for three days work.[96]

Stories based on events that took place at least a year prior continued to appear.

For example, the *Galena Times* reported that "Marshal Toes" and his rather large posse of fifty men hunted Christie, a man "wanted for a dozen murders and many other crimes," in the "Choctaw Mountains." "Toes" and company finally thought they cornered him in "a large stone fort which is the headquarters for the gang." In this bit, "Toes" destroyed the "fort," but not before he captured Christie's wife, who would not tell him the whereabouts of her husband who had disappeared before the posse somehow ruined the "stone fort"[97]

A few months later, Christie's name appeared connected to yet another violent crime. On December 9, 1891, resident William Shirley walked past the property of Wed Shirley, located about twelve miles west of Barren Fork, and saw the body of Deputy U.S. Marshal Josiah Poorboy, a Cherokee, lying in the road in front of the house with a gaping and brain-splattered exit wound in his forehead and close by, the body of government detective Thomas Whitehead, a man deemed by the papers as of "good address." A few days prior, Poorboy and the twenty-three-year-old Whitehead were told by accused Alabama murderer John Brown that whiskey was being sold by members of "Ned Christie's gang" close to Wed Shirley's property.[98] The *Muskogee Phoenix* yet again dragged Christie's name into an event by stating, "These two unfortunate men were lead into the death trap by John Brown, an ally of the notorious Ned Christie."[99]

As it turned out, the two lawmen were killed by sixteen-year-old Waco Hampton (seen as "Wakoo" in Fort Smith records), who papers claimed had "a record as bloody as any criminal in the Territory." Hampton emerges as an interesting outlaw character. Newsmen persisted in describing him as not only a cold-blooded murderer, but they also speculated on what could have been: "The handsome, countenance of the youth impresses one that there might have been a chance for an intelligent and manly career had his associates been of a law-abiding and elevating class."[100] And he is similar to Christie in that he is deemed "handsome." One paper, the *Watertown Daily Times,* stated that Hampton killed his cousin Bill Christie, but thought he was shooting at Ned Christie.[101] The *Telephone* stated that Hampton was Ned Christie's nephew and therefore "is part of a notoriously desperate and murderous family." His father, William, had been sentenced to ten years in a Detroit prison.[102]

Our Brother in Red attempted to ignite excitement by writing a rousing story about Waco and his uncle Christie:

> Before Ned Christie became an outlaw young Hampton endeavored to kill him. He killed his cousin in thinking it was Ned. Soon after this

Hampton, assisted by his father, killed an old man. For this crime father and son were tried a few years since for the last named crime. The former being sentenced to 21 years and the latter, on account of his youth, given 10 years in the house of reformation, from which institution he escaped. He is a nephew of Ned Christie and young as he is, can discount his uncle in crime. These two leading criminals are said to be deadly enemies, and as they range in the same locality they may meet in deadly combat among the hills of their native home.[103]

The *Dallas Morning News* summarized the crime situation in the Cherokee Nation: "There are a dozen desperadoes in these hills who have notches on their gun stocks showing the number of lives they have taken. The death average is four. The gang knows every hog path in the almost impenetrable country and have a system of signals by which the movements of the officers are communicated to members of the gang as they travel these paths and public highways." The paper claims that their "hilly rendezvous" was situated between Tahlequah and the Arkansas River. The writer asserts that one of the passes in the "mountains" leads to a tent village, where the bandits go for rest or when too closely pushed by the authorities." Of course, there are no mountains in that area, only hills with the highest elevation being around eight hundred feet, and there are no other reports of a "tent village."[104]

Steele writes that shortly after Maples's death, Christie called his Keetoowah friends together and they formed a "small army" and posted sentries "at several miles distance around his home." He states that "his army of supporters grew to such an extent that it was suicidal for anyone to attempt to capture Christie."[105] There was never an "army" of dangerous sentries and protectors around Christie's land. If there had been such a defense force, Christie would never have been attacked, much less killed.

As seen in the plethora of newspaper stories, layers of information about Christie, ranging from possibly accurate to certainly manufactured, emerged on a regular basis. Only the *Telephone* managed to write something undebatable: "Considerable excitement has prevailed here since the affair, and rumor after rumor are only contradicted by a subsequent one."[106]

CHAPTER 5

THE FINAL FIGHT

Ensconced in his storm port he bid defiance to all comers, and had
dynamite never been discovered, would yet be a live man.

ARKANSAS GAZETTE, November 5, 1892

By fall of 1892, Ned Christie had managed to elude frustrated posses for four and a half years. Steele asserts that Judge Isaac Parker faced "tremendous pressure from Washington to bring Christie and the Cabin Gang to justice" and that the citizenry lived in fear of the gang and demanded that Parker stop Christie and his "growing outlaw support."[1] However, no one in the Cherokee Nation expressed fear of Christie or demanded that he be dispatched. It is true that the deputy U.S. marshals were anxious over Maples's death and wanted someone punished for it, so they pushed Fort Smith to finance their forays onto Christie's land. And, as evidenced by Yoes's letter to Miller, they would receive payment for doing so.[2] Further, Ned's ability to thwart the officers resulted in what Steele said was "a great source of embarrassment for Parker."[3] That is only one reason why Parker might have willingly financed further expeditions.

Even stronger motivators for the irritated lawmen to confront Christie yet again were events occurring not within the Cherokee Nation but within the neighboring Choctaw Nation, which is much closer to Fort Smith. As among the Cherokees, political divisions within the Choctaw Nation often proved dangerous and deadly. The Choctaw Nation made national news in the months leading to its volatile election of 1892. The Nationalists and Progressives had sniped at each other through editorials, letters to editors, and face-to-face shouting matches. Name-calling, slander, and libel were commonplace, culminating in the scandalous 1892 election, which ultimately went to the Progressives. Furious, on September 10, a group of fifty Nationalists embarked on an assassination spree led by full-blood Silon Lewis, a Nationalist similar to Christie in that he held various prominent tribal positions, including sheriff of Tobusky County. The new and vindictive Choctaw chief, Progressive Wilson N. Jones, illegally removed Lewis from his position and replaced him with one of his cronies. Silon and other Nationalists then swept across the countryside killing several men, including the sheriff of Gaines County, Joe Hukolutubbee. The man called in to help quell the insurrection was Indian agent Leo K. Bennett, the white man who married Bub Trainor's sister Anna, and whose office was located in Muskogee, just thirty miles from Tahlequah.[4] Bennett knew very well the happenings in not only the Choctaw Nation but also the Cherokee Nation, and he communicated the situation back to officials at Fort Smith who sent messages to Washington.

The federal government monitored closely how the Choctaws handled the murders of Choctaws by fellow Choctaws, because if the tribe did not control the situation adequately in tribal court, the government remained poised to step in. Since violence among residents in the Choctaw Nation continued to attract attention, many Cherokees remained understandably concerned about how they would be perceived. After all, the two nations bordered each other and there were real fears that the Choctaw Nation might be put under martial law. Plans were already in motion to create the Dawes Commission (passed on March 3, 1893) and the federal government would have been pleased with more reasons to disband tribal governments, including the Cherokee Nation.

The government did not have legal authority over Silon Lewis and the other Choctaws who participated in the murders, but it did have control over the arrest of anyone accused of killing a white man, just as it had jurisdiction over any Indian who had killed Dan Maples. Parker knew of violence in the Choctaw Nation and he could do nothing about that, but he could do something about Christie.

A month after the assassinations in the Choctaw Nation, on October 11, 1892, Creekmore, along with eight others, including C. L. Bowden, Dave Rusk, Charles Copeland, D. C. Dye, Joseph Bowers, and John Fields, tried to accost Christie. Some papers beefed up the account by adding that Christie had a variety of men inside with him. The *Pittsburg Daily Headlight* stated that Walkabout (Arch Wolfe) and Bear Paw, "who are both desperate murderers and fugitives from justice," were with Christie. The teenager Arch was in the house, but not Bear Paw.[5] Reports that Ned's half-brother Ball were with him were also untrue.[6] A story in the *Omaha Herald* revealed that Marshal Yoes had sixty men with him and the Cherokee Nation contributed twenty more men, excitedly predicting that "there is certain to be bloodshed and a spirited battle."[7] Another version was the Ned's fort had been "burned over his head," but the desperado and his "20 men" escaped.[8] There were only five people present in the Christie home: his wife, Nancy; her son, Albert; Ned's daughter Mary; Arch Wolfe; and Charles Hair.

The early morning raid reportedly caught Ned eating. Creekmore asked Christie to surrender and Christie answered by shooting Joe Bowers in the foot and Fields in the neck.[9] Some papers erroneously claimed that "the women and children" were ordered out of the house and arrested. The posse set fire to an outbuilding and tried to dynamite the house, but the fuse failed to light.[10] Milo Creekmore sent word to Marshal Yoes via telegram that read, "Send deputies to Ned Christie's. We have him surrounded, but have not enough men. Joe Bowers and John Fields, of our party, are wounded. Fields will die." Yoes responded, "Have wired everywhere for deputies. You will have lots of help tonight. Hold the fort by all means and get him this time." He sent men from Fort Smith and West Fork.[11]

According to one paper, Chief Mayes ordered High Sheriff Harris to help gather men to assist Creekmore. They did, but upon arrival they discovered that Christie and the others had already left.[12] The *Muskogee Phoenix* reported on October 27, 1892, that John Fields died after being shot through the neck by Christie because he had suffered without medical attention.[13] The *Cherokee Advocate* stated that Bowers, "it is hoped, will fare better than his predecessor Achilles, who was also shot in the heel and died from the effects."[14] As it turned out, Field's neck wound improved as did Bowers's heel.

The *Morning Star* paper in Rockford, Illinois, published the same story, adding only that "the fort will be so surrounded that that outlaws must be surrender or die like rats in a trap."[15] Other papers, including the *New Haven Register,* added their own commentaries, such as that the Christie cabin was set afire and Ned "leaped" through the flames and escaped to the "woods, the bullets aimed at him falling harmlessly."[16] The house did not burn. The *Dallas Morning News* fabricated a story that marshals searched Christie's home and, according to only that paper, reportedly found "a quantity of goods that had been stolen from a store across the Arkansas line a short time since."[17] The marshals did not search the home because they could not gain entry to the building.

There were no other stories of Ned visiting Arkansas. His name is not mentioned in any court record regarding theft of a store, although other Christies are. In February 1893, George Christie, Arch Wolfe, Jack Wolf, Jackson Wolf, and Jim Christie were indicted for stealing eight pairs of boots, six hats, fifty yards of calico, fifty yards of domestic, twenty dozen spools of thread, twenty yards of velvet, and twenty brass pins from David N. Moore. They allegedly stole the goods on September 18, 1892, two weeks before Ned was killed. Three months after Ned died, the accused called a variety of witnesses to attest to their innocence and they were not prosecuted.[18]

Writers needed only to read the Christie name to associate Ned with the crime. Perhaps spurred by the thought that Ned had committed a heist, the lawmen grew eager to attempt another assault. Ned felt a sense of foreboding. He expected a formidable posse to try and kill him, so he asked Nancy to cut his long hair with the kitchen knife, then they wrapped it with otter string and prayed before burying it on the east side of their home.[19] Among many tribes, cutting one's hair is a sign of mourning. The Christies felt that his time to die had come.

November in Oklahoma is beautiful. Temperatures can range from the 30s to highs in the 70s. One might have to contend with mosquitoes on a hot day, and by afternoon a fast and cold wind could sweep in, dropping the temperature to the 30s in a matter of minutes. This is the time of year when leaves change color, transforming the leaves into a landscape of red and gold. Cherokees gathered nuts, harvested corn, squash, and other garden produce. Deer are in rut in November, making it prime hunting season. An 1894 study of killing frosts in Oklahoma suggests it frosted the morning of November 3. We know the day warmed a bit, because the posse men wore light jackets in pictures taken after their encounter with Christie.[20]

John G. Caelti wrote in his *Adventure, Mystery and Romance: Stories as Art and Pop Culture* that stories of increasing violence are necessary in order to honor the Code of the West, that is, "the classic resolution of the shootout."[21] Therefore, accounts of the final siege are as various and exaggerated as every other Christie-lawmen encounter. What is known for certain is that a posse had retreated after the unsuccessful attempt to capture Ned in October but was not deterred. On November 3, Yoes and twelve men started for Christie's house along with Cherokee Goingsnake Sheriff Ben Knight.

Tales about the posse's preparation for the encounter are also integral to the mythology of Christie. In *Iron Men*, McKennon has the posse encounter an array of supporters along the road in their quest to get Christie, including the "portly" man, Summers, who told the posse before giving each of them two cans of sardines for their trip that Christie "raided my store twice, and I don't mind telling you I was plenty spooked both times. He is a tough-looking jasper since he got smashed in the face with a rifle ball."[22] There are no reports of Christie raiding any store except the dubious claims of Catherine and Lucinda Sanders Wilhite.

Also in the Christie saga is the requisite "Indian scout" of western lore, the Cherokee Ben Knight, who was willing to turn against one of his own. In this case, Steele describes Knight as not sympathizing with the Christie cause. Bonnie Speers copied that assertion and wrote that Knight came along as a guide to Christie's home because he "did not condone Christie's increasingly violent activities."[23] To the contrary, the posse already knew the location of Christie's property because some of them had just been there weeks prior. That does not stop western writer Erin H. Turner from reiterating assertions about Knight in *Rotgut Rustlers*, stating that Knight was "no partisan of Christie" and "agreed to guide them into the heart of Christie's lair."[24] All were wrong. Knight was a full-blood, a Nationalist, and a Keetoowah. He served as translator to ensure that Christie understood all instructions given by the posse leaders.[25] Still, writers persisted in creating Knight as Christie's adversary as well as a Cherokee lawman as formidable as Christie the Outlaw. McKennon describes Knight: "A full-blooded Cherokee, he moved with the sureness of a born athlete, and his well-worn six-gun and rifle eloquently indicated his active profession."[26]

A list of those in attendance at the siege can be pieced together from the letter Yoes wrote to the attorney general after Ned's death in combination with Larry Kraus's analysis of photographs taken shortly after the event:

> Deputy Marshal A. B. Allen
> Deputy Marshal James Birkett (Poteau)
> Oscar Blackard (Clarksdale)
> Tom Blackard (Clarksdale)
> Deputy Marshal James Wesley Bowman
> Eli Hickman "Heck" Bruner (Siloam Springs)
> Deputy Marshal Harry Clayland (Clarksville)
> Deputy Marshal Charles E. Copeland (Siloam Springs)
> William Ellis
> Vint Gray (Clarksville)
> George Jefferson (Bentonville)
> Deputy Marshal Thomas "Tom" B. Johnson (Fayetteville)
> Cherokee Sheriff Ben Knight
> Mack Peel (Bentonville)
> Cook Frank "Becky" Polk
> Deputy Marshal E. B. Ratteree (Hartshorne)
> Deputy Marshal Dave V. Rusk

Frank Sarber (Clarksville)
Deputy Will Smith (Fayetteville)
John Tolbert (Clarksville)
Paden Tolbert (Clarksville)
Captain Gideon S. "Cap" White[27]

Some writers and informants created lists that confuse the 1892 siege with previous attacks on Christie.[28] Some include names such as U.S. Marshal Hitchcock, Joe Payne, Holden Pedford,[29] Dick Bruce,[30] and Annis Mills.[31] Henry Andrew "Heck" Thomas did not participate.[32] Nor did Sam Maples, the brother of the murdered deputy Maples.[33] And neither did E. P. Parris, a Cherokee who one Indian Territory resident claims participated in all three attacks on Christie's home.[34] Reflecting the need to portray Christie as an enemy of his own people, the *Salina Daily Republican* claimed that "twenty good and true Cherokees"

The posse that killed Christie. *Front row (left to right):* Dave Rusk, Heck Bruner, Paden Gilbert, Charles Copeland, and Captain G. S. White. *Back row:* Wes Bauman, Abe Allen, John Tolbert, Bill Smith, Tom Johnson. *C. B. Rhodes Collection, Oklahoma Historical Society.*

accompanied the "six deputy marshals" to the house of Ned Christie.[35] There was only one Cherokee in the group: Ben Knight.

After the encounter, Yoes wrote to W. H. H. Miller, attorney general of the United States that "I am sorry to say that he had to be killed in the attempt to capture him."[36] But in that same letter Yoes approved of a newspaper article he enclosed entitled "Ned Christie No More" that stated the men left for Christie's "for the purpose of either capturing or killing Ned Christie."[37] The mail carrier who worked in the Caney Mountain area close to Christie's house reported seeing a wagon laden with ammunition and other provisions en route to Ned's home.[38] Yoes's statement rings hollow considering that the large posse of heavily armed men brought along deadly firepower, including a cannon and dynamite. He had every intention of killing Christie. One cannot overestimate the desire of lawmen to avenge the death of one of their own.

During that brisk November morning the posse surrounded Ned's home, hoping to surprise him when he awoke. We do not know what was said, although the creative McKennon offers some Indianspeak from Knight to the posse in his contrived narrative: "Just over hill, Ned Christie fort. Move in closer when Dave Rusk come. He meet here. Leave horses tied here, but move wagon closer later. Keep quiet."[39]

Ned's wife, Nancy, and her son, Albert; Ned's daughter, Mary, and her daughter, Charlotte; and Ned's son Jim were in the home, along with Arch Wolfe and Charles Hair, a twelve-year-old who had worked for Ned. Charles Hair has a rather complex family. A woman named Lucy Spade had a son with a man named Stitchie, or Stitch Canoe. That son was named Charles Hair. Lucy later married a man named John Hair, also known as John Harris or Tahneyuhlee. John previously had a wife he called Aggie, but who was also called Betsy Chicken or Cluyahua. John and Betsy had a son they named Charles Hair the same year the other Charles Hair was born.[40] That means John was father to one Charles Hair and stepfather to the other Charles Hair. The child born to Betsy Chicken was known also as Charles Soldier Hair and that individual was the Charles Hair who stayed periodically at Christie's home to help the Christie family maintain their small farm.

By four o'clock in the morning the posse settled in around Christie's "fort," which was actually his home, and watched as a few women came outside, looked around, but did not see the hidden officers.[41] According to a newspaper version endorsed by Yoes, as the day broke Arch Wolfe emerged and was told to surrender. Wolfe responded by firing; the posse returned his fire, and was then "pierced by nearly a dozen bullets."[42] As it turns out, however, Wolfe was not hit and it is unclear if he even fired a shot. In fact, one man recalled in 1937 that Charles Copeland told him that the only two males present were Christie and Hair.[43]

Yoes wrote in his letter to Miller that they called to Ned and told him in English to surrender and that Knight reiterated that command in Cherokee. Christie responded by firing a few shots. The posse returned his fire.[44] Amid the shooting Ned told the women to take the children out through the root cellar. They later tried bringing ammo to Ned but the posse held them back.[45] Yoes heard Christie whoop.[46] Roy Hamilton says that Ned did not whoop. He could, however, imitate a turkey gobbling, which is not the same thing.[47]

In "Blood in the Cookson Hills," author Rand has Christie sound like James Cagney as he yelled at the marshals from inside his "fort": "Fire all you want, you dirty rats. You couldn't knock a tin soldier down with that cannon."[48] Paul Kirchner, in his 2001 essay, "Ned Christie," is the only writer to state that one of the men involved in the siege "made up some flaming arrows, slender sticks tipped with oil-soaked rags, which he launched with an old .45–70 Springfield. The deputies cheered when one stuck in the fort's wall, but its flame was too feeble to ignite the logs."[49]

The posse decided to retrieve a cannon some of them had heard was located at Coffeyville. The blacksmith who built it agreed to ship it along with forty "conical projectiles" by train to West Fork, Arkansas. The cannon made its way by wagon driven by Gus York and Enas Mills to Christie's home. The cannon weighed only three pounds with a four-foot barrel and one-inch bore. They rigged a mount for it: "for elevation, the barrel had a screw wheel, but windage adjustment would have to be accomplished with a crowbar. There were no wheels on the gun carriage." Using a metal cup, Tolbert and White loaded the cannon's muzzle with powder. They placed a "projectile" inside, then rammed it in with a stick. Another bit of powder was placed in the touchhole. Tolbert used a stick wrapped with cloth and dipped into kerosene to light the powder. Despite the noisy blast, the projectile did not make a dent into the fort. They repeated the process several times but the shots proved good only for shaking the house.[50] One paper claims that the posse fired at least two thousand rifle bullets and an astonishing thirty cannon shots at Christie. There are no other reports to back up the claim that the cannon was fired more than a few times.[51] Harry Sinclair Drago uses the most interesting imagery by writing, "The cannon vomited its supposedly lethal load."[52]

Wes Bowman states in his 1952 interview that the cannonballs just "bounced off, barely missing us deputies." He also says that "the man in charge decided to use a heavier charge of power. He packed it in and then fired the weapon. But the charge was too heavy and the cannon was blown to pieces."[53] Still, the concerned Christie moved to the first level of his house and for a while took refuge under the home through a trapdoor. The shooting resumed and Yoes recounted that the men grew hungry, weary, and discouraged. Everyone perked up after the arrival of Dave Rusk and Charley Copeland and the fighting recommenced, continuing until dark.[54]

Clouds obscured the moon. Will Smith and Charlie Copeland took advantage of the darkness and slowly made their way to a wagon that sat about twenty feet from the house. With cover from the wagon they built a "fortification" with fence rails, and even though Christie spotted them, they completed the project and then slipped back to continue firing until four o'clock Friday morning. White states that they continually tried to communicate with Christie, telling him that if he and his companions surrendered they would be treated well. Christie ignored them and continued to resist. White also recalls that the women "made sport" of the officers for attempting to arrest the men, a claim repeated in the much-exaggerated *Chicago Daily Tribune* story. At four o'clock, the posse decided to destroy the structure. According to most reports, while some of the posse continued to shoot, Charlie Copeland made his way to the house with a heavy metal shield in front of him under cover of the wagon barricade and placed one dynamite boom under the edge of the corner of the house. The fuse was lit and the tremendous explosion "raised it high and let it down again." Papers exclaimed that the explosion could be heard from twelve to thirty miles away.[55]

Another version is that Charles Copeland ran to the front of the house and laid six sticks of dynamite under the house. After retreating, he shot the sticks, resulting in an explosion that destroyed the front of the fort.[56] The *Arkansas Gazette* reported that it "knocked out one corner" of the house.[57] But the posse tried a new tactic. Paden Tolbert and William Smith approached the house to the right, while William Ellis and G. S. White ran to the other side as all began firing. One man states that the eighteen-year-old John Waters crawled to the house and put dynamite under the floor.[58] Not to be outdone, the *Guthrie Daily Leader* remembered that day in a 1900 reminiscence about "the old Cherokee outlaw" and stated, "Finally Copeland volunteered to blow up the house with dynamite, and, taking off his shoes, and carrying the dynamite in his hands, he made a rush for the house and with great daring succeeded in placing the dynamite and lighting the fuse. The explosion shattered the house and set it on fire and Christie came out, his eyes blazing like a demon, and fell fighting to the last gasp."[59] Why

Copeland felt compelled to remove his shoes on a cool November morning is not addressed.

The *Chicago Daily Tribune* also dramatizes that vignette by telling readers that Copeland, "as reckless a white man as ever walked," crawled up to the house and tried to place the dynamite into a crevice under a log. The hole was too small, "so Copeland squatted down alongside the wall and proceeded to knead that dynamite stick between his knees until it was flat enough to slip under the log." Obviously, this is a foolhardy maneuver and a dubious claim considering that if the stick already had a cap on it, friction could sometimes cause it to be set off. And Copeland had at least six sticks, not just one.[60]

The blast blew a large hole in a wall and set the heavy logs ablaze. Events happened very quickly and versions of Ned's death are as plentiful as number of the bullets fired. The commonality among these stories is that Christie is described as almost flying out of his home, guns drawn, before it is destroyed. Rand is more specific, telling us that "out of the hole came Ned Christie, stumbling awkwardly, all his clothes blown from his body. He staggered only a few feet and fell dead. Seven bodies of his men were found in the fort."[61] In reality, the only male with him at the end was Charles Hair, aged twelve.

Yoes admits that no one knows who actually killed Christie, although a host of people have taken the claim for firing the killing shot and many people claim they know who did. Gilbert Fallin puts it succinctly when he said in 1968, "Course, a lot of officers say 'I'm the one that shot him.' Anyway they were after him. I know they talk about the Pollock down there, he was with the posse that killed him back there. He was down around Tulsa someplace. And he said, 'We never did know who shot him but we'us all shootin' at him.'"[62] If the house really was blown up at four o'clock in the morning, then the sun had not yet come up and shots were fired in the dark without accuracy. Still, that reality has not stopped others from taking credit for the kill.

One says Heck Bruner killed Ned.[63] Still another names Marshal Kale Starr.[64] Tolbert and some of the other men were some distance away when they heard two shots. Tolbert ran toward the sound when he heard pistol shots. According to this fabricated story, it was Bowman who shot Christie "behind the ear" and killed him after they almost ran into each other when Christie bolted from his burning home, but it was Sam Maples who stood over the dead Christie and said, "Maybe I didn't kill him, but he sure as hell was heavier with lead. I've been waitin' five years to throw lead into him." Maples then "went berserk . . . [and] he stood there emptying his gun into the lifeless form."[65] Maples was not present at this event.

Another vignette has Ned running out of ammunition, then sprinting out the door with his rifle as if it were fully loaded. He made it to the gate, then "started running down the road by the side of the fence like some scared fox before the hunter's hounds."[66] The *Arkansas Gazette* states that after the roof fell in, Arch Wolfe emerged, "nearly roasted," then Ned followed, "firing in every direction"; he stumbled, fell, and, "before he could arise, was killed by the officers." Charlie Hair was found dead.[67] A *Chicago Daily Tribune* reporter wrote, "Up into the air sailed Christy's cabin, ripped into blazing kindling-wood. But Christy popped out of the explosion alive, his Winchester going full speed. He started off across the clearing, running like an antelope, whipping his rifle first over one shoulder and then over the other and letting it go at every jump."[68]

Yoes wrote to Miller that when Christie emerged from the burning house, he yelled, "Damned white marshals," while firing his six-shooter, not his rifle.[69] One former deputy marshal who served with Heck Bruner asserted that after Christie left his home, "only one officer in that crowd was shrewd enough to know just what would happen if Christie did make his escape." In this version, Heck Bruner is the one who fired the fatal shot and also has Isibol [Isbell] being wounded in the shoulder instead of during the 1889 siege.[70] Cherokee William Ballard, a deputy marshal who was not involved with Christie, nevertheless stated in 1937 that Christie "sprang out the door as the house blew up and was shot down by Kale Starr, Marshal."[71] R. Y. Nance stated the same year that Charles Copeland told him that he was the one who shot Christie dead.[72] Yet another version is that after the initial explosion, Christie ran out of the house and "the officers filled his body full of bullets and he fell among the rocks between two blackgum saplings. The blood stain from his bleeding body remained on the rocks for many years after."[73]

The siege on Christie's fort was immediate and exciting news. Papers around the country alerted readers to events as fast as they could publish them. Ned and the men and women with him were maligned, but the marshals and deputy marshals continued to be hailed as heroes. C. B. Rhoades, a man who neither participated in the attack nor knew Christie but who had strong opinions about him, described the lawmen as possessing all the "cunning of the animal in pursuit and location of fugitives."[74] It is no wonder that over time the list of men who participated in the siege of Christie's home has lengthened.

Wes Bowman, who was twenty-three years old when Christie died, lived the longest of the lawmen. Apparently, the lawman who lives the longest gets the last word. His enhanced view of his role in the Christie killing grew into legend, at least in the newspaper world. He claimed in 1952 that the very last shot Christie fired missed him, but managed to burn his face "by the rifle blast and particles of powder [that] were imbedded in my skin."[75] In 1967, ten years after Bowman's death, the *Milwaukee Journal* included a bit taken directly from McKennon's *Iron Men,* which also came out that year: "A few minutes later young Wes Bowman was peering watery eyed into the smoke when he spied a tall, shadowy figure sprinting toward him. It was Christie, but before Bowman could react, the Indian fired a missing shot at such close range that the lawman's face was peppered with gunpowder. Racing on past, Christie was almost away in the woods when Bowman fired his rifle from the hip and killed him with a shot behind the ear."[76]

McKennon seemed convinced that Bowman pulled trigger. He creates the scenario in which a crowd of schoolchildren missed classes to see the shooter after he arrived at Fort Smith: "'Fellows,' boomed Copeland to the crowd, 'since you are skipping school to see the man that got Ned Christie, here he is, Deputy Marshal Wess Bowman.' Then Judge Parker commended Bowman for killing the outlaw: 'I see,' the big jurist had said, his piercing eyes twinkling, 'that you had a good Winchester!'"[77]

The version accepted by Yoes is that Christie fired his "six-shooter" only once and was hit in the shoulder, head, and side. Christie lay still for almost five minutes before the posse became aware of his death. They were preoccupied with getting the youth Hair out of the burning fort. Ben Knight yelled at Hair in Cherokee to come out, but the boy stayed until the fort started to fall down around him. He managed to run from the burning building with burns on his head, face, hands, and back.[78] The record for how many times possemen shot Christie comes from the *Grand Lake News Online*: "To demonstrate that crime does not pay, Christie's body, allegedly shot 117 times, was displayed on Judge Parker's courthouse steps in Fort Smith."[79]

Christie was dead, but what of his family? Papers took information from short news stories sent out from Tahlequah or Fort Smith and then spun them into drama. The *Daily Illinois State Register* rightfully admitted in a November 5, 1892, story that "it was impossible to get accurate particulars last night," but nevertheless proceeded to include phrases such as "desperate battle," "Christie and his gang," "Cabin fort in the Caney mountains," "Deputy Marshal White, reputed one of the bravest men in the country," "a perfect fusillade of firing," and "their orders are to get the gang dead or alive."[80] Other papers quickly flung out stories such as "They found the body of Charles Wolf, the man who had been shot earlier in the day, burned in the ruins of the home."[81] Charles Hair tried to escape and was arrested. Wolf's body was found, burned to a crisp or "burned up."[82]

Ultimately, Hair suffered a few burns and Arch Wolfe made his way out of the house and away from the gunfire at some point during the melee. He may have made his way out by accessing a trapdoor and crawling out from under the building.[83] The posse loaded Christie's body into a wagon, along with the burned Charles Hair, and rode to Fort Smith where they arrived around two o'clock in the afternoon.[84] The possemen took Christie's rifle and pistols. No one in the Christie family saw the rifle again until it went on display at the Fort Smith National Historic Site. Christie's pistols disappeared, and according to descendant Roy Hamilton, someone later purchased what were supposed to be his pistols at a Georgia auction. The authenticity of the rifle and the pistols remain in doubt.

Jacob Yoes wrote to the attorney general, stating that "he was sorry to say that [Christie] had been killed in the attempt to capture him." He also sent word—"an identification" of the body of Christie—to the court at Fort Smith along with a request that Gus York please be paid the sum of $1,000 as a reward for himself and his men for bringing in Christie. He noted that subduing Christie was expensive, at least three times the amount of the reward. The effort proved difficult and dangerous, he said, and it was done "in the interest of the government." Yoes stated that after Christie healed after being shot in the head in 1889, he had returned to his "career of crime" by bringing in whiskey "by the wagon load" and "robbing stores with impunity."[85] The *Muskogee Phoenix* concurred, opining that "the amount is $1000, to which will be added $300 offered by outside parties. This will be divided among the captors, sixteen in number. The amount is not commensurate with the trouble incurred in capturing the desperado."[86] Besides a few statements by confused pioneers, there is no evidence that Ned engaged in any kind of organized crime. Yoes blatantly used false claims of criminality to rationalize Christie's death and the posse's reward. Christie did not instigate any of the encounters between him and lawmen. The latter started every confrontation, yet in order to rationalize his death, writers had to concoct scenarios in which Christie robbed, killed, or peddled whiskey, and Yoes was the first to do so.

Hair was taken to St. John's Hospital, the first hospital built in Fort Smith, known today as Sparks Regional Medical Center. Papers reported that Hair "lay for weeks" in a hospital bed, but there is no mention of what happened to him after that.[87] I. N. McCabe, Simon R. Walkingstick, C. W. Carson, John Williams, and Joseph Hogner [sic] swore they knew Christie and positively identified his body.[88] Deputy Hugh Harp placed his personal rifle in Ned's hands in an effort to make him look more like an outlaw. Harp then said, "This feller died by the gun, he ought to have his picture made with one."[89]

Pride writes in his story "The Battle of Tahlequah Canyon" that Christie was photographed "with the celebrated rifle in the traditional upside down position of the defeated."[90] The butt of the rifle may be slightly higher than the muzzle in this photograph because that was the only way to fit the weapon into his hands, but it is not "upside down." An upside down rifle symbolizes a soldier killed in action. Regardless, Christie did not surrender, and he did not brandish his rifle when he died. He held a pistol.

Ned's body was photographed and viewed by gawkers. The *Muskogee Phoenix* reiterated the description of the scene from the *Ft. Smith Call*: "Yesterday the corpse was placed on the front entrance of the U.S. jail and the public were allowed to see the disfigured tenement of clay so recently occupied by a more contorted soul."[91]

In twentieth-century stories about Christie, he is described as being an imposing six feet four. After Christie's death, reporters who looked at his body were surprised that he seemed to be "about 5 feet 7 inches in height and weighing about 140 pounds."[92] This is logical because his mother, Lydia, is described as "tiny."[93] Joe Pride asserts that either Bruner or Thomas stated, "For a little guy, he sure raised a lot of hell."[94] The "death photograph" of Christie reveals that the rifle in Ned's hands is a Winchester measuring forty-three inches in length, a longer weapon than Christie's Winchester Centerfire .44, model 1873 saddle-ring carbine that is on display at Fort Smith. Taking into consideration that Christie's ankles are a bit buckled in the death photo, a measurement reveals him to be around five feet eight inches. One book states that the Fort Smith men broke Christie's legs so he would fit into the coffin, but there is no source given for that account.[95] Coffins were generally at least six feet long. The one Ned rests in was made by his brother Goback who knew his brother's height. There would have been no need to desecrate his body.

After crowds of gawkers streamed past Christie's body, he was turned over to his father Watt on Sunday night. His family buried him one hundred yards southwest of the Bidding Springs School, on Highway 51. It is probable, however, that in order to protect the integrity of his grave, Christie lay someplace other than next to where his headstone now stands.

On April 25, 1893, a passerby found the body of George Dick, the husband of Jennie Grease (and niece of Watt Christie), his throat cut amid signs of a "desperate struggle." His horse, with two cuts on the right shoulder and stab wounds in its side, stood nearby. In an attempt to keep the excitement about Ned Christie going, the *Evening Kansan* offered a vague report in which two drunken men,

Ned Christie, dead and holding Hugh Harp's rifle, and the posse that killed him. *Courtesy National Park Service, Museum Management Program, and Fort Smith National Historic Site*

"Dick and Christie" (the latter actually Ball Christie), a brother of Ned, departed Tahlequah after trading at Johnson Thompson's, then embarked in a knife fight. Christie cut Dick's throat "from ear to ear," and because he was nowhere to be seen, it was assumed he had killed his colleague and then departed for the "Christie neighborhood." Just as papers had written about Christie, writers asserted that "if they find Christie a fight will take place, because he will die rather than surrender to an officer." A posse was organized the next day.[96] The *Muskogee Phoenix* continued to take advantage of Ball's name to stir up some exciting news: "Christie is a brother to the notorious Ned Christie, who in his day murdered more men than the celebrated Tom Starr."[97] Ball Christie was found guilty of murder and after several reprieves, he contracted tuberculosis. Chief Joel B. Mayes sent Ball home to die of tuberculosis, rather than to be hung. He died on Friday, December 13, 1895.[98]

Ned's family suffered more grief on July 4, 1893, when the mutilated body of his and second wife Peggy Tucker's seventeen-year-old son, James "Jim" Christie, was found on the road twelve miles east of Tahlequah, shot in the back of the head, beaten extensively with a rock, his throat cut and body stabbed numerous times. Some papers reported that he had been decapitated. Papers painted him as a killer "like his father and uncle," Ned Christie and Ball Christie.[99] Jim Christie was no killer. He had been murdered by Sam Mayes (son of Tallow Mayes, the half-brother of Chief Joel B. Mayes) who made his confession in Cherokee through a translator before he was hanged.[100]

Yoes resigned as U.S. marshal on May 29, 1893.[101] He continued to live comfortably after Ned's death. He bought one thousand acres of land and accumulated wealth from his mercantile stores along the Frisco Railway and plantations on the Arkansas River. He built a cotton gin, sawmill, gristmill, warehouses, as well as a large home. He died in 1906 at age sixty-seven and was buried at Fort Smith.[102]

On November 4, 1894, almost exactly two years after the death of Ned Christie, Silon Lewis, the Nationalist Choctaw, was executed for his role in the deaths of Progressives, although many argue that he was murdered. On June 23, 1893, a Progressive Choctaw jury had found the Nationalists, including Lewis, guilty of murder. This ruling caused an uproar among the Choctaws, who believed the jury was biased, but also raised concern at the federal level—not for the condemned, but that the executions would trigger more intertribal violence. The dozen or so men who had initially been condemned to death were exonerated, and Lewis was the one left to pay the price. He could have run after the date of his execution was set, but he promised to get his affairs in order and to return to be shot through the heart. And return he did to Wilburton in November 1894, where he was blindfolded. The local physician concluded that for some reason, Lewis's heart was located on the right side of his chest; therefore, the shooter Lyman Pusley, a repeat criminal and known killer, shot him through a lung. Silon suffered intensely for fifteen minutes until an impatient sheriff smothered Lewis to death with his handkerchief.[103]

A year later, on November 20, 1895, Jesse Bates swore to the court at Fort Smith that on November 16, Bub Trainor cut him with a knife and "that while he was assaulting and cutting me, he was declaring that he would kill me."[104] This case never went any further because within a few weeks Trainor was found shot to death "with buckshot and bullets in the darkness of night."[105]

Deputy marshal Charles L. Bowden, who had been reported dead in 1891, was readministered his oath as a federal deputy on October 27, 1894.[106] In November 1895, Heck Thomas was sworn in as deputy marshal of the Western District of Arkansas.[107] In 1896, Thomas led a posse against Bill Doolin, an active criminal who rode with the Daltons and the Cooks, then served as the first Lawton, Oklahoma, police chief. He appeared in the 1908 movie *The Bank Robbery* and died of heart failure in 1912.[108] On June 21, 1899, Heck Bruner perished while attempting to cross the rain-swollen Grand River after a man he was chasing. He made it only halfway across the river when witnesses watched him flounder, then disappear. They recovered his body downriver the next day.[109]

Lands of the Five Tribes were allotted from 1897 to 1906. Many Keetoowahs who refused their allotments were jailed. Daniel Gritts, leader of the Keetoowahs, along with five other men, finally relented and reportedly accepted their allotments only after the prison barber was ordered to cut off their long hair. Gritts died in 1906.[110] In April 1903, Goback Christie was released from jail after three months for refusing to accept his allotment. Chief of the Creek Nation, Pleasant Porter and Coming Deer, a full-blood Cherokee, posted his bail.[111] The *Muskogee Daily Phoenix* elaborated, stating that in contrast to his brother Ned, Goback "has always led a quiet, peaceable life, and was regarded as a law abiding citizen until his arrest for resisting the authority of the commission." The paper stated that Goback's counsel, John Coming Deer, posited that he is "the dupe of unscrupulous and designing men of his own race."[112]

Zeke Proctor, the man many writers portray as a vicious killer equal to Christie, served as a deputy U.S. marshal from 1891 to 1894 under Judge Parker and as sheriff of Flint District in 1894. There is no record that Zeke was assigned to capture Ned. He may have had physical difficulty riding and walking because in November 1901, Proctor applied for an invalid pension because he was deaf, "lame" in both ankles, and suffered from rheumatism in his right shoulder as the result of an injury while a U.S. scout for the Second Cherokee Home Guard. Ezekiel Proctor joined the National Senate in November 1903, and died four years later, on February 23, 1907, at age seventy-six from pneumonia. He is buried in Johnson Cemetery in West Siloam Springs in Delaware County. The town of Proctor, fifteen miles east of Tahlequah, was named in his honor.[113]

Wauhillau became known as a "picturesque" and place to vacation, with cool weather and many waterways providing "the finest bathing in the world." A year after Ned's death, entrepreneurs organized the Wauhillau Club and built fifteen cottages, without "fancy flubdubbery" for those willing to pay to spend hot summers under the shade of the dense forests and in the coolness of the Illinois River's streams.[114] The private Wauhillau Outing Club is not in Wauhillau, but in a nearby wooded area of Cherokee County. The Wauhillau Store operated until the 1970s. From 1952 to at least 1968, Mr. and Mrs. Edwin Willis ran the operation, which by that time had to compete with larger grocery stores. Harrison Leach ran a strawberry processing and tomato canning plant next to the store, but moved to Texas for lack of business.[115] The town of Christie, located twenty-five miles east

Ned's repaired gravestone. The inscription reads:
Ned Christie
Born
Dec. 14, 1852
Died
Nov. 3, 1892
He was at one time a Member of the Executive Council of the C.N.
He was a blacksmith,
and was a brave man.

The inscription in the Cherokee syllabary at the bottom of Christie's headstone
means "Nede Wade"—Nede, son of Watt. *Photo by author.*

of Tahlequah in today's Adair County, is not named after Ned's family; rather it is
named after John Francis Marion Christie.[116]

The Watt Christie Cemetery has been through some hard times and by 1968
had badly deteriorated. Headstones have been toppled and broken, and the few
trees were carried away sometime after 1968 by a tornado. In the late 1970s, someone stole Ned's headstone to use as a tabletop. One of Roy Hamilton's cousins
located the headstone, then had to purchase it from the thief to get it back. It has

been broken several times since and Roy continues to epoxy it back together.[117] One day we visited the cemetery; a Christie descendant who lives on the property reported that the night before she witnessed a drunken man attempting to topple one of the larger headstones but who ran away when he saw her. In the past few decades, visitors from around the country as well as from Japan, Germany, and other countries have journeyed to see Ned's grave. Some leave artificial flowers. Another left a set of marbles and horseshoe. The Cherokee National Historical Society has replaced some of the headstones, but the old ones remain.

Nancy married Ned's brother Jack, and they had five children. One son, Joe, fought in World War I. He spoke no English. His brother George enlisted, but died while training in Kentucky. Nancy did not approach the Dawes Commission

Joe (*left*) and Tom Christie, sons of Nancy and Jack (Ned's brother), whom she married after Ned's death, c. 1910. Joe died in France during World War I and another brother, George, died in Kentucky. They were interred in the Jack Christie Cemetery that was bulldozed and destroyed by the Nolan family. *Roy Hamilton Collection.*

to enroll for allotment and neither did her husband at the time the rolls opened, Jack Christie. Instead, a man named Benjamin Johnson answered the interviewer's questions about them. He testified that he had known Nancy since she was a little girl, yet for unknown reasons he maligns her name by also stating rather flippantly that "she was the wife of Ned Christie and a dozen others perhaps. She was telling my wife a while back that this was her twelfth child." Nancy had one child with Adair and after Ned's death, five children with Jack. She and Ned had no children who survived infancy.[118]

One evening in 1921, Nancy told her family that she felt cold. She lay down in front the fireplace, fell asleep, and died. Even after death, she had to deal with indignities. Nancy and her sons Joe and George were buried in the Jack Christie Cemetery. The land was sold to the Thornton family, who also established a family cemetery on the property. The land was sold again, this time to the Nolan family, and the patriarch of that family bulldozed the Jack Christie Cemetery, including the bodies, caskets, and headstones, into a pond. Roy Hamilton managed to salvage few pieces of headstones. The Thornton cemetery, however, is still there.[119]

Goback Christie and his son Harold Amos making chairs at their sawmill. December 9, 1937.
Thomas-Foreman Home Collection, Oklahoma Historical Society.

CHAPTER 6

YOUNG MEN LOST

ARCH WOLFE AND CHARLES HAIR

Previous to the opening the asylum this unfortunate class of Indians
were without care or attention. None of them were wanted anywhere,
nor by anybody. They were a great burden to their relatives or friends.

OSCAR A. GIFFORD, Superintendent of Canton
Asylum for Insane Indians, 1903

In November 1892, eighteen-year-old Arch Wolfe and twelve-year-old Charles Hair (listed as Wolfe and Hare on court documents) were charged with assault with intent to kill Captain Gideon S. "Cap" White, one of the posse members who assisted in killing Ned Christie.[1] A year later, however, Arch found himself indicted for a total of five charges: one for selling liquor, two for introducing liquor, and two for assault with intent to kill. He pleaded not guilty to all of them.

That long day in November 1992 ended with Christie being dispatched, yet that did not seem to be enough revenge for this group. The officers had been relentless in their pursuit of Ned and they assessed any associate of Christie as fair game. In addition, Arch Wolfe had been charged with larceny in 1892 and had a warrant out for his arrest.[2] And recall that a year and a half earlier, on June 8, 1891, William Adair made the accusation that Arch Wolfe, Tom Wolf, and Ned Christie had shot him three times. Adair addressed his letter to the same Gideon White. That White made the same charge immediately after he and the rest of the posse attacked Ned's home was not a coincidence. White and the others decided to take advantage of Arch's larceny warrant and a pre-vious—and dubious—assault accusation to ensure that the courts punished anyone associated with Ned Christie, even if Arch Wolfe had left the scene prior

Arch Wolfe in shackles after the death of Ned Christie. He was sentenced to prison
in Brooklyn and died at the Canton Asylum for Insane Indians in South Dakota in 1912.
Courtesy of the Cherokee National Historical Society, Tahlequah, Oklahoma.

to gunfire and even if the other male present was a child. Lawmen agreed that
only one of them was needed to step forward to ensure that Wolfe and Hair
were dealt with and they had an obvious choice in Gideon White. Any one of
the posse members could have made the assertion, but only one accuser was
needed to convict the two.

Wolfe and Hair were quickly charged afterward, but Arch Wolfe did not
appear at court in Fort Smith until December 1893. Steele claims in *The Last
Cherokee Warriors* that Arch somehow made it all the way to Chicago, where a
few months later marshals arrested him in an unnamed hotel lobby. It is unlikely
that Wolfe managed to get the almost seven hundred miles to Chicago.[3] The
teenager needed money, food, and clothing for the rapidly changing November weather. He could have traveled on the Chicago, Rock Island and Pacific

Railroad, but he would have had to pay for it. In January 1893, the *Muskogee Phoenix* included a short blurb: "Arch Wolf, the desperado, who was supposed to have been burned in the Ned Christie fort in the Cherokee Nation at the time of the killing of the notorious Christie has turned up alive and is giving the officers trouble." The paper, however, does not say what sort of "trouble."[4] If this is true, Arch remained in Indian Territory, not Chicago, for at least three months after Ned died.

Once Arch arrived at Fort Smith he had to face more than one charge. The accusation made by William Adair, that Arch tried to kill him in June 1891, remained to be addressed. The brief court document states that Arch denied attempting to kill Adair and he requested that William Christie, Ollie Cochran, Nancy Grease, Mary Christie, and George Wilson appear as witnesses on his behalf. Arch argued that he was several miles away from where William Adair was shot and he was at that unnamed place when he learned about the shooting. In regard to the charge of assault with intent to kill Gideon White, Arch stated that he could prove that he was not present at Ned Christie's home when the marshals set the home on fire on November 3, 1892. Mary Christie and Nancy Grease were in the home at that time and Arch claimed that they could state that he was not there, but he also said that he "is poor" and unable to pay for those female witnesses to travel to Fort Smith.[5]

Arch may have been with Christie up to the time the posse arrived, but it appears that he had left Christie's home before the gunfire began. Newspaper accounts of the final attack on Ned's home vary as to Arch's whereabouts during the melee. Papers stated that he "burned up" or "burned to a crisp," while others mentioned that he escaped. Jacob Yoes, in his recounting of the event to Miller, does not even mention Arch Wolfe. Instead, his statement runs counter to the more stirring newspaper accounts that claim Arch came outside, looked around, then went back in or that he started shooting and was shot multiple times. Yoes also seems to be more concerned about getting paid for killing Christie than he does in giving a detailed account of the event. In addition, most papers fail to mention that Charles Hair was a child and the man in charge of this attack, Yoes, does not mention Hair at all in his letter to Miller. Yoes and the posse were probably embarrassed that a child stood with Christie, so Yoes simply did not mention him, but they apparently got over that concern in order to accuse Hair of attempted murder.

Arch's witnesses never arrived at Fort Smith. Witnesses in other cases never made it, either. The roads to Fort Smith were poorly maintained, bridges often were impassable and thieves and murderers were known to prey on travelers. A freight hauler who often carried goods between Indian Territory and Fort Smith stated in the late 1880s that he often saw dead men on the road.[6] Witnesses were not reimbursed for any travel expenses, such as food or hotel, and they only received fifty cents per day for their time. Indian agent Tufts commented, "This court is located so far from the settlements of these people, and the expense of attending being more than the fees and mileage allowed, in some cases the witness is punished as much as the criminal."[7]

According to the *Fort Smith Elevator,*

> A deputy marshal goes out into the Indian Country at his own expense, and risks his life in his endeavors to bring criminals to justice. He gathers up five to a dozen and of course must summon a number of witnesses in each case. These witnesses must leave their business of crops and obey the summons of the government, or lay themselves liable to a heavy fine. They come perhaps two or three hundred miles at their own expense, go before the commander, and after being discharged present their check to the marshal for their pay. He has no funds, and is compelled to put them off with a marshal's check or voucher, and in order to cash it they must discount it to some merchant or speculator for 50 cents on the dollar.[8]

There were indeed many factors to consider for a potential witness called to Fort Smith. Wagons could break, horses might become lame or throw a shoe, gardens and crops could fail, in addition to the very real possibility of facing thieves, rapists and killers. Witnesses who traveled to Fort Smith often did so in groups to ensure safety, as did the witnesses for John Hogshooter and Charles Bobtail in 1887.[9] But by the time Arch Wolfe stood before Parker at Fort Smith in November 1893, Mary Christie and Nancy Grease were facing the arduous task of making a living and a long trip did not seem feasible. Their home had been destroyed and they continued to grapple with the loss of Ned, Nancy's cousin George, and the vicious death of Ned's son Jim. Agent Tufts also stated that while the court is "respected by these people they feel they have no cause to complain against the action of the court or its officers."[10] The Christie family did "respect" the court because it represented the power of the United States government. And the witnesses for the prosecution were Paden Tolbert, William Smith, A. B. Allen, and Charles Copeland, the same men who fired upon the Christie home where Mary and Nancy lived. They all saw each other. Perhaps Mary and Nancy could have enlisted the traveling company of Ned's father, brothers, or male cousins, but another factor surely weighed on them: fear of how they would be received by the court.

Without the aid of witnesses, there was not much hope of Arch finding freedom. Arch and his attorney made the decision to plead guilty to the charge of assault with intent to kill Gideon White so the district attorney would drop the vindictive charge of Arch having attempted to kill William Adair.[11] There are two additional charges listed against Arch, both for "Introducing Spirituous Liquor," but on February 8, 1894, the prosecutor entered a nolle prosequi decision for one of them; that is, he stated he would not prosecute Arch for one of those liquor crimes.[12] That deal did not ultimately come through because Arch was prosecuted for three crimes.[13]

On March 21, 1893, a jury found the now- thirteen-year-old Charles Hair guilty of assault with intent to kill. There is no information about where Hair spent his year before sentencing. After his stint in St. John's Hospital, he could have been imprisoned at Fort Smith, although it would have been irresponsible for Judge Parker to insist that the young Hair mingle with older and hardened criminals until he was sentenced. Regardless of where he had been for the previous year, on that day, Parker sentenced him to reform school (probably the Reform School of the District of Columbia). By order of the attorney general that ruling was set aside on May 25, 1893, and Charles was instead sentenced to three years hard labor at the Illinois State Reformatory (changed from Illinois Reform School two years prior) in Pontiac beginning May 31, 1893.[14]

There is a question as to the fate of Charles Hair. Records of inmates do not start until 1895 and Charles Hair (or Hare) does not appear on any prisoner list.[15] The *Indian Chieftain* newspaper stated on September 26, 1895, that after his three-year term at Pontiac, he returned to Fort Smith on September 25 before traveling back home. According to the paper, he possessed a "letter from the reform school superintendent, giving him a good name." He apparently had a support group of "persons familiar with the case [who] were interesting themselves in his behalf yesterday and will make up an amount of money sufficient to pay his fare to Tahlequah, near which his family lives."[16] This story does not make sense considering that Hair was sentenced to three years beginning on May 31, 1893, which means he would not have been released until the end of May 1896.

Given the *Indian Chieftain*'s track record of incorrect reporting, it could be that Hair did not even leave Indian Territory. Or he served only a partial sentence. Regardless, what is known is that in 1902 Charles Hair was twenty-two years old. In his interview for the Dawes Commission he stated that he had never been out of Indian Territory, but if the *Indian Chieftain* story is correct, then Hair was less than truthful about his travels. He may have believed that admitting he had been convicted at Fort Smith might not endear him to the Dawes Commission. According to the Cherokee Nation census card, he died in 1907 at age twenty-seven.[17]

Arch's story is much more complex. All of his indictments were scheduled to be tried by jury on February 5, 1893, but records show that the trial did not take place until a full year later. There are no records indicating that he posted bail, so he probably lingered in the unpleasant Fort Smith prison among reprobates of all races, ages, and temperaments. During his ordeal, he would have been forced to contend with intimidating men. He slept on a wooden cot, washed his face in a "slop pot" and occasionally his entire body in a communal barrel. Because there was no running water, an open urinal tub served as a toilet, and in summer after the floor was rinsed with water, the steam produced an environment not unlike a steam bath. Even Judge Parker stated that the smell permeating through the courtroom floor from the prison a floor below distracted him.[18]

The *Muskogee Phoenix* on February 8, 1894, wrote that Arch Wolfe's trial would be one of the most interesting in Parker's court that month. Indeed, his connection to the now-infamous Nede Wade Christie made him a celebrity of sorts. Because of the deal made with the district attorney, Arch did not face punishment for the accusation made by William Adair. It is unknown what happened to Tom Wolf other than that he died November 9, 1895.[19] Gideon White, however, along with Paden Tolbert, William Smith, A. B. Allen, and Charles Copeland, served as witnesses against Arch and Charles Hair. There are no court testimonies to tell us if the defense argued that Hair had run from Christie's home before any gunfire or if any shooting done by Hair and Wolfe commenced out of self-defense. After all, they were completely surrounded by lawmen brandishing firearms, explosives, and a cannon. With the lawmen determined to find him guilty and with no witnesses of his own, Arch was at the mercy of the court.[20] Parker sentenced Arch to two years of hard labor at the Kings County Penitentiary in Brooklyn for the crime of assault, another eighteen months for the misdemeanor of "retail liquor distributing," and then on the heels of that sentence, he received yet another eighteen months for "introducing spirituous liquor."[21]

Yoes stated in his November 12, 1892, letter to Miller that he concurred with a newspaper story out of Fort Smith that stated, "There were no serious charges in this court against Arch Wolf, his gravest offense being his connection with Christie and resisting officers in their efforts to capture the outlaw. There are no charges here against the boy Hair, except that he was with Ned and assisted him in resisting the officers."[22] This indicates that the liquor charges were not deemed "serious," but two eighteen-month sentences—each only six months less than the two-year sentence for the charge of assault with intent to kill—for two charges of selling whiskey implies that Parker either did indeed deem them a serious transgression or wanted to punish Wolfe as much as the law allowed.

Arch Wolfe served two years at Kings County Penitentiary in Brooklyn. The penitentiary had been established around 1848. Its grounds consisted of a workhouse for inmates convicted of misdemeanors and petty crimes with a penitentiary housing those convicted of felonies.

The prison gained notoriety for its brutality toward prisoners, deplorable living conditions, and corrupt supervisors who kept monies meant for prison supplies. Prisoners were fed substandard food, including spoiled fish, "tainted meat, rusty pork and sour bread." One report stated that marrow was extracted from meat bones intended for the prisoners' soup and instead was sold for profit by kitchen workers. Some prisoners were confined in dark cells for weeks, flogged with rawhide, and forced to drag iron rollers and weights attached to their legs by chains. A broken sewer pipe dumped its contents directly into the cellar.[23] In 1888, a reporter toured the prison and stated that "I had not been inside the gates of the Penitentiary more than two hours, but I had already been impressed with the feeling that despair must indeed seize upon the minds of the unfortunate criminals incarcerated there."[24]

After a year and a half at the prison, on August 29, 1895, the twenty-one-year-old Arch Wolfe was sent to the first Government Hospital for the Insane (later named St. Elizabeths Hospital, without an apostrophe) in Washington, D.C.[25] The circumstances under which Arch left the prison are indeed bewildering. On August 29, 1895, a year and five months into his sentences, the *Brooklyn Daily Eagle* included a story entitled "Two Insane Federal Prisoners Leave the Penitentiary": "Deputy Marshals McManus and Koch left the penitentiary at 6 o'clock this morning with two insane federal prisoners, who are to be placed in the asylum for government prisoners near Washington. The convicts were Arch Wolf, an Indian, from the Indian Territory, who was sentenced two years ago to five years' imprisonment for horse stealing, and Joseph La Mafea of New York, who was given two years by Judge Benedict for counterfeiting. They were adjudged insane some time since but the order for their removal was received only yesterday from Attorney General Harman."[26]

Arch had not been sentenced because of horse stealing and it is curious that the paper did not mention the serious charge of assault with intent to kill. There are no records of Arch at the prison so we do not know the exact time allotment in the phrase, "They were adjudged insane some time since." Nevertheless, the Government Hospital for the Insane admitted Arch, and the physician declared him suffering from "acute melancholia," the cause of his affliction being "prison life."

Arch became homesick. In addition, he had been through the traumatic event that claimed the life of Christie, the man who often assumed the role of his father. Just as significant, if he had indeed languished in the prison at Fort Smith prior to his trial, he became despondent before he even walked upstairs to Parker's courtroom. Arch had three and a half more years left in his sentence. Either he did not think he could tolerate prison life any longer and fell into depression, or he may have thought he could go home and serve time in the Cherokee Asylum for the Insane, Deaf, Dumb and Blind. That institution opened in March 1877, six miles south of Tahlequah and Ned's brother Senator Jim Christie sat on the insane asylum committee.[27]

That would have been preferable to what Arch was about to face. In 1887, the *Cherokee Advocate* wrote, "No one who has seen this institution but will agree that it is by far the most beautiful of our public institutions." Workers kept it clean, the foliage in the yard trimmed and highlighted with bright flowers, and trash promptly removed.[28] The management of the Cherokee asylum proved to be quite different from the asylums where Arch Wolfe found himself. The administrators of the Cherokee asylum were not intent on keeping inmates who were not actually insane or those who were desperate to leave. In 1887, one young woman left the premises and Dr. Adair reported, "We learned that she is improved to such an extent—that she will not return again, as an inmate—Let her go—and joy be with her."[29] Other asylum superintendents had diametrically opposite viewpoints about releasing patients.

In 1905, the insane asylum had been moved to the Cherokee National Jail in Tahlequah to make room for orphans after the orphan asylum burned in November 1907. Sending Arch to the Cherokee asylum became a moot point because Oklahoma became a state in 1907, and early in 1908 the remaining ten patients were transferred to a hospital in Norman. Still, that Norman locale would have been preferable to where Arch ended up.

The Government Hospital for the Insane opened in 1855 as the first psychiatric hospital operated by the federal government. The initial goal was to provide services for indigent mentally ill patients in the District of Columbia, and for those persons in the U.S. army and navy deemed insane. The western wing was built for black patients and during the Civil War it became a hospital for navy patients. The eastern portion was used by the U.S. army for wounded soldiers. That portion took the name St. Elizabeths Army Medical Hospital. The west wing housed patients with mental illnesses.[30] Dr. William Whitney Godding had served as superintendent for eighteen years when Arch arrived.

There is no way of knowing Arch's emotions. There is no diary or letters from him to his family. There are, however, a few letters in Arch's file from his family to the hospital that reveal they became distraught at the lack of information about him. The earliest letter in the file is dated 1896 from his grandfather Arch Christie who wrote a brief inquiry about his grandson:

W. W. Godding
Superintendent

You will please let me know what they gone do for him my grandson Arch Wolf. They gone hold him till time out or they gone turn him out.

Want you let me know that.

I am your friend.

ARCH CHRISTIE
Wauhillau, Ind. Ter.

The second letter (with no date) pleads with doctors to clarify a letter written to them:

Wauhillau Cherokee Nation, IT
Dr. C. H. (illegible)
Assistant Physician
First Government Hospital for the Insane

Dear Sir

Yours of Sept. 11 '95 is at hand, saying Arch Wolf is in a critical condition in your hospital and not likely to recover. Will you kindly write inform me, his grandfather of his condition if yet alive. This will greatly oblige yours truly

ARCH CHRISTIE
Wauhillau Cherokee Nation, IT

This letter is puzzling, because Arch had been diagnosed with "melancholia" upon admittance, not a dire physical ailment that would lead to him being in "critical condition."

Arch's family persisted. There are no copies of letters written back to them from the hospital, so it is unknown if and when they received correspondence. They did, however, get at least one letter from Arch, or rather from someone who probably wrote for him because the next letter indicates his family still wanted word about his health:

Jan. 6, AD 1896

W. W. Godding
Superintendent
Government Hospital for the Insane

Will you please let me know how Arch Wolf getting along. We never hear from him long time. Last time we heard from him was getting better. You will please let me know what they gone do with him. If he gets well send back home or send back to New York.

If they will send back let us know it in a short time by writing.

When ever you write direct your letter to

Chas. E. Young's
Wauhillau post office Cherokee Nation Indian Territory.

Please write soon.

Still no reply, so Roach Young (who signed his letters Charles E. Young), Arch's stepfather, wrote a few more letters also asking for information. The shortest letter reflected the family's frustration:

July the 6th, 1896
Wauhillau Cherokee Nation, Indian Territory

W. W. Godding, M.D.
Superintendent
Gov't. Hospital for the Insane
Washington, D.C.

Dear Sir,

Please want you inform me how Arch Wolf getting along or is still there
yet or sent somewhere else. We wrote to him about four weeks now we
never heard from him yet. That is reason want you let me know soon is
possible as you can.

And oblige yours.
CHAS. E. YOUNG

Please write me.

Young apparently received no response, so the next letter came from attorneys at Barnes & Mellette in Fort Smith, Arkansas:

Dr. M. M. Godding
Washington, D.C.

Dear Sir,

The relatives of Arch Wolf who was sent from the U.S. Court here for
assault with Intent to Kill for five years, but who has been transferred
to the institution to your charge, have requested that we write you
for information as to the condition of Wolf. They want to have him
pardoned if he is in such a condition as that he could be safely released.
They think he would get better if he could get to his native country.
Please give us your opinion about the matter. The Cherokee Nation has
an asylum for the insane, but of course they get no such care as you give
there. However they want him back if possible.

Truly,
BARNES & MELLETTE

The last two sentences are poignant in that Arch's attorneys really did not know what sort of care Arch received in Washington, D.C., yet apparently felt compelled to ingratiate themselves with Dr. Godding so he might have Arch sent home.

Less than a year after his arrival at the Government Hospital for the Insane (and after only twenty-seven of the sixty months he was to serve as a prisoner), Godding sent Arch's file to the Department of the Attorney General, either asking for Arch to return to jail to complete his sentence or to be released to the insane asylum in the Cherokee Nation. By March of that year, Arch would have already served his two years for the assault charge as well as three of the eighteen months for his first liquor charge. The *New York Times* reported on June 30, 1896, that Arch Wolfe was one of twelves prisoners denied clemency by President Grover Cleveland.[31] The response of the pardon attorney, William C. Endicott, Jr., dated June 29, 1896, reiterated President Cleveland's decision: "Denied.—If this convict is still insane as appears to be the case, he perhaps ought not to be discharged in any event. He certainly should not be in the absence of the most satisfactory assurance that he will be properly cared for outside of the asylum where he is now confined."[32]

There are no letters from Dr. Godding to Arch Wolfe's family in Wolfe's file, and because the family continued to send letters asking about him, one might surmise Godding did not send them any. One letter written by Arch's stepfather, Charles E. Young, in February 1898 came across as particularly distressing, stating, "We heard is dead. If it so or not. We uneasie since we heard is dead. Please let me know soon as possible as you can."[33] Another in January 1900 implies that the family had communication with Arch sometime in the previous two years because Young stated, "We was looking for him. He thought his time out last September. . . . Be sure write to me soon is you can to his old folks. So good, good bye."[34]

The last letter in the file suggests that Godding wrote to the family, because in response, Young seemed to assume that Arch would be released: "Arch Wolfs mother and grandmother are poor not able to send any one after him. Cannot you place him [in] charge of conductors and send him to Stillwell I.T. this is near to us."[35]

There are no more communications in the file.

There is no letter telling us what Godding wrote to President Cleveland about Arch. The statement by Endicott to Godding about Arch in 1896, "as appears to be the case," suggests that Godding told Cleveland that Arch was indeed insane and should not go back to prison. That might explain Cleveland's decision, but it does not explain why he could not go to the Cherokee Insane Asylum. There are, however, two other explanations for keeping Arch away from Indian Territory and the Cherokee Insane Asylum.

By 1896, the Cherokee Nation government was headed for dissolution. In 1893, the Cherokee Outlet had been filled by opportunistic Sooners on their land run, and although the Curtis Act would not be passed until 1898, the federal government already had planned its course of action, which was to take complete control of the tribe. In 1900, for example, President McKinley overturned the Cherokee National Council's decision to allow the highly qualified Cherokee Female Seminary's principal, Ann Florence Wilson, lifelong tenure in that position. It had become clear that the tribal nations were about to be controlled by the new state of Oklahoma, and McKinley probably wanted to keep the Cherokee Nation from making long-range decisions.[36] It seems logical that Cleveland thought along the same lines four years earlier and did not want Arch back among his people who might let him leave the asylum. The other reason for disallowing Arch to leave Canton is that Cleveland knew of Arch's convictions. News stories about Ned Christie appeared in papers across the country, and considering that Christie had been labeled the killer of a deputy U.S. marshal, Cleveland would be loath to allow someone associated with Christie to leave confinement.

Godding's diagnoses reflect the notions of the day about mental health. The definition of insanity in 1895 varied, depending on who used it. Courts could declare a problem person "insane," while doctors defined the term more broadly to include persons who were depressed or those who were "idiots" or deranged. Some declared those suffering from epilepsy or "mutism"—that is, not speaking at all or not speaking to anyone besides oneself—insane. According to Roy Hamilton, Christie family members never described Arch Wolfe as having a peculiar or combative personality; rather, he was "fine." The ward notes on Arch Wolfe from November 1900 to December 1903 do not reveal anything unusual about this young Native man confined to an institution far from his tribe and who had experienced significant emotional trauma. In fact, the almost-daily log could be about almost any person experiencing a bout of depression. For examples:

November 15, 1900: "Patient seems quite well. Helps around the ward. Has very little to say. Appetite good. Sleeps well."

December 6, 1900: "Stays in bed very quietly and seems comfortable. Appetite fair."

December 7, 1900: "Cod liver oil and whiskey t.i.d." [Three times a day.]

December 8, 1900: "Strych- gr 1/30 t.i.d." [That is, 1/30 of a grain three times a day. Strychnine was used as a stimulant, laxative, and for stomach problems. It could be that Arch was given strychnine because he often seemed lethargic. It is toxic, however, and today is used as a pesticide and to poison rodents.] "Quiet day. Seems comfortable. Very fond of reading. Appetite poor."

December 16, 1900: "Patient says he spit up a quantity of blood. Complains of feeling weak. Stays in bed quietly."

December 27, 1900: "Appetite improved. Sleeps well. Seems comfortable."

January 8, 1901: "Seems rather weak. Appetite poor. Continually asking for pills or medicine of some kind. Sleeps fairly well. Habits tidy. Breath very bad. Lips dry and parched."

It is no wonder the description for January 8 states that his breath merited mention. There was no dental care at the asylum, and reportedly, inmates did not use toothbrushes. The entry also suggests dehydration. Interestingly, Godding stated that he did not believe in perpetual medication. He believed rest was crucial for all patients and stated, "A full stomach, labor, active exercise in the open air, warm baths, darkened rooms, all these are often found good substitutes for drugs in inducing sleep."[37] Still, interspersed among Arch's days are lapactic pills, castor oil, and whiskey dispensed for constipation. Arch also had bouts of vomiting, usually after a dose of colocynth or "Blue Mass." This is not surprising, either. Colocynth is an herb containing curcubitacin, a chemical compound found in plants such as cucumbers, gourds, and pumpkins that functions as a deterrent to animals inclined to eat the plants. For humans, curcubitacin from the fruit of the flowering desert vine plant *Citrullus colocynthis* (known as colocynth, bitter cucumber, bitter apple, or wild gourd) has been used to treat constipation; but it is an overcure. The Food and Drug Administration banned its use in 1991 because small amounts of colocynth can result in paralysis, convulsions, and death; at the very least it will damage the kidneys, mucous membranes, the linings of the stomach and intestines, and can result in bloody urine or prevent urination.

Blue mass is a mercury-based pill containing a variety of other ingredients, such as glycerol, licorice, or rose honey and was used as early as the late 1600s to treat syphilis. Later, doctors dispensed blue mass to relieve toothache, parasites, and constipation, the latter a problem Arch probably did have, unless perhaps the physician and nurses were not satisfied with how many times a week he visited the water closet.[38] Blue mass also had been prescribed for Abraham Lincoln for his "hypochondriasis," a term that included everything from melancholia to constipation. As researchers have since discovered, a main component of blue mass was mercury, and it is probable that mercury poisoning accounted for Lincoln's "bizarre behavior," extreme mood swings, tremors, and conversations with himself.[39]

On January 29, 1901, a physician diagnosed Arch with chronic bronchitis, but he seems to have recovered in a few weeks.[40] Proceeding through his file, one can see that observers reported that he slept well, cleaned his area, helped around the hospital, walked outside, read a lot, and did not talk much. Most days he was "doing nicely" and his condition "remains unchanged."

For examples:

February 12, 1901: "Getting along nicely."

February 20, 1901: "Seems to be feeling quite well. Helps around the hall. Appetite fair."

May 4, 1901: "Condition remains the same. Goes out walking and has nothing to say [to] anyone."

December 7, 1901: "Getting on nicely. Talks at times to himself. Helps in ward. Very willing and obedient. Appetite very good. Sleeps well."

Throughout 1902, Arch continued to read, stay quiet, sleep soundly, and assist in the ward. On other occasions he was seen "muttering" or "talking quietly" to himself, and one observer commented in July 1902 that he "mutters and laughs to himself a great deal" and seemed "very childish in manner and habits." If he had been speaking Cherokee, then obviously no one would understand what he was saying. According to Susan Burch, who has researched the Canton Asylum for Insane Indians, the staff at Canton seemed to be focused on the patients talking to themselves. She assesses that concern as "pathologizing any Native language use."[41] Obviously, Arch had no other Cherokee speaker to converse with. At Canton where he would later live, the population was comprised of Indians from around the country, but their languages were different. If the patients did not speak English, who else were they supposed to talk with besides themselves? And there is nothing in Arch's file to indicate that he behaved like a child other than this one comment.

By 1903, Arch had been away from his family and home for nine years. Bonnie Speer states in *Killing of Ned Christie* that Arch was released in 1903 and returned home because the word "Discharged" is in cursive handwriting in the last of Arch's ward notes, dated January 15. Sadly, and contrary to Speer's assertion, Arch never made it back to Indian Territory and he never saw his family again. In fact, he was among the first Native patients sent to the new Canton Asylum for Insane Indians in South Dakota.

Canton Asylum, also known as Hiawatha Asylum, was the only psychiatric facility of the Bureau of Indian Affairs. Canton opened in 1903 after Congress was convinced of the need for an Indian asylum after a survey of forty-three Indian agents stated they observed fifty-five "insane" Indians and perhaps fifteen to twenty "idiotic Indians." The agents stated that they had no facility to treat them. They did not mention if the tribes in question had medicine men or women who might address what the agents deemed mental illnesses. The commissioner of Indian affairs voiced approval of a separate asylum for Indians, although Dr. Godding argued that such a building was unnecessary. After all, he had only five insane Indian patients at St. Elizabeths (one was Arch Wolfe) and he believed an asylum for "African citizens" more important.[42]

Arch's file reveals that from October until his discharge in January 1903, he was "doing nicely in every respect." His appetite remained good, he slept well, and he worked in the ward. There is no mention at all of him misbehaving or engaging in abnormal behavior. What is puzzling is that scattered throughout the daily commentary is that his "condition remains unchanged." Unchanged from what? The file does not elaborate on any malady except constipation and talking to himself. And, interestingly, there is not a single mention about Arch being "Indian," much less a Cherokee, in his St. Elizabeths file, other than Godding's mention that in 1897 that there had only been five Indians admitted to the hospital to that point.[43]

Regardless, after Canton Asylum for Insane Indians opened, Arch along with other Native men were admitted to that facility: Miguel Maxcy (Mesa Grande) and John Woodruff (Sioux-Mulatto) both of whom also suffered from melancholia; Chu-rah-rah-he-kah (Pawnee) diagnosed with "chronic mania"; Joseph D. Marshall (Rose Bud Sioux) and Robert Brings Plenty (Pine Ridge Sioux), both with "chronic epileptic dementia."[44]

How and why did this happen? Why would Arch be transferred to another asylum for the insane? There is no clear answer. Dr. Godding died in May 1899 was replaced by Dr. A. H Whitmer who died just one year later. Whitmer's replacement was Dr. A. B. Richardson, who had the responsibility of managing an institution that cared for 2,076 patients, 500 more than it was intended to house. Some male wards were built to hold eighteen men, but instead, forty-four had to fit into the small spaces. The women's wards experienced similar overcrowding. Richardson died in June 1903, six months after Arch had been transferred to Canton.[45]

It could be that because of overcrowding Arch would be a logical choice to transfer out, especially since the Canton Asylum for Insane Indians had opened. Indians on reservations could be committed to Canton by authorization of the commissioner of Indian affairs, but investigations into Canton reveal no documents pertaining to the inmates' commitments to Canton in the B.I.A. offices. State courts could commit Indians to custody of the secretary of the interior and placed in Canton.[46] And filling the facility with "insane" Indians would prove that the Canton asylum was good and necessary.

In his report to the commissioner of Indian affairs in August 1903, Oscar S. Gifford, the superintendent and special disbursing agent at Canton, recounted the opening of the Canton asylum on January 1 and provided a summary of the first patients. He claimed that "the condition of the larger number of these patients, mentally and physically, when received into the asylum, indicate extreme neglect in their former care and treatment. This may be due to several causes. Some of these unfortunate people have no relatives nor friends who are responsible, either legally or morally, for their care or support, and some Indians are quite superstitious regarding insanity and will have nothing to do with an insane relative or friend, except to get rid of them in the quickest and easiest manner possible."[47]

While this might have been true among some groups, the Cherokees had an insane asylum, and Arch had friends and relatives. There were twenty-four Indians that Gifford met at the time of writing the letter, representatives from nine tribes: Cherokee, Comanche, Osage, Pawnee, Mission from California, Winnebago (Ho-Chunk), Chippewa, Shoshone, Fort Totten Sioux, Santee Sioux, and four other unidentified Sioux tribes. He also claimed they suffered from a variety of ailments such as paralysis, tuberculosis, pneumonia, influenza, syphilis, edema, and eczema. Arch had none of these medical issues.[48] Gifford further stated that "the establishment of the asylum was certainly a humane and proper thing to do. Previous to the opening [of] the asylum this unfortunate class of Indians were without care or attention. None of them were wanted anywhere, nor by anybody. They were a great burden to their relatives or friends, or to the agency or school officers, as the case might be, or they were neglected altogether."[49]

In regard to Arch Wolfe, the claim that he was unwanted could not be further from the truth. His family repeatedly wrote heartfelt letters to W. W. Godding at the Government Hospital for the Insane begging for information about him, asking for his return to the Cherokee Nation, and even suggested ways that he could come home. Although the Cherokee asylum did not have the same financial support as the government's asylum, there is no indication of the stringent patriarchal authority and questionable medical diagnoses as exhibited by the Washington, D.C., asylum and certainly at Canton where Arch died. And Arch's family would have been able to visit him.

There is no daily log of Arch's life a Canton. In 1907, however, a short description of Arch reads, "Arch Wolf 34 Cherokee 1/03 Union Paranoia (Terminal Stage) Systematized delusions of expansive tendency, incoherent, has parole, causes no trouble, but potentially dangerous."[50]

A closer look at this description reveals a few things. By 1907, Arch had been separated from his family and tribe for fourteen years. In 1910, only four other patients at Canton were Cherokee. If he did not converse with them, then he did not speak Cherokee with anyone else. The physicians at both the Government Hospital for the Insane and at Canton could have deemed him "incoherent" because of his language. Arch had not been diagnosed as paranoid, delusional, or dangerous at St. Elizabeths, yet Canton physician Dr. John F. Turner declared him so.

According to the American Journal of Insanity, "Terminal stage paranoia" at that time meant that the patient had developed mental weakness with "gradual fading of delusions and hallucinations." There were, however, no descriptions in the ward notes at the Government Hospital for the Insane of Arch suffering from delusions or paranoia. Systematized delusion is an "organized delusion, which fits into an overall plan that within itself maintains logic, order, and consistency, even though the logic is based upon false initial assumptions."[51] His diagnosis is quite a leap considering that the quiet and "incoherent" Arch did not impart any of his thoughts to the doctors.

Finally, the assertion that he is "potentially dangerous" might only have emanated from the reality that he was sent to prison fourteen years prior for assault with intent to kill. And even that charge was questionable. Granted, the hospital staff would not have known that. Still, he exhibited no signs of violent tendencies while St. Elizabeths and even the Canton description of him includes the statements "causes no trouble" and "has parole," denoting that he had "parole of grounds."[52] This also means the staff either allowed a delusional, paranoid, and potentially dangerous person to roam the asylum property—or the diagnosis was a sham.

In 1909, Gifford had resigned under duress because of scandals, including his not making note of a patient becoming pregnant by another inmate and another incident of his disallowing a Canton doctor from performing gallbladder surgery on a patient who later succumbed. The twenty-nine-year-old Dr. Harry Hummer, a former senior assistant of Dr. White at St. Elizabeths Hospital, replaced him in 1908, remaining in that position until he was finally removed in 1933. Hummer's tenure got off to an inauspicious start with a number of serious complaints from staff against him for mistreating patients, keeping nonviolent patients locked in their rooms, not distributing proper rations, among other things. An investigator recommended that Hummer should be removed, but the chief of the Indian Health Service disagreed, so he stayed. His abrasive and autocratic behavior persisted. Employees resigned, transferred, or were dismissed.[53]

Arch died in 1912. On July 2, Dr. Hummer wrote this letter to the commissioner of Indian Affairs:

Department of the Interior
United States Indian Service
Asylum for Insane Indians
Canton, South Dakota, July 2, 1912

The Commissioner of Indian Affairs
Washington, D.C.

Sir—

I have the honor to report that Arch Wolf, an insane full-blood Cherokee Indian, who was admitted into this institution January 17, 1903, died at 8:25 this morning of diabetes mellitus and pulmonary tuberculosis.

Superintendent Kelsey has been notified by telegram.

The remains will be interred in the Asylum cemetery unless I receive instructions to the contrary.

Very respectfully,
H. R. HUMMER, M.D.
Supt. & Spl. Disb. Agent.

There are no stories telling us how Arch's family received this devastating news or if they wrote back inquiring about details. Workers buried Arch in the asylum cemetery, "Tier Number 4, fourth row from west side, beginning at north and Canton Asylum Cemetery, All Males." Arch lies in plot 27, between a Tohono O'Odham from Sells and a Chippewa from Leech Lake, Minnesota. There are no markers.[54]

In 1910, Hummer reported that only one patient suffered from diabetes, 18 from respiratory problems, 14 of those from tuberculosis. Of the 182 total deaths at Canton, 63 were from tuberculosis, a number much higher than those who died of the same disease in the surrounding town of Canton, probably because the asylum inmates were confined to crowded and poorly ventilated rooms.[55] There had been no mention of Arch suffering from diabetes until this letter. While he lived in the Cherokee Nation, his diet probably resembled Ned's: wild turkey, deer, chicken, eggs, seasonal fruits and wild plants, garden produce, and occasional store-bought wheat flour. The basic diet he ate for two years at the prison included bread, coffee, and some meat. For the eight years he lived at St. Elizabeths, patients were fed a "plain and substantial" diet of meat, butter, potatoes, fresh vegetables and fruits in "great abundance from the farm and garden." The hospital did not serve many sweets, "the amount of pastry and cake is small."[56] Still, his bouts with constipation occurred only during winter, which suggests that fibrous foods from the garden were served only in warm months.

The food provided at Canton had to have been an ample departure from those diets to have caused Arch to develop diabetes. According to Canton records, the ten-acre farm supplied the kitchen with a variety of plant foods, as well as milk and pork from the dairy and hog herds.[57] Gifford claimed in 1903 that all the new patients who arrived at Canton craved meat and sweets, so he allowed them sweets but little meat.[58] Still, records reveal that the only person who had diabetes in 1910 was Arch, signifying that Hummer simply assigned a random diagnosis to further rationalize his death.

In 1926, a team of investigators was assigned by the secretary of the interior to investigate the conditions and affairs of the socioeconomic, educational, industrial, and medical aspects of the Bureau of Indian Affairs and American Indians on tribal lands. The result of that study, the 847-page Merriam Report, found a plethora of problems in Indian country. Among the findings of the seven-month investigation were disturbing problems at Canton. The cooking range and bakery oven did not work, there were not enough utensils, and hot water was in short supply. The dining room, bakery, laundry, power plant, and dairy barn were found in "great disorder." Some patients had to sleep on "the springs of a bed on the floor," no precautions were taken to prevent the spread of disease, the food was inadequate, and some patients ate off the floor. One young "retarded" boy was kept in a straitjacket and in seclusion for three years.[59] Any sane person who entered Canton either died there or emerged emotionally traumatized. From 1908 to 1933, Hummer served as the only physician at Canton. He made all the diagnoses, decided treatments, and prescribed medications. He truly had free rein to determine the fate of hundreds of patients.

There have been plenty of investigations into the egregious treatment of the Canton asylum inmates. Psychiatrist Samuel A. Silk, the medical director of St. Elizabeths Hospital inspected the Canton asylum in 1929 and 1933. Both times he found the facility and treatments woefully inadequate and conditions under which the patients were held "sickening" and "intolerable." There were no ward records, no data about suicides or accidents. Some patients suffered long periods of confinement, were restrained by metal shackles and wristlets, and all were locked up at night without access to toilets. There was no occupational schooling or therapy offered. Further, Silk expressed concern that there had never been a patient who had been allowed to go home on parole or on a "trial visit."[60] In October 1933, John Collier dismissed Dr. Hummer for "misfeasance and malfeasance of extreme character . . . and of practically complete failure of medical administration." And the asylum was closed the next year.[61]

So, if Arch Wolfe was not deservedly confined, why was he there? The same can be asked about other Canton patients. Bradley Soule and Jennifer Soule wrote in their 2003 article, "Death at the Hiawatha Asylum for Insane Indians," that Indians deemed troublemakers could be redefined as "mentally ill" by Indian agents. This strategy could be applied to those who butted heads with Indian agents, those who refused Christian overtures, or, as Silk discovered, perhaps a man or woman who had an argument with their spouse or a fight with a white man. The Canton asylum really did appear to be "a warehouse for cultural/political prisoners."[62]

As we can see in Arch Wolfe's ward notes at the Government Hospital for the Insane, it would be a stretch to diagnose him as "insane." After Silk inspected Canton, he came to the same conclusion about the patients there, stating that there was no justification to merit keeping many of the patients incarcerated. He asserted what many descendants already know, that some patients were there because they had argued with a spouse or were merely troublesome to an Indian agency.[63]

Silk suggested that Dr. Hummer essentially acted as a jailer, overseeing bothersome Indians who were sent to Canton from Indian agencies around the country. If that is true, then it would be up to that physician to create mental illness diagnoses to justify the inmates' incarcerations. Therefore, Hummer came up with a spectrum of ailments, including some form of melancholia or dementia, plus a host of other maladies from "hysteric angina pectoris" to "sporadic cretinism" to "epileptic idiocy." Hummer came to these conclusions about people that he admitted he knew absolutely nothing about as individuals (and certainly he knew nothing about the various cultures they represented), nor could he communicate with them because many of them did not speak English.[64]

The Bureau of Indian Affairs basically allowed Hummer, a man with numerous and serious allegations against him from the beginning of his tenure, to act in any manner he pleased. Hummer had no intention of allowing those he had control over to leave unless he saw fit. While he agreed with Silk that perhaps some of the patients really had no symptoms of mental illness, he still argued that they were "below normal" and that they needed to be sterilized. Since he had no way to accomplish that task, he kept them. Reading through the letters, reports, patient assessments, medical treatments, his dismissals of his patients' life stories, and earnest letters of complaint against Hummer leaves one wondering if Canton was the inspiration for horror movies featuring insane asylums.

Arch Wolfe, the Cherokee who had been convicted of assault with intent to kill and of whiskey selling, had been sentenced to prison for only five years, yet he ended up spending seventeen years—almost half his life—in insane asylums. More than one person decided Wolfe's fate. Vengeful lawmen, newspaper writers with a flair for sensationalism, Judge Parker, Dr. W. W. Godding, President Grover Cleveland, Superintendent Oscar Gifford, the Bureau of Indian Affairs, and Dr. Henry Hummer all contributed to Arch's miserable existence. One might even fault Ned Christie for running from the law in the first place and allowing Arch (and the twelve-year-old Hair) to stay in his home when he knew an armed posse could arrive at any time.

Gideon White, the man who accused Arch Wolfe and Charles Hair of attempting to kill him, became a schoolteacher and taught for twenty years. He contracted typhoid and died two years after Arch. His funeral at the La Veta, Colorado, Cemetery positioned him as an honored soldier, a Civil War veteran. Nineteen military guards served as honor guard detail.[65] Dr. Harry Hummer opened a private practice in the Canton area and died in 1957 at age seventy-nine. He was buried with honors in the Congressional Cemetery in Washington, D.C.[66]

CHAPTER 7

THE HUMPHREY THEORY

*Christie was a horse thief who killed
Marshal Dan Maples and others.*
"OUTLAW INDEX: NED CHRISTIE"

Twenty-five years after Christie's death, two newspaper stories and one letter to the editor appeared in Oklahoma newspapers. All three say basically the same things, but with different names. One in particular has served as the foundational rationale for Christie's innocence.

First, on March 5, 1917, the *Tulsa World* looked to reignite interest in Christie and published a sketchy story with no author and no sources credited. The article explained that on the night Maples was shot, Christie and Bub Trainor visited "old lady Schell" and bought a quart bottle of "firewater" from her. Later, Christie stood at one end of the crossing log with the bottle of whiskey in his hand about to take a drink when Trainor said, "There's Sam Manus. Shoot him." Christie then drew his pistol and shot Maples. The paper alleges that Christie had an argument with Manus a few days prior and that Trainor knew the man was not Manus.[1]

Manus was Ned's brother-in-law and there are no family stories about an argument. It appears that this letter writer got the idea about Manus from the 1892 story in the *Indian Chieftain* claiming that Christie attempted to shoot Manus and instead hit Maples. And Nancy Shell testified after Maples's death that Christie had come to her house before Maples was shot, but she did not say he came with Trainor nor did she say they purchased liquor. Deputy Marshal J. F. Stokes testified after the murder that Bobtail made mention of "some women who were selling whiskey," but did not reveal them by name.[2]

Two months after the publication of that *Tulsa World* story, D. E. Ward, a Cherokee who claimed to have been in Tahlequah at the time of the shooting, wrote a letter to the *Tulsa World* to say the Manus version was incorrect. Ward explained that on the night of the shooting, Maples used the new telephone at the J. W. Stapler and Sons store to call Fort Smith. A man whom Ward identified as "Jones" listened in on the phone call and heard Maples request that warrants be issued for bootleggers "Old Lady" Shell and Mandy Springston, a person heretofore not mentioned in any document. Jones told "Bud Trainer" of the phone call and Trainor then relayed that message to John Parris's brother Taylor Parris. John Parris and Bub Trainor then went to the log crossing "just below the deep hole." As they crossed, Trainor noticed Christie drunk and asleep, his coat next to him. Trainor put on Christie's coat and waited for Maples. It so happened that the "darkey" blacksmith, "Humphrey," watched from a distance as Trainor shot Maples and kept watching then as Trainor shook the still-drunken Christie to wake him to give him back his coat. Christie wandered east to sleep in a thicket while Trainor went west. Ward states that the next day Christie met friends in town who told him that Maples had been killed and Christie was deemed the culprit. Those friends told him to "go on the scout" and Christie fled the area. But Ward also writes that Christie hired E. C. Boudinot and R. M. Wolfe to work on the case and he came to town every few days to talk with them. Christie planned to face a Fort Smith trial, but the violent September 1889 encounter with Thomas and Isbell changed his mind. Ward asserts that Maples fired one shot that broke a bottle nestled in the pocket of Christie's coat worn by Trainor. The neck of the broken bottle fell to the ground. He claims that Shell could identify the bottle as the one she sold to Christie because it had no stopper and she used a torn piece of her dress instead. Ward concludes that the broken bit of bottle was the evidence needed to indict Christie.[3] There is no explanation of why Parris and Trainor felt compelled to shoot Maples, although it might be assumed they were angry at the potential loss of their whiskey dealer.

Nothing more was written until a year later, on June 9, 1918, when the *Daily Oklahoman* published "Cherokee Indian, Killed for Murder He Didn't Commit, Exonerated after 30 Years." The *Daily Oklahoman* makes it appear as if it broke this story, when in fact, this oft-used story is directly copied from Ward's 1917 *Tulsa World* letter except that instead of "Jones" the paper changed the eavesdropper to "Winn" and, the story states that Humphrey was afraid of Trainor so he did not inform authorities what he witnessed.[4] Whom did Humphrey tell? None of the papers say. Steele writes in *The Last Cherokee Warriors* that this story actually broke in 1922 in "a Tulsa, Oklahoma newspaper" within an article written by former lawman Fred E. Sutton. In this story, Sutton claims that Dick Humphrey told him that he had witnessed someone other than Christie shoot Maples. What makes this claim interesting is that Steele apparently did not see the previous *Tulsa World* and *Daily Oklahoman* stories that had already mentioned Humphrey. It might be assumed that Sutton copied from previous stories without mentioning them and decided to take the credit for the Humphrey concept. That remains to be seen because Steele does not properly cite this newspaper story and it cannot be located.[5]

All of these stories are unlikely. Nancy Shell was born in 1849 and was only thirty-eight years old at the time that Maples supposedly requested a warrant for "Old Lady" Shell. Neither Shell nor anyone else mentioned a bottle, much less a cloth bottle plug, during their court appearances. And, there are no other reports of anyone questioning Shell about how she stopped her bottles. The first *Tulsa World* story also contradicts the testimony given by Christie's brother-in-law Sam Manus in 1887, when he swore that he saw Christie after the shooting and he was standing. Further, if Christie had issues with Manus, he had ample opportunities to confront him in daylight and Manus made no mention of conflict between him and Christie.

Did Christie wear a coat or a light jacket? Although weather records begin at 1900 and we do not know the temperature the May evening that someone shot Maples, the average high temperatures in early May are from the 70s to the low 80s during the day and the coolest temperatures are in the 50s.[6] Christie would not, therefore, be wearing a heavy coat; instead, he would likely have worn a light jacket. The *Daily Oklahoman* writer did not like the letter from Ward that stated Christie's coat was on the ground next to him, so he changed that scenario to "Bud [Bub] Trainor, who wore a white shirt, stepped up to the sleeping man and drew the coat from his body." What this means is that not only did Trainor not consider the evening cool because he did not wear a jacket, but that he actually took Christie's coat off of him while Christie lay passed out on the ground. It can be difficult enough to remove clothing from a sleeping child, much less from a grown man. One also wonders about the bottle in the "inside pocket" that was broken by a bullet, but that bullet did not hit Trainor. There are no Christie family stories about a bullet-torn coat. Along that line of inquiry, the bottle managed not to fall out of the coat pocket as Trainor struggled to get the coat off of Christie.

The story says that Christie bought a "quart" bottle from Shell. Also according to the *Daily Oklahoman* story, the bottle fit into his coat pocket. A light jacket would not have an "inside pocket" to hold a quart. Even if Christie had a smaller flask of whiskey, it is unlikely that he became unconscious from drinking, say, eight ounces of whiskey from a bottle small enough to fit into a jacket pocket. It depends on how much he had eaten beforehand and his degree of hydration.

If the bottle was empty, why would Christie put it back in his pocket? If the bottle still had whiskey in it, the liquid would have gotten all over Trainor after it burst from being hit by a bullet, and anyone around Trainor, and then Christie the next day, surely would have noticed the smell. And if Christie lay on the ground, the bottle would be horizontal and the whiskey would have flowed out through the cotton material from Shell's skirt. If the bottle Shell sold to Christie had no cork and she had to use material from her dress to stop it, that means she also used dress material to plug the other bottles that she sold. What would have been left of her dress at the end of a night of whiskey selling?

Indeed, Ward's claims in his letter do not mesh with Shell's testimony that she heard shots thirty minutes after Christie left her place, seemingly too short a time for a man to absorb enough whiskey to pass out, especially if he shared the bottle with another person. The portrayal of Ned as a hard-drinking character is crucial not just to Wild West writers who need to portray their outlaws as irresponsible sozzlers. This image also is essential to those writers wanting to prove Christie's innocence. In order for the theory that he was unconscious at the time of Maples's shooting to work, Christie had to be a habitual drinker who unsurprisingly passed out.

Witnesses stated that Christie and his uncle Grease were together, yet the *Daily Oklahoman* story ignores the reality that Ned was not alone. Sam Manus testified that he saw Ned Christie at Nede Grease's home after Maples was shot, which contradicts the *Daily Oklahoman* story that states Christie was passed out all night and did not realize what had transpired until the next morning. Nede Grease lived just a few short blocks from the site of the shooting. Christie always stayed at his home when he came to town for council meetings and it would be unusual for him not to stay at Grease's that night. Christie had a bed just a short distance away, but according to these stories, he just lay down on the ground. Nede Grease would not have allowed him to stay outside overnight and, even if Christie had passed out, Grease knew Maples had been shot and would have looked for his nephew. Christie would not have been difficult to find. In addition, the *Dallas Morning News* reported that at least twenty shots were fired. A person cannot stay asleep through such a firestorm occurring right over his head.

The *Daily Oklahoman* story also states that Humphrey was "old" at the time of the shooting in 1887. "Old" is a relative term and if Humphrey was, say, seventy—an age deemed "old" in 1887—he would have been 101 in 1918. Speer states that

Humphrey was eighty-seven when "he told his story to the *Daily Oklahoman*," but she gives no reference as to where she found his age.[7] She copied this vignette from Steele, who refers to the elusive 1922 "Tulsa, Oklahoma, newspaper."[8] Richard A. "Dick" Humphrey or Humphreys is not listed on any Cherokee Freedmen rolls (Wallace, Kern-Clifton, or Dawes; the latter closed in 1907), on any Cherokee census record, nor is he mentioned in any Works Progress Administration or Doris Duke oral history interviews. There is, however, listed on the Wallace Roll, a "Richard Humphries" who was sixty-four in 1890, making him ninety-two in 1918.[9] If Humphrey talked in 1922 (and that is highly unlikely) he would have been ninety-five years old. "Dick Humphries" is also mentioned in a short article about "darkeys" selecting a burial ground "a mile above town in the timber near Dick Humphries."[10]

Questions of age aside, Shell and Manus testified that they heard shots "after dark." The *Daily Oklahoman* story tells us that Humphrey stood "away down the creek on another foot log, concealed partially by a bend in the creek." In other words, the paper wants readers to believe that Humphrey not only was positioned around "a bend" (which meant he had no direct line of sight), but he saw what transpired from a distance, who did the shooting, and how that affected the victim, Maples. This took place after sundown, in the dark, under a dark tree canopy.

Bub Trainor was shot in 1896 by "negroes," either as he sat at a table eating, or at a "negro dance" on Rab's Creek outside of Oologah after he threatened one man. The alleged killers were Jack and Nick Rogers and Tat Hawkins.[11] The *Daily Oklahoman* referred to them as some Cooweescoowee "bad niggers."[12] This is a direct contradiction of the story's first paragraph that states, "The man who is said to have been the cause of the murder being committed is still alive but far away from Tahlequah, the scene of the murder." Trainor had been dead twenty-two years when the *Daily Oklahoman* article appeared, so who did the editor expect readers to believe killed Maples? Trainor's 1896 death leaves the obvious question of why did Humphrey not tell what, if anything, he knew at that time. He probably did not come forward at all, but that has not stopped writers from using this story.

Steele, Speer, and subsequent writers have used the Humphrey Theory as the accepted reason why Christie should be considered exonerated. Speer claims that Humphrey had approached the *Daily Oklahoman* editor to tell his story, but Steele asserts that it was Fred E. Sutton who wrote it for the *Tulsa World*. The article used most often, from the *Daily Oklahoman*, however, does not even say that Humphrey was interviewed, much less when or where. Sutton fixed that troublesome problem by attributing the interview to himself, even though the supposed interview took place four years earlier. The information contained in Ward's letter and the *Daily Oklahoman* is not buttressed by other documents or witnesses. Speer states about the *Daily Oklahoman* article, "I was delighted to find that details were supported by other records in the National Records."[13] To the contrary, not a single document she lists in her bibliography supports the "details," or any of her other discussions, for that matter. She also concocted a quote, attributing it to that story, that Christie had left Shell's house, "considerably drunk," when no such phrase exists in the paper or in the court testimonies. She also states that marshals Carroll and Curtis found the broken bottle after Maples died, yet that assertion is attributed to a source that does not mention a broken bottle or the two officers. Once again, Speer slyly takes information about the broken bottle from one source—the *Daily Oklahoman*—and attributes it to another source to lend more weight to the argument. She then asserts that "Curtis told Carroll that many people believed that John Hawkins or Jackson Ellis had been the intended victim," but the reference she cites is untraceable.[14]

Numerous other versions of what happened the night of the shooting appear in newspapers, journals, and books. Since the Humphrey Theory is faulty and does not hold together, the question remains: Did Christie shoot Maples?

First, one must consider what Christie may have done after leaving Shell's house. Shell did not state to the court that anyone bought whiskey from her, although it is reasonable to assume they did because she was a known whisky seller, and it is doubtful that she would admit that to Judge Parker even if he already knew her business. Christie probably did purchase whiskey from her. He had no other reason to go to her home.

Christie was with Nede Grease, so walking back to his uncle's home seems a logical scenario. If the two men did go back to Grease's home, which was located a few blocks from the spring, they surely heard the gunshots from inside the house. If they did not hear shots, then it is understandable that Christie would have been surprised to learn what happened the next morning. That is a moot point because Manus stated that he saw Grease and Christie after Maples's shooting, which means they did hear the shots. And Manus's testimony negates any claim that Christie had passed out or learned about the shooting the next day.

If Christie had been with Nede Grease during the Maples incident, that means Grease could have said exactly that in court. Grease, however, did not travel to Fort Smith when called to testify about John Parris, but then again, neither did the other summoned witnesses. Why did Grease not talk to the papers and defend his nephew? He may not have wanted to talk to reporters or Judge Parker for the same reason that Christie never did. Both Nationalists Keetoowahs were of the same mind about the U.S. government and were concerned that they would not be believed. Parris and Trainor were not Keetoowahs, however, and they were not known for making any negative commentary about the federal government.

The theory that the Christies were so leery of the government that Christie refused to defend himself is not easy to accept. Most innocent people accused of murder would want to protect themselves and one would think their relatives would want to help. But the overriding factor for Christie was his fear of the U.S. court system and that may indeed have proven the main obstacle to his coming forward. Parris, Bobtail, Trainor, and Hogshooter managed to wriggle out of the charge because there was another man in the vicinity of the killing and that man refused to discuss his side of the story. And Judge Parker did not forgive those who tried to elude him. The hardened judge probably believed that if a man ran, he must be guilty. Christie should have defended himself immediately. Too much time had passed. Being accused of murdering a white deputy U.S. marshal and then convincing others you did not do it would take some serious strategy and good attorneys.

What if Christie had appeared in Parker's court? Other than pleading not guilty, one can speculate about possible scenarios. Parris and Bobtail might swear that Christie did it. Christie could have summoned witnesses who would say he did not shoot Maples, most notably his uncle Nede Grease who would testify that he was with him at his home. If Humphrey had appeared at court at that time (and provided the *Daily Oklahoman* story were true), he might have been challenged by a prosecuting attorney for claiming to have seen what had transpired in the dark. Christie could say that, yes, he had been drinking, but that he had only a bottle small enough to fit into his jacket pocket. Perhaps Christie would call witnesses who could swear to his good character as one of the tribe's political leaders. Still, because no one seems to have seen what happened, except for the killer (and maybe the man who stood next to him while he shot Maples), Christie might be discharged because of reasonable doubt.

If Christie did not kill Maples, who did? Either John Parris or Bub Trainor, and both knew who pulled the trigger.

The case for Trainor being the culprit is that there was little bad press about him and his family. As previously discussed, there is a big difference between what happens to the reputations of Ned Christie and Bub Trainor. Hawkins, the Cherokee high sheriff, had shot Bub's father, the white man Thomas Trainor, Sr., in self-defense. Trainor Sr. will be remembered as being a sloppy and loud drunk, and despite his attempt to murder a man, he is still considered "harmless" as well as "an affectionate father and loving husband."[15] Trainor also fathered Bub, who proved to be relentlessly ill-behaved, yet the misdeeds of the son also were pushed into the background. The Trainor family escaped character assassinations probably because Bub's mother, Lucy, served as a courier for the Cherokee Confederates during the Civil War. Bub's sister Anna attended the Cherokee Female Seminary and grew up to be one of Indian Territory's prominent socialites, seemingly the token "Indian maiden" used for social events. She first married Muskogee-Creek Albert Stidham. After he left Indian Territory in 1894, she married Dr. Leo K. Bennett in 1895, the Indian agent for the Union Agency. They led an active social life, reportedly mingling with President McKinley and his wife. After Bennett died, she wed Warren R. Butz. He quickly died and she married Mark Matheson who died a year later.[16]

In 1907, Anna served as "Miss Indian Territory" for the "symbolic marriage" between Miss Indian Territory and Mr. Oklahoma Territory—that is, between the two territories sometimes called the Twin Territories—at Guthrie's Carnegie Library, then did it again at the twenty-fifth anniversary of Oklahoma's statehood, as well as at other events.[17] Oklahoma statehood is not an event celebrated by traditionalist Natives of either territory, certainly not by Keetoowahs. Bub probably escaped more personal prosecution from the powers that be in Oklahoma because of the prominence of his sister.

Parris is the more likely culprit. Bobtail had immediately accused him of being the shooter after the men were taken to Fort Smith. Unlike Trainor, who continued to live in the area and behave badly, Parris made himself scarce after he left the Little Rock penitentiary in 1890. His brothers stayed in Indian Territory, but there are no more mentions of John in the documents. Bub had the confidence to continue his wayward life. Parris may also have done so, but he lived it elsewhere, away from any possibility that attention might turn toward him as the killer of Dan Maples.

CHAPTER 8

CREATING OUTLAWS AND THE HEROIC HEROES WHO KILL THEM

Storytelling is the oldest form of entertainment there is. . . . It is one of the most fundamental ways humans have of making sense of the world.

THE NEW YORKER, December 29, 2015

Ned Christie, the noted Cherokee outlaw, was one of the most dreaded of his class, and the full history of his many crimes will never be recorded.

D. C. GIDEON, *Indian Territory*, 1901

Stories told about Christie the outlaw, whom the forces of good (lawmen) chased and dispatched, are part of the larger western storytelling tradition that includes attributes of manliness, outdoor adventure, American expansionism, and rugged individualism. As Michael T. Marsden wrote in 1978, "In the Western, issues are placed within the context of a fixed, historical world in which the final outcome is never in question, only the means to reach the outcome are."[1]

There are two endings for Christie: one is that Christie killed Maples and the men who retaliated against Christie remain above reproach; the other is that Christie did not kill Maples and he died an innocent man who stood up for his tribe. How writers created their conclusions is alternatingly fascinating and disconcerting. For the most part, they simply wrote what they wanted to be true. Details within a story can be created by anyone with an imagination and, indeed, versions of Christie's story contain plenty of what Michael L. Johnson refers to as "post-frontier hallucinations."[2]

....

Christie has been demonized in two ways: as an outlaw and as an Indian outlaw. Interestingly, while some news stories describe Christie as a "Cherokee outlaw,"[3] many news stories do not mention that Christie was an Indian, much less a Cherokee. The common theme of Indians as members of an uncivilized race that is inherently inferior and inevitably doomed to fall to the advance of democracy and Protestantism does not appear in stories about Christie. There are few racist descriptions of Christie the Indian and only a couple from newspapers published within the tribal nations.

For example, the *Chicago Daily Tribune*'s November 1894 story is notable not only for its audacious descriptors of lawmen and outlaws and its insulting descriptors of females but also for its repetitive errors. In this odd piece, the writer refers to Christie as both "Christy" and "Starr" and Charles Hair is called "little Nick Wolf." The women are called "squaws" and we are informed that, during the last siege on Christie's home, "Christy during the lulls in the fusillade yelled and hooted at the deputies and called them unpleasant names in two languages. By and by he sent his two wives out just to get them out of the way. They were taken in charge by the deputies. They amused themselves all day by reviling the Deputies and telling what their Ned was going to do to them unless they got back to Fort Smith in a hurry. The two squaws seemed to look on the whole affair as a joyous picnic."

As for "little Nick Wolf," the writer created a typical scenario for the "little wild Indian" who behaved like an animal: "The boy was pretty well singed, but he revived fairly well to be carried back to Fort Smith as a trophy. They put him in the jail there and he crouched for weeks in the darkest corner of the hospital glaring at everybody as wildly as any caged catamount."

The strange story continued, describing Christie's "gobble" as "the pet Indian style of expressing defiance or a yearning for blood. When your Indian man gets full of bad whisky, when he wants a fight, when he is really feeling good, he 'gobbles.' It is a weird performance—an imitation of the war notes of the turkey cock. As these Indians do it, it is enough to scare the fight out of most men. Christy gobbled and bellowed away all day in a most terrifying manner." Then the paper cites Deputy White, who says, "The critter made me feel real nervous."[4] Once again, here is an early reference to Christie as a drinker and in this case, an early-morning imbiber.

That is the exception. Most papers outside of Indian Territory do not describe Christie in the same manner they do other Natives. For example, the *Waukesha Journal* wrote about Big Foot's men before they were massacred at Wounded Knee, South Dakota, on December 29, 1890: "When the savages at Wounded Knee turned their carbines upon the soldiers these troops faced the awful fire."

This is the same edition that referred to Christie as "a negro outlaw."[5] And from the *Deadwood (S.D.) Daily Pioneer Times*: "General Carr is rushing through a plan whereby he will give the treacherous, bloody horde a fight that will be their last this side of the phantom hunting grounds. These devils have one and only one alternative now, either to lay down their arms or be shot down carrying them."[6] Something similar appeared in the *Spearfish (S.D.) Queen City Mail*: "Col. Forsyth says he counted ninety-two dead bucks, and while pursuing the Indians through a ravine he saw several more dead bucks, but which he didn't stop to count. He believes they killed nearly all the bucks of Big Foot's band."[7] No one referred to Christie as a "buck," and no one wrote that Christie had a "band" with him; rather, he had a "gang of desperadoes."[8] Arch Wolfe is called "a tough customer and a desperate man."[9] And Christie hails from a "notoriously desperate and murderous family."[10]

The "Apache Kid," or just "Kid" before he gained notoriety, was born at the San Carlos Agency around 1860. He served as a first sergeant of scouts at the agency and was court-martialed for desertion and mutiny because he left the area to kill another Apache who had murdered his grandfather. After serving five years at Alcatraz, he then was convicted of murder in a civil trial and sentenced to the Arizona Territorial Prison in Yuma. He escaped on the trip to jail in 1899, and then disappeared into the west. When and where he died remains unknown.[11] Like Christie, Kid was a complicated and mysterious figure whom newspapers described in the same derogatory terms as Christie and accused of a spectrum of unsubstantiated violent depredations.[12] A report out of Washington, D.C., printed by the *Newton Daily Republican* referred to "the Apache Kid," as a "restless redskin" and "wily savage" for eluding lawmen, but in the column next to that is a report from Tahlequah that refers to Christie only as "the desperado."[13] A month later, the *Salina (Kansas) Daily Republican* printed a story from Deming, New Mexico, that described "the Kid and his band of Apache renegades" as savages thrice, and two columns over, Christie is described by a Tahlequah report as "the notorious outlaw," "a perfect specimen of physical manhood," and "before becoming an outlaw was an experienced gunsmith."[14] The story does not mention that Christie was an Indian.

There are only a few racist descriptions of Christie in local papers. The *Muskogee Phoenix* reprinted a short piece from the *Ft. Smith Call* that stated, "Christie was a full-blood Indian and his countenance and general make up is about an ideal, one would have of the original blood thirsty savage of the 'Western Wilds.'"[15] This particular story is not surprising because the *Muskogee Phoenix* sided with Progressives at every opportunity and proved especially deleterious to Christie, the Nationalist. That paper had a penchant for biased and tabloid-type news and is assessed by Jerry Akins at the Fort Smith National Historic Site as the *National Enquirer* of its day.

As did newspapers outside of Indian Territory who wrote inflammatory stories about Christie, the *Muldrow Register* did the same. It had no reason not to. Christie and his fellow Keetoowahs and Nationalists were vehemently against the unethical intruders onto their tribal land. After the November 1890 raid on Christie's home, the paper maligned his name once again:

> He is perhaps the most notorious outlaw and desperado in the Indian Territory. . . . Christie has turned up alive and may cause trouble yet; is said to be on the war path fiercer than ever and vows vengeance on the marshal and his posse. Ned Christie is perhaps the most desperate character in the territory and there is a large reward offered on his head. He has killed a number of men, among whom might be mentioned the Squirrel brothers, also considered "tough men." He is said to be a dead shot, has eluded the officers of the law for about four years and says he will not be taken alive.[16]

The majority of newspaper stories about Christie say that he is a bad man resembling Jack Wilson, the villain in the movie *Shane* (1953). Wild West stories including Christie were penned by writers who did not know anything about Christie other than what they read in other papers: that he killed a lawman. Marsden writes that in westerns, there is the "epic confrontation between the gunfighter/messiah/hero (who redeems the town/civilization/mankind through cleansing violence) and the villain who may be a disembodied abstraction of evil or a more concrete form of savagery."[17] Writers made up descriptors of a generic evil criminal and applied them to Christie, but writers who knew that he was Cherokee did not know how to identify him. Christie was not like Goyanthlay (Geronimo) or Sitting Bull. He lived in a different world from the Apaches and Plains tribes. He may have been a traditionalist, but he also was educated and read and wrote in English, served as a tribal council member, and dressed like white men in the Territory. Christie did not fit the standard image of people most Americans believed to be "wild Indians." Murderers, thieves, rapists, and swindlers pervaded Indian Territory, and casting Christie in the same light as these criminals may have been easier than to describe him as an educated Indian criminal who appeared different from the "uncivilized" Indians.

As early as February 1895 the *Cherokee Advocate* attempted to debunk outlandish tales, presumably referring to fabricated stories printed in the *Globe Democrat* about Henry Starr, Belle Starr, and Ned Christie. The *Advocate* reprinted stories stating that Christie "led many a daring raid years ago," and that Henry Starr "alone killed over seventy men, fully a dozen of his victims having been felled with a single blow of his mighty fist. He was a Cherokee with a tinge of Seminole blood, nearly 7 feet tall, massively built, and with an arm and fist like a sledge hammer." In response, the *Advocate* admonished, "We publish the above in order to show what wonderful liars some correspondents are. . . . Ned Christie was wanted for murder but never led any raids . . . and was in no way connected to any band of outlaws."[18] Writers ignored this statement and persisted in comparing him to various outlaws or used his name to enhance the reputations of lawmen.

That Christie happened to be an Indian rendered him prime fodder for some writers who took advantage of his situation. White Americans clamored for land in Indian Territory and the convenience of having a bad Cherokee at large gave further justification for extreme action against him. Dan Maples, a white marshal, had been shot and because the case against Christie was shaky, there needed to be more crimes attributed to him. Killing Christie, the Outlaw Indian, would be doubly justified. Nontribal papers discussed Christie and seemed eager for him to be eliminated. But kill him in order to save whom? One vague statement could mean either Cherokees or Indian Territory residents in general: "and while he possessed many warm friends in the nation, he has been the cause of much anxiety and fear on the part of others."[19] A few papers put forward statements that Christie needed to be killed to safeguard the *white* people who inhabited tribal lands. In order to make him appear doubly dangerous, papers added that Christie also posed a threat to Cherokees. Several papers, therefore, ran the same line: "All the Cherokees join in denouncing the murderers and stand ready to volunteer their services to crush the bloodthirsty outlaws out of existence."[20] The *Salina Daily Republic* said that "twenty good and true Cherokees" participated in the final assault on his home.[21] The *Chicago Daily Tribune* published a story, "End of the Reign of the Bad," that reads like a precursor to the later Wild West stories: "He killed Maples, then gathering three or four companions, he set out to follow the old road of crime. Horse stealing, robbing country stores, and whiskey peddling employed his talents until the deputies crowded him too close." The paper continued by stating that Dave Rusk and Charlie Copeland recruited a "small army of friendly Indians" to "dislodge the desperate man," but failed.[22] And as previously mentioned, Speer and Steele tell us that Ben Knight acted as a Good Indian Scout to show lawmen where Christie lived because he did not approve of

Ned's behavior.[23] Here we see the "friendly Indians" at work—those men who are deemed "good" because they rally behind the white lawmen against their "bad" brethren.

On the other hand, some writers attempt to show that the "good" Indians are rare because Cherokees sided with the murderer Christie. McKennon wrote that "the Cherokees rallied with silent vigor to protect Ned."[24] Steele claims that Christie and his Keetoowah friends created an army to surround and protect him.[25] Another story claimed that "the tribe hid Christie on top of a hill about a mile north of his burned out house, and for shelter built him a rough fort nestled among boulders and foliage."[26] The Cherokees did not hide Christie. Keetoowahs may have kept an eye out for posses coming his way, but Christie knew where to go and he stayed on his land. Christie's hiding place stood in plain sight.

....

Berkhofer writes that Indians usually served as the backdrops for western plots, not as the center of attention. To completely focus on Indians, and in this case, Christie, "would have discarded simplicity for complexity and violated the premises of popular culture production. If the Indian was to be taken seriously, his motives and his culture would have to be presented as alternative values and lifestyles to White civilization . . . since introduction of Indian culture would imply the questioning of White values if not the criticisms of White actions in history."[27]

Therefore, we do not see much discussion about Christie's life before Maples's murder except for the usual manly descriptors, such as he knew gunsmithing, was a crack shot, stood tall, attracted women just like his father, and behaved aggressively. We do not see in the newspapers much about the men who were with Christie the night of the killing: Bub Trainor, John Parris, and John Hogshooter, with Trainor and Parris being particularly unruly individuals who engaged in unscrupulous behavior before and after Maples's death. Until the 1918 *Daily Oklahoman* story about Humphrey, few papers bothered to debate Christie's guilt or innocence. The sensational stories ignore the reality that there were numerous people in the vicinity of Maples's shooting. There is a reason for this: the papers also would have to explain how Christie became a guilty murderer, not merely a suspect.

For the five years that Christie attempted to stay away from lawmen, Cherokees engaged in serious debates about events that would alter their land base and sovereignty. News reports about Christie's encounters with the lawmen usually originated from Tahlequah and found their way across the country. Not mentioning that Christie was a Cherokee would be a logical omission. With few exceptions, papers in the territory did not exaggerate stories about him because, until the death of Maples, Christie and his family were prominent and well respected. Pondering his guilt or innocence would have to include his position as a national councilman. Serving on the council and creating acts and laws for a sophisticated tribal nation that patterned its system of governance after the United States was no small responsibility. Making more of the Maples's killing than occasional news flashes would only draw attention to the Cherokee Nation and might cause readers to wonder about how a murderer found his way into an important tribal position.

During the last two years that lawmen were closing in on Christie, Sitting Bull was killed, soldiers massacred 256 Sioux at Wounded Knee in South Dakota, and the Apache Kid escaped. Newspaper writers could not take up space explaining the complexities of how an educated Indian (who probably knew more about U.S. policy than many white people at that time) would have such a significant role in tribal politics. It was more essential to sell copies. Besides, most newspapermen did not know much about Cherokee culture. Descriptions of the realities of Tahlequah, with some mixed-blood Cherokee women in Victorian dresses and carrying parasols alongside Cherokee men dressed like eastern attorneys, were not exactly the images most Americans held about Indians. Newspapers would have too much explaining to do.

Any discussion of Christie's possible innocence would necessarily also bring up issues of federal criminal jurisdiction in Indian Territory, which most tribespeople believed intrusive. There also would be revelations about Christie's cultural and political allegiances and the latter, especially, might be polarizing. After all, Oklahoma statehood, allotment, and the ending of tribal governments illustrated the government's willingness to break treaties, cast aside tribal concerns about culture retention and sovereignty, and spotlighted the government's negligence in not stopping the tidal wave of white intruders onto lands that were guaranteed to tribes. Indeed, any later analysis would reveal unfair and racist policies and most newspaper editors were unwilling to criticize the government.

....

A common theme of Wild West literature and western movies is that the action takes place in the wilderness, away from civilization. Writers of that day did not depict outlaws and lawmen as men who sat around philosophizing or pontificating. The bad guys and the good guys who pursued them were depicted as men of action.[28] As such, the active males are always riding horses, hunting, shooting, chasing outlaws, or preparing to do all those things in a challenging, unknown landscape void of the refinements of American culture.

Portraying Christie as a man skulking around in the wilds satisfies two criteria for the Wild West genre. First, he is a "child of the forest," a Noble Savage, who is most comfortable away from civilized people. He lives in a dangerous and mysterious wilderness, what Frederick Jackson Turner referred to as "the meeting-point between savagery and civilization," an environment that for that moment many white people fear.[29] Simultaneously, he is a villain who cannot normally function in civilized society so he must live far away from it. Therefore, a commonality among stories about Christie involves his residence that is set away from settled towns. There was nothing mysterious about where Christie lived with his family in Wauhillau. They had a home and outbuilding, along with a garden, a few horses, cows, dogs, and chickens, just like the majority of residents in Indian Territory at that time. Even after a posse burned his first house, the one he rebuilt was not as spectacular as some writers describe. His normalcy did not matter. By 1892, the year Christie died, the last tribes had been sent to reservations (Sioux tribes to the Dakotas and Apache tribes to the Southwest), white settlements had been established from coast to coast, the bison were almost gone, and the wilderness was quickly fading. There needed to be some excitement about the vanishing frontier in the news and Christie provided it. As Michael L. Johnson writes in *Hunger for the Wild*, "Americans were loath to let go of their frontier mythology."[30] Newspapermen and Wild West writers have been happy to oblige.

The *Chicago Daily Tribune* expresses how many felt about the Indian Territory "wilderness" in the late nineteenth century: "Then there are great areas of utterly wild country, well timbered; the population is an inextricable mixture of Whites, negroes, and Indians—what better range could the bad man ask? He has come hither from everywhere—old veteran desperadoes, convicts, every kind and condition of criminal. So horse thieves, train robbers, killers, highwaymen, bootleggers, and whisky peddlers are thick enough in the Territory. It has a red history, this strange land."[31]

Writers therefore turn the modest Cookson Hills into "mountains" dotted with "hundreds of caves" and valleys are instead labeled "box canyons," as if Christie were eluding John Wayne amid the red rocks of Sedona. Two of Christie's structures, his sturdy log home and ten-foot-high stone lookout, are referred to as part of the landscape: "a mountain fortress"[32] or an "an impregnable fortress" against a "sheer rock face." Rand also wrote that Christie hid in "the box canyons north of Tahlequah, where it was almost impossible to find him." Rand attempts to depict the same type of three steep-walled canyon with only one entrance and egress often seen in the West and used to trap wildlife—or as used in movies, to corner outlaws or outlaws' victims. In this scenario, Rand attempts to conjure the possibility that any lawmen trying to capture Christie would have to ride into the mouth of the canyon and become trapped and vulnerable to being shot by someone along the top of the steep cliff walls.[33] Other papers refer to Christie's home base as in the "Caney Mountains," "the mountains," or the more dramatic "storm port" or "cabin fort in the Caney mountains."[34]

The unknown dangers that might lurk in the imposing wilderness are not enough to keep the resolute heroes from confronting their personal fears. Anderson and Yadon describe the arduous path Isabel and Fields took to get to Christie's home in 1889: "It took three days of skulking over craggy cliffs, quietly easing aside thousands of spindly, ensnaring, thorny branches of briar bushes, wading through swift-running creeks, and above all else, avoiding the many silent alarms that were Ned's friends and neighbors."[35]

They do not say exactly where these "cliffs" are located, much less the "swift-running streams." It is true that the area was heavily forested, but one also needs more information about the "thousands" of thorny briars. Perhaps they mean blackberries or saw greenbrier. Looking at the area today from the vantage point of Google Earth, one can see how much has been cleared for ranching and farming. Granted, during Christie's lifetime, trees and underbrush covered the area. Navigating that landscape in the late 1880s would not have been easy and anyone who wanted to approach Christie's home would need a good sense of direction; otherwise, one could become lost. Still, although the landscape was indeed forested, it was not impossible to traverse. It does not matter, really, because the message is clear: with American fortitude forged from sheer grit, the manly representatives of the law—the white law, that is—forge ahead to protect the weak, cowering citizenry from the threat of the fugitive Christie who concealed himself in the lands beyond.

The "caves" of the Cookson Hills are an integral part of the 1964 story Jack Forbes authored about the Cherokee "mad killer" Mose Miller for *The West* magazine. Mose Miller is like Christie and Pigeon, a Keetoowah, with plenty of wild stories told about him. Forbes wrote that Miller operated as part of a gang and in this unsubstantiated tale, Miller could escape into "those Hills where a hundred caves offered perfect hiding places."[36]

The *Dallas Morning News* played off the December 10 *Muskogee Phoenix* story about the Poorboy and Whitehead murders committed in 1891, the same time that lawmen were stepping up their attempts to arrest Christie. The paper was obviously referring to Christie when it wrote, "There are a dozen desperadoes in these hills who have notches on their gun stocks showing the number of lives they have taken. The gang knows every hog path in the almost impenetrable country and have a system of signals by which the movements of officers are communicated to members of the gang as they travel these paths and public highways. It is known that one of these passes in the mountains leads to a tent village, where the bandits go for rest or when too closely pushed by the authorities."[37]

There were no "tent villages" or mountain passes. Situating Christie in the wilderness helps to separate him from trappings of civilization such as literature, music, and reading.[38] Stories such as Rand's depict the uncivilized Christie emerging from his dark backwoods to kill random people, then retreating to the mysterious hideout. The hardy white lawmen, however, know how to negotiate Christie's rough country and the stories serve to illustrate the lawmen's talents and resourcefulness in defeating their enemy, who is at home in the wild. Ned Christie died on his homeland where he grew up; it was not in a fortress, box canyon, hideout, or cave, but outside of the home that he built, in the company of his family.

....

Christie's actions, as described by some newsmen, were fast, vicious, and unrelenting. In the realm of western outlaw and lawmen literature, Christie made his decision not only to resist arrest but also to become a criminal. He is not conflicted. Someone had to rescue innocents from the diabolical brigand and any man who went after the fiend needed to be tougher than Christie and mightier than the average marshal. Anything Christie the outlaw could do, the marshals would have to do better. These are precisely the men readers got. All narratives about lawmen of the West describe dominating, almost superhuman marshals who die only because of old age, ambush, or in Heck Bruner's case, drowning during an attempt to cross a river to catch a criminal.

Richard E. Meyer states that when analyzing the lives of outlaws and lawmen, writers must take "the factors of distortion, embellishment, and fabulation at face value, as phenomena indicative of a 'truth' equally as viable as literal historical veracity."[39] Indeed, every lawman associated with Christie continues to be described repeatedly and consistently in manly terms: tough, dead shots, determined, independent, resourceful, honest, efficient, and they never disobey orders. Even lawmen who granted interviews to newspapers seem to be aware that they are legends in the making and they contribute personal folklores to the creation of their mythologies. Christie shoots, wounds, and thwarts the intrepid officers, but they refuse to give up. They eventually kill their quarry after blowing up his home with dynamite and they stand next to his dead body. The pictures are posted on multiple outlaw and lawmen sites. There is no regret expressed by any of them in any publication that came after. Judging by the plethora of writings that continue to be published about them, these men will forever be immortalized with guns in their hands.

From the perspective of Fort Smith lawmen and those who faithfully support them, Maples is the main victim in the Christie saga. Maples even garnered the legend of a friendly bird landing on his shoulder—an avian attempt to warn him of impending doom. In 1964, Maples's grandchildren spoke to the *Northwest Arkansas Times* writer Pat Donat regarding their grandmother's tales about her husband, Dan Maples. They claimed that Dan Maples traveled to Tahlequah at the behest of the residents "who asked for a man who was not afraid because the lawless element had gotten out of hand." This article only offers a few new statements about Maples from his grandchildren because the majority of the article rehashes news from previous newspaper stories and articles. There are no reports anyplace else that Tahlequah residents requested Dan Maples to come rescue them. Cherokees had their own marshals. But because Maples did not have the opportunity to show us that he was a stalwart lawman, newspaper stories retroactively make him so.

The story reads that Mrs. Maples died in 1934 and she "never forgave the Indians for killing her husband." Donat then snarkily proclaims, "The Indians apparently didn't forgive themselves for they offered a reward and promised to do all in their power to catch and bring to trial the slayer."[40] While residents of Tahlequah did indeed compose the indignation letter, not all of the people who signed it were Indians. And saying that Indians "didn't forgive themselves" for the transgressions of another Indian would be the same as asserting that white people did not forgive themselves for Billy the Kid's behavior, which is hardly what Donat had in mind.

Tall tales of the heroism of deputy U.S. marshals appeared within a few years of Christie's death, and through the decades bragging contests emerged to see who could one-up the previous imagining. The first revolved around Copeland. The *St. Louis Republic* claimed that Copeland single-handedly dispatched Christie after camping for a week around his "fort" and, when Christie left his home, sneaking in and placing dynamite in the cellar. He waited until Christy returned "and then exploded the bomb." The paper further asserts that Ned never received a decent burial and besides, "his friends could not find enough of his body to hold a funeral."[41]

Yet another yarn appeared in the *Cleveland Plain Dealer* paper based on a letter written to them posted from Wichita, Kansas. According to the unknown letter writer, who claimed to have interviewed Copeland, the latter said, "I've had many a good Indian fights, but the hottest one I ever led was in the attack on Ned Christy and his gang." Besides the usual Wild West boasting—"We were on the edge of the reign of terror down here then in those days before Judge Parker had cleared the Indian Territory of its gangs of desperadoes"—Copeland claims that inside the fort with Christie was his "gang," consisting of Red Eye Scraggy, Red Cloud, Browne, Rattlinggourd, and Ike Rogers. Copeland assessed Christie as "the nerviest Indian I ever met," then asserts that "in the six months that gang operated he killed six deputy marshals, four express messengers, and ten other men who had the misfortune to stand guard over money that he wanted." Copeland claims he led the attack on the fort and hired Smith, Bruner, and Ellis. He declared he had ridden the 160-plus miles to Fort Smith, then another seventy miles to Tahlequah. He described Christie's home as a "hut" and referred to his wife, Nancy (who came outside to look around prior to the fight), as an "old squaw." His version is that "three of the gang dashed out" and they were quickly "laid out." Bill Smith and White were shot and incapacitated, as was Heck Bruner. Copeland says he crept up to the cabin with the dynamite, the building exploded, and when Christie appeared at the door, Copeland shot and killed him.[42]

In 1937, C. B. Rhoades gave a rousing testimonial to lawmen that he called "Lest We Forget":

> The writer again wants to state that no braver set of men ever lived than the old Indian Territory deputy marshals. They possessed all the cunning of the animal in pursuit and location of fugitives, again the writer wants to state the night was never too dark, the weather too severe the roads and trails too rough or crooked for the old deputy to fail to act and they had all those conditions to contend against. Not a public or Section line road, not a bridge across any river, and very few ferries. Yet the old deputy received call for his services at midnight save as noon, and he went.[43]

What is notable about this tribute is that he refers to these men as "old" yet they continued doggedly in their quest to kill or capture badmen. Apparently, they had no desire to just sit by the fire for a spell with their feet up. The "Lest We Forget" romantic diatribe of the eternally determined aged lawmen, however, is the section immediately before his "Capture of Ned Christie" interview, which includes exaggerated claims, such as two thousand rifle bullets and thirty shots of the cannon fired, all to no avail until the six sticks of dynamite blew up the house. With two exceptions, the men who participated in the siege were under forty, most were under thirty, and two (Clayland and Sarber) were teenagers.[44]

Illustrative of newspapers attempting to celebrate the gutsy lawmen and to catch readers' eyes is the extravagant headline in the January 8, 1911, issue of the *Daily Oklahoman*: "Little Stories of Men Whose Lives Overflow with Danger; Wildest Tales of Adventure and Excitement Never Equalled the Real Histories of United States Marshal and Deputies Now Working in State of Oklahoma."

This article contains the reminiscences of "grim, dead-shot manhunters": Allen "Al" G. Goff, Chris Madson, "Scissors Tails" Henry "Heck" Thomas, John Paul Jones, and D. A. Haden, who told tales about Christie, the Verdigris Kid, the Daltons, Bill Doolin, Scar Face Bill, and others, including Cherokee Bill (Crawford Goldsby), whom John Paul Jones called a "human hyena" and Heck Thomas referred to as "that nigger-Indian mixture of all that was bad."[45]

John R. Abernathy, sometimes known as Wolf Catcher and Catch 'Em Alive Jack, also has emerged as a rather fantastic historic figure. He was born in 1876 to Scottish parents in Texas, and grew up Sweetwater. His various professions included a U.S. Secret Service agent, a wildcat oil driller, and from 1906 to 1910, deputy U.S. marshal. Abernathy's real talents lay in wolf catching; but not with a gun. Instead, he forced his hand into a wolf's mouth, thereby stunning it. He earned fifty dollars per wolf "by eager ranchers" and caught the attention of President Theodore Roosevelt. According to his autobiography, "I have caught over a thousand wolves with my hands, and I suppose I have ridden that many bad horses. During my career as an officer of the Government, I captured hundreds of outlaws single handed and placed seven hundred and eighty-two men in the penitentiary."[46] One might question these rather dubious claims, but further exploration into his tales would sully his image.

Marshal Heck Bruner, who participated in the final siege on Christie's property, was not only credited with killing Christie but also with having "done more to rid the territory of desperadoes than any other marshal in the territory." That claim was made even more impressive because the paper also misstated that Christie used a Gatling gun to keep lawmen away from his home.[47] Yet another paper claimed that Bruner "had a hand in bringing to justice every notorious outlaw that struck that country during his term of office." In order to make Bruner appear powerful yet reasonable, the paper added, "He never shot a man unless he was forced to do so, but he would perform his duty at all hazards and get his man dead or alive."[48]

In Phillip Rand's frenetic narrative, "Blood in the Cookson Hills," Deputy Jim Brand was shot to death when he attempted to accost Christie. Enter the thirty-two-year-old Heck Bruner, whom Rand calls one of the "great United States marshals of the West," to deal with the outlaw. Rand goes even further by writing that during the final moments of the siege on Christie's home, Bruner was the one pushing the cannon and Christie shot him in the shoulder. A few seconds later Christie shot Bruner in his leg; "he went down but came up weakly." Bruner kept pushing the cart, then Christie shot his chest, and Bruner fell. Apparently, those wounds were not enough to impart to readers Bruner's sturdiness, so Rand adds that the explosion caused "rocks and splinters from the blasted logs" to rain down on the valiant Bruner. He made a remarkably fast recovery in a Fayetteville hospital.[49]

Bruner's death offered the opportunity for writers to rehash the man's life and their contrived tales included the outlaws he vanquished. The *Daily American Citizen* published such a story, claiming not only that Heck Bruner killed Christie with his "sure aim" but also implying that Christie is buried in an unmarked grave in the "Heck Bruner Graveyard" section of a Vinita cemetery alongside the other "bandits and dangerous outlaws" that Bruner dispatched.[50] Wright contends that heroes possess at least one "exceptional ability."[51] Those who rode after Christie had more than one. They were not only exceptional marksmen, riders, and trackers; they were also physically irrepressible.

Bass Reeves has drawn praise for his efficiency as a deputy U.S. marshal and also for being one of the first black lawmen in the West. Reeves never encountered Christie, but because one news story in 1890 falsely claimed Reeves attacked Christie's fort and almost killed him, that scenario has been cited repeatedly for 125 years, mainly by Wild West writer Art Burton. The Bass Reeves legend has grown through the decades and it could be that, in the words of one long-time Fort Smith National Historic Site curator, "Art Burton created Bass Reeves."[52]

Many residents of Indian Territory desired to place themselves firmly in the midst of the grand western epic, that is, to be remembered for their manly exploits and having taken part in the transformation of the American landscape. Therefore, many residents claimed to have known or encountered Christie. In 1897, the *Wichita Beacon* featured a story about C. S. Bowden who commented about Christie, "Ned sent a bullet through my hand. . . . He was the hardest man I ever tackled. . . . He shot to kill, and he was a shooter. . . . Bullets came thick and fast." He also seemed a bit sympathetic: "Talk about outlaws, bandits, and desperate characters of this territory, but Ned Christie discounted them all. With a large standing reward on his head he never ran away, but staid at home with his family and met all comers, and was only overpowered and killed by overwhelming odds."[53] A hitch to this story is that there was no "C. S. Bowden" in any record associated with Christie, but there is a "Bowden, Charles L., D.U.S. Marshal" on a list of Oklahoma's U.S. marshals, deputy U.S. marshals, and possemen.[54] Even if the paper is mistaken and this is actually C. L. Bowden, there is no other report of Christie shooting him. There is, however, the case of John Fields, whom Ned shot in October 1892 during the attack on Ned's home. Fields was the nephew of Bowden and it could be that Bowden took that shooting story for himself.[55] In 1937, C. B. Rhodes commented that "some of the men wounded in previous battles with Christie carried their hurts permanently until their death."[56] Rhodes makes it sound as if there were a host of men shot by Christie when in fact the only men who had injuries were Isabel and Fields.

In 1921, yet another "pioneer peace officer" who "reigned as a terror to criminals" appeared in the news. J. J. "Uncle Bud" Ledbetter, who at the time of the story was seventy years old, stated without any trace of humility that he not only captured Al Jennings during the "wild and wooly times long passed," he also "jumped Henry Starr," "had it out with six-shooters" with Cherokee Bill, and "caught Ned Christie." In addition, he "smashed enough whisky to float a dozen battleships."[57] There are no records of Ledbetter having any connection to Christie.

Fifty-five years later, the eighty-three-year-old J. W. "Wess" Bowman spoke about Christie in Gilbert Asher's Wild West story that appeared in the *Tulsa Daily World* article "'91 Gunfight with Outlaw Still Vivid." This story is replete with adjectives—"rough," "tough," "dangerous outlaws"—in addition to claims about Christie, including that he was "one of the most feared outlaws of that or any era." And the oft-repeated claim that "Christie had ridden a crimson trail through the area, leaving in his wake the bodies of murdered men and the rifled strong boxes of business firms and private citizens" makes an appearance. The 1952 story never mentions that Christie was a Cherokee.[58] Bowman's legend continued to grow because fifteen years later he was credited with killing Christie. Thirty-two years after that, the late Bowman appeared yet again as a feature in the *Fort Smith Southwest Times Record*. The paper expanded the previous stories to state that Bowman and other marshals fired cannonballs "all day long" at Christie's "fortress," and that finally, "a flash of powder fired by 23-year-old deputy U.S. marshal Wes Bowman brought Christie to his end." And afterward, the paper claims, "as Parker looked at Christie's corpse, he praised Bowman for shooting Christie."

Even the headline states that Bowman killed Christie: "Deputy's gun did what dynamite couldn't." The paper also states that Ned stood six foot four inches tall and twice refers to him as a "big Indian." Again, this comes from McKennon, who wrote it first. The paper also makes an important statement about the inherent dangerousness, yet righteousness, of lawmen: "Bowman decided at 18 that it was time to make a living for himself. He had little education and believed there were few professions at which he could succeed. A skilled gunman, he saw two choices: being an outlaw or a lawman."[59]

Despite all of this self-congratulation among lawmen, the *Cherokee Advocate* office recognized it years earlier for what it was. Crime continued to flourish in the territory and tribal police played significant roles in killing or capturing criminals. Many were taken to Fort Smith, while Indian criminals were tried and convicted in tribal courts. The *Cherokee Advocate* took exception to the commonly held idea that Cherokee lawmen did not receive credit for their work:

> It seems that some people are so prejudice and narrow minded that they can not see anything that is good in the Indians. Even when a Cherokee officer captures or kills an outlaw the papers in the states says the work was done by United States deputy marshals. Recently Sam McWilliams and John Sanders were killed by Johnson Manning and—Stephns, officers of the Nation and in giving acc't of the killing a Fort Smith paper says the marshals did the work, when in fact there was only one marshal present, and he was disarmed by the outlaws and had it not been for the Cherokee officers he never would have recovered his gun. The entire Cook gang was captured or killed by Cherokee officers and citizens of this Nation, except Bill Cook, who was captured in New Mexico. It is discouraging to Cherokee officers after risking their lives to capture outlaws to have the honor given to some deputy marshal.[60]

....

Curiously, some writers vilify Christie as a murderer and thief, but they also describe him as "a perfect specimen of manhood," possessing "more than ordinary intelligence";[61] "one of the bravest men in the southwest";[62] and "as cool as a dancing master."[63] One of the earliest descriptions of Christie's physicality appeared in 1902, when the *Chicago Daily Tribune* refers to him as a "big, handsome, smooth featured Indian."[64] More than half a century later R. H. McKennon understood that dangerous men needed to be physically intimidating. Therefore, he elevated Christie to six feet four in *Iron Men* (1967): "Christie was a striking figure of manhood, dark features, snapping black eyes and he wore his hair in long black locks contrary to most Cherokees. He was six feet four inches in height, and he had the catlike agility of his forebears."[65] That feature is repeated by Philip Steele and in numerous newspapers and western literature, such as Dorman's *It Happened in Oklahoma* and Clyde Good's essay, "Ned Christie: Determined Cherokee Renegade," in which Good takes that impressive descriptor even further by adding that "the 6-foot, 4-inch Indian served as bodyguard to Principal Chief Dennis Bushyhead."[66] Anderson and Yadon describe Christie as "having always been a strikingly good-looking specimen."[67] The phrases about his masculinity and intelligence first appeared in November 1892 newspapers after word came from Tahlequah that Christie had been killed and these descriptors have been adopted by dozens of writers since. None of the newsmen who copied these descriptions offer any elaboration, but given their obsession with height and appearance it meant he stood tall and was easy on the eyes.

Gail Bederman, in his *Manliness and Civilization,* notes that by the 1890s among the middle class, the ideal male body was no longer the "lean and wiry" look of the 1860s; rather, the new ideal was larger with well-defined muscularity. Team sports and exercise grew in popularity and football became a fierce expression of masculinity.[68] Writers geared their material toward middle-class males and expressed this appreciation for manly appearances and behaviors by using masculine terminology to describe outlaws and lawmen.

This concern about masculinity is clearly illustrated in the descriptions of Christie's physicality. Descriptions of Christie's height and distinctive physical appearance in western lore is crucial, just as are the physical images of strapping western movie actors Clint Eastwood, William Smith, Gene Hackman, Charles Bronson, John Wayne, Lee Van Cleef, and many others. Not surprisingly, the late Creek actor, the imposing six feet five Will Sampson, was supposed to play Christie in a 1970s movie that derailed before it got started. In order for McKennon's portrayal of Christie to work—that is, Christie as the huge and formidable bad guy—he had to ignore the reality of Christie's real size. In fact, in order to keep up the "David and Goliath" comparison, McKennon describes Bowman as having a "slender figure" in the same paragraph he describes Christie as "an extremely tall Indian." He also reminds us multiple times that lawman Dave Rusk was only five feet four, and of course, others repeat that.[69] He does not mention anything about Christie's probable height in *Iron Men*, and neither do other writers who can clearly see the differences in stature between Christie and the possemen who killed him.

He may have been a "perfect specimen" but that is all we get—nothing about his beliefs, any code of honor he may have held, or how he treated his family. Of course, those things were not especially interesting to the readers who just wanted him dead, but before his demise, he needed to be a worthy foe for lawmen. Many people were pleased he died, but some of those same people also admired his resourcefulness and perceived him as a rugged individual, traits highly revered. These contrasting images of Christie as savage brigand and at the same time a tall, handsome, talented gunsmith, outstanding fiddler and marble player, Cherokee councilman, deadeye, and defender of his homeland in many ways mirror the romanticism of the charismatic Tecumseh, the Shawnee who attempted to unite midwestern tribes against the United States in the 1790s. To make Tecumseh even more sympathetic, the Rebecca Galloway legend was created: even a white woman could be attracted to the Noble Savage. In short, although Tecumseh was definitively anti-American, his masculinity, independence, and intelligence also served as a role model for white men.[70]

We see this admiration for other outlaws. Papers described Jim Starr, who repeatedly found himself in trouble in the 1880s, in similar ways as Christie: "a splendid specimen of the half-breed, tall, powerfully built and courteous in manner. He possesses some excellent natural traits."[71] The *Arkansas Gazette* complimented criminal Tom Starr: "the Cherokee Nation produced a remarkable lot of desperadoes in its time, the most wonderful of whom was old Tom Starr."[72] The *Philadelphia Times*, however, included a story about the romanticism of Frank James and how his cell in the Independence jail had been "transformed into a regular drawing room." The paper expressed dismay:

> The people make a lion of him. His name is upon everybody's lips. Women grow sentimental over him. Young girls carry him bouquets of flowers, and the boys imagine themselves a Frank James in embryo and emulate his deeds in miniature. It is a sickly kind of sentiment which pervades the air of Independence. It is anything but a good lesson which is being taught Young America. Instead of painting Frank James as the murderer, assassin, train robber and bandit that he is, people sympathize with him, use their influence with the Governor for a pardon, and talk about him as if he had never been such a very bad man after all.[73]

Writers like Rand viewed Christie as a villain with no redeemable traits. Readers may have wanted to see Christie die for what he supposedly did to Dan Maples, but they sure did admire his rugged individualism. Others consider him a hero because stood against colonization and many perceive his five-year run from the United States lawmen an injustice, but also brave on Christie's part, as the title of Lisa C. LaRue's book, *He Was a Brave Man: The Story of an Indian Patriot*, tells us. Still others believe Christie was innocent of killing Maples, but possibly had a hand in the deaths of Palone and Grimmet, and shot lawmen Fields and Isbell. To them, Christie is still a hero, capable of violence yet wrongly accused of the serious transgression of murdering a lawman. Still, he ran from the law and that made him an outlaw, regardless of whether he killed Maples.

All heroes have flaws. Richard E. Meyer analyzed the stories about Sam Bass, Jesse James, Billy the Kid, and Pretty Boy Floyd and concludes that these "outlaw-heroes" possess certain characteristics or "elements in the conception of the outlaw as a peculiarly American folk type." Christie also fits into Meyer's "elements" that define a folk hero:[74]

He is a "man of the people," identifies with the common people, stands in opposition to certain established, oppressive economic, civil, and legal systems peculiar to the American historical experience.

Christie's story resonates with Cherokees and other peoples whose history includes oppression and persecution. Inherent in the Cherokees' view of Nede Wade Christie is that he stood against allotment, Oklahoma statehood, and the pilfering of tribal resources by outsiders. Cherokees state that Christie regularly spoke out against white intrusions onto Cherokee lands. Chief Bushyhead and editors of the *Cherokee Advocate* knew this and they supported his appointment to the National Council.[75] The killing of Christie was not just a way to eradicate the threat of violence. His death also meant eradication of an opinionated voice concerned about white encroachment on tribal lands.

Phillip Steele also understood this, but he expresses the sentiment incorrectly. Among the many problems with his book is the title, *The Last Cherokee Warriors*. This implies that after Proctor and Christie died, no more Cherokees went to war. To the contrary, not only have Cherokees fought to preserve their lands and culture since contact with colonizers, thousands of Cherokees have participated in wars after the two men died, from World War I to those currently serving in a spectrum of roles in the U.S. military.

In his preface, Steele states about Proctor, "Through an unusual set of circumstances a half-breed Cherokee named Ezekiel Proctor became the tribe's leader in its last revolt against the United States interference in the Cherokee judicial system." Steele also states that Proctor was the only individual in history to sign a treaty with the U.S. government, yet he also asserts several times that such a document does not exist and he assumes that it must. He then cites a 1967 letter from Congressman Ed Edmondson to A. D. Lester: "Since records of the 19th Century were very incomplete, it is possible that a newspaper clipping will be the most reliable source of news of this type. They cannot find records of this specific grant of amnesty, and said that an inquiry to the National Archives by them turned up no records on it there. The Library of Congress said that a news clipping often was the most reliable record in those days, and they also advised that you should use it as your substantiation for the grant."[76]

This is an amusing stance because as we have seen time and again, while some newspaper stories were accurate, others were—and are—among the least reliable sources of information. Steele states that "hundreds" of newspapers stated that Proctor was granted amnesty by Grant, but, newspapers in the nineteenth century usually took a flash of news that arrived and editors either copied it verbatim or added supplementary aspersions. In this case, papers from around the country used the one—elusive—story from Fort Smith and reprinted it.[77]

Steele also claims, "By most Cherokees they [Proctor and Christie] are remembered as the last of their tribe to stand up for their lands against the encroachment that resulted in the eventual loss of a proud nation." Again, Steele is incorrect. The Cherokee Nation has never been lost. Proctor and Christie may have had strong concerns about the changing world around them and about how socioeconomic policies were affecting their tribe, but they were hardly the only ones leading "a personal war for what he believed in." They were not the "last warriors," regardless of how one defines the term. Roy Hamilton's book title, *Ned Christie: Cherokee Warrior*, is more on the mark. As with other tribes, there exist serious issues within this large nation, including political factionalism, identity appropriation, land use, climate change, health problems, and poverty, and there are plenty of Cherokee scholars, attorneys, activists, environmentalists, educators, traditionalists, health care workers, business people, and grassroots movers and shakers who are engaged in protecting their nation. "Warriors" is an apt term for the modern Cherokees who fight for tribal sovereignty and treaty rights. Christie and Proctor did this, but the struggles did not stop with them.

The outlaw-hero's first "crime" is brought about through extreme provocation or persecution by agents of the oppressive system.

The descriptions of the lawman Heck Thomas as being "genial, harmless and likeable" illustrate another trait of heroes: the ability to behave ruthlessly when necessary to destroy evil, resuming their normal placid and acceptable behavior after the threat is gone. In this genre, the villain Christie is not allowed to be normal. Perhaps he once was an upright citizen of the Cherokee Nation but like the once gentle Old Yeller, his behavior became unalterably changed and he had to be put down. He had reverted from being a semicivilized Indian National Council member to a cold-blooded savage.

Certain influential events started Christie on his course of outlawry; what those events were depends on who is writing the story. One is the shooting of Maples. After Christie's death, the *Arkansas Gazette* reported that "he was once a quiet, peaceable man, but his career of crime commenced when he killed Maples. He was possessed of a deadly hatred for Deputy Marshals, and woe be the luckless officer who crossed his path." In this story, we are not told why Christie hates deputy marshals, only that he does and that he killed Maples. But this newspaper story also states that "he never had a practice of robbing people," thus negating its claims of Christie embarking on a career of crime.[78] More importantly, in order for this scenario to make sense, there must be a reason for his encounter with Maples. The paper does not give us one. Steele takes his cue from that newspaper story and writes that Christie turned from a "beloved, jovial, and peaceful citizen" after shooting Maples into a "belligerent outlaw" who "struck out against the invaders."[79]

Another newspaper writer analyzed Christie: "His frequent conflicts with the officers plunged him deeper and deeper into the meshes of the law until he soon arrived at that stage of the game where he either had to hang or shoot it out, and he chose the latter."[80] Pride asserts in his story "The Battle of Tahlequah Canyon" that Christie "turned his back on his family, friends and everything he had stood for" before embarking on "a six-year spree of outlawry."[81] Speer writes that the bullet that hit his face in 1889 not only caused "grotesque facial features" but also caused him to never again speak English and resulted in a dramatic personality alteration: "he became vicious and driven by hatred of all White men."[82] Anderson and Yadon also write this, citing O'Neal, who does not mention how Christie felt about being shot. Nevertheless, they add their own adjectives: "Christie was more than a little put out with Thomas's shooting that day; so was the bridge of his nose and his right eye. The bullet left a fierce scar to Christie's classic, chiseled Native American face. That bullet inspired an incessant, fermenting hatred for Whites."[83] Stories that rely on the Disfiguring Bullet assert that not only did Christie's personality change for the worse after being shot but that those who destroyed his handsomeness would eventually kill him. The facial wound was not nearly as devastating as writers describe. In order for the psychological change story to work, however, Christie needed to be significantly disfigured.

Yet another contribution to the Christie legend, albeit completely incorrect, is provided by Robin Stann, who combines all the above events. In the middle of "that night," impatient marshals who could not find Christie snuck to his home that was occupied by his wife and children. They set fire to the home, causing the occupants to flee into the darkness outside, and his thirteen-year-old son was shot and killed in the melee. Seeking revenge, Stann said, "Christie defied the marshals and turned from the once fine and amiable, law-abiding citizen that he had been and became a killer, for in his heart was a bitter hatred towards the marshals who had killed his child and burned his home and he came into the open and sent the marshals word where he was and told them if they thought they could capture him to come and he would shoot it out with them. For two years Ned Christie lived hunted like a rabbit."[84]

In 1937, Eli Wilson told his opinion, although it is a typically vague *Indian-Pioneer Papers* reminiscence:

> This officer [Maples] thought it smart for him to hail an Indian Councilman and embarrass him [Christie] by hailing him before a court. Christie thought this man was an intruder or ahold up instead of an officer. He just drew his own gun that he always carried for self-protection, as it was during the days when self-protection was a common law. He thought himself lucky when his opponent fell but on further examination found he had slain an officer of the law and at that Christie became excited and just rode home to his family. He really did not know what he should do in case of this nature.

Wilson also claims that Christie "stated to me that after he had time to realize that he would be charged with murder he thought it no benefit to try to beat a murder case under the existing Cherokee laws. He just decided to die at home fighting."[85] There are no reports of Maples confronting Christie, and Wilson does not explain what he means by "intruder." Also, Christie had no issue with Cherokee laws; rather, it was U.S. laws he feared.

In *The Last Cherokee Warriors*, author Steele attempts to find commonality between Christie and Proctor by molding both men's images into "two angry men," that is, "Cherokee warriors." Virgil Berry also assessed Proctor as perpetually "angry"—if not furious: "It is a peculiarity of the American Indian that when he becomes an outlaw against society his hatred of the human race knows no bounds."[86] Conversely, a man who knew him, Stanley Clark, commented that Proctor had a smile" that would illuminate his whole face."[87]

Another incident that changed Christie's life was when he decided not to travel to Fort Smith and instead "went on the scout" to evade the law. As Eli Whitmire explains it, "Christie had no way of proving his innocence."[88] Parris and Trainor could not prove their innocence either, but they appeared at Fort Smith and that made all the difference. Because of Christie's decision to run, he shot Isabel and Fields in self-defense after the two men attempted to arrest him at his home in 1889. But running from the law and trying to remain peaceable is not the same behavior as evading officers, and then purposefully killing and robbing. Newspapers preferred the latter because the actions of a thief and killer make a more marketable story than deputy U.S. marshals hounding an innocent man.

Wilson's last sentence, "He just decided to die at home fighting," might be true. Christie could have left the Cherokee Nation and even Indian Territory, but instead he stayed among his extended family and fellow Cherokees. He had to have known in 1887 that there was a possibility he would be prosecuted, but by 1889 when lawmen came firing their weapons, he realized there was no way he could survive much longer. One might assume he told his family and friends to stay away from him for their own safety, but they made their decision to remain and support him. Arch Wolfe and Charles Hair definitely felt the repercussions of their choices.

The outlaw-hero steals from the rich and gives to the poor.

There are only a few stories about Ned attempting to "right wrongs" after the shooting of Maples. One, found at *The Spell of the West* website, describes Christie as a Robin Hood who stole to give to the poor despite there being no evidence of him being a bandit.[89] There also are no other stories about Christie bestowing any booty that he may have collected to anyone because he never stole any.

An elderly Oklahoma resident in 1972, however, made a statement about Christie being generous as well as protective, and this provides a rationale for why Christie shot Maples:

> I've been told that Ned Christie didn't kill the man [Maples] he was sup-posed to have killed. There was a man and his wife at the spring at the foot of Northeastern College entrance. People used to come to the spring and get water in barrels and take it home in wagons. There was a Cherokee man and woman there at the spring and she was pregnant. I was told that

this man [the father to be] killed some man and Ned Christie was there, and said he [Christie] did it to protect this man from going to jail. He [must] have known these people and been their friend.[90]

The outlaw-hero is good-natured, kind-hearted, and frequently pious, and during his career he is helped, supported and admired by his people

Residents of the Cherokee Nation testified about Christie's charisma. Christie was a social man who played marbles with his friends; Roy Hamilton recalled that his aunts told him that at gatherings Ned danced and friends always asked him to play his fiddle.[91] Eli Wilson claimed in 1937 to be so close to Christie that after the various encounters with lawmen at Christie's home, Wilson and his siblings ran over to Christie's place to pick up the empty shells to see how many men he had killed. After shooting whoever attempted to accost him that day, Ned would not only take the time to ascertain if the cows needed milking or the horses watering, he also would sit down and play marbles with Wilson while laughing "very heartily." Wilson stated that a lot of his neighbors always came to visit him and "express their joy that he had come through safe once more. You see Ned was a nice neighbor, and a very intelligent man to talk with."[92] Another man stated, "He stood and walked as straight as an arrow which was typical of his race, always truthful and reliable and never known to betray a friend."[93] And as Roy Hamilton wrote, "He is a man which many people greatly love and remember fondly—including myself."[94]

Many outsiders did not think kindly of Ned, but they did of his brother Jim. In May 1894, a rather intrusive minister named Milton A. Clark wrote in the newspaper *Our Brother in Red* about his visit with Ned's brother Jim and his wife, whom he does not bother to refer to by name. "Jim is very different from Ned," wrote Clark. "He is an industrious, quiet, peaceable Indian." He then recounts the array of vegetables Jim's family cultivated and animals they raised. It is curious that he also states, "It is a rare sight to see cards, spinning wheel and loom in a home these days, but we saw all these at Jim Christie's." To the contrary, many Cherokees played cards and many utilized looms. Clark also recounted a previous visit in which he did his best to convince Jim and his family to become Christians, but that effort was to no avail. During that visit, he also learned that the community did not want him to return.[95]

According to a multitude of newspaper stories and books that copy those tales, family members and Keetoowahs warned Christie of approaching lawmen, and to a certain extent, they did. In 1969, Jack Kilpatrick stated, "The Cherokees indignantly deny every charge in unison and go right on believing that he was a just and honorable man who fell victim to the monstrous injustice of the White man."[96]

In 1970, Jefferson Tindall summarized Keetoowah sentiments: "The White man tried to make a Ukaga out of Ned, as they have all the other Indians for 1400 years, and it still does not work. The memory of a good man forced into a way of life he did not want, is wonderfully preserved in the hearts of his people. The memory of thousands of White men who were great in their time, but have long since been forgotten. But not this one."[97]

The outlaw-hero is characterized by the audacity, daring, and sheer stupendousness of his exploits.

Eli Whitmire provides probably the most reverential statement about Christie: "He was a man of steel and iron, who feared no man."[98] A foundational aspect of the Christie legend is that he consistently evaded the frustrated lawmen who had difficulty accosting their prey. Steele refers to this five-year period of evading posses as "his personal war with the United States."[99] Shirley says, "He fought a greater number of battles with government officers than any other outlaw in the history of Judge Parker's court."[100] But did he, really? Christie did not run all over the Cherokee Nation, much less Indian Territory, desperately trying to outrun posses. Nor did he keep up a running gun battle along the inner ring of defense after posses managed to break through the outer ring that was supposedly provided by Keetoowahs. Every time he confronted lawmen, he did so on his property and, when he died, he did so outside his house that stood in the same area where he was born and raised. Creating stories about an evasive Christie who disappeared into the vast wilderness certainly sounds better than admitting that lawmen were incompetent. Recall that McKennon fabricates the story of how Christie and his "gang" rode over seventy miles round-trip without encountering any lawmen in order to tar and feather the hapless William Israel.[101]

What we do read about is Christie being a dead shot with his rifle. Steele writes in *The Last Cherokee Warriors* that "before he was ten years of age Ned was ranked as one of the best marksmen in the Cherokee nation, and his elders marveled at the lad's ability."[102] What we do not see any place, however, is the "ranking," that is, who else is on that Cherokee Nation marksman list and who kept track of who shot what with accuracy? Portraying Ned as a sharpshooter at a young age accomplishes at least two things: it sets the stage for how he is able to defend himself after 1887, and his precociousness with a weapon suggests that killing—for good or bad—was his destiny. Clyde Good wrote in 1975 that because Christie was "an excellent marksman" and stood so tall, Bushyhead used him as a personal guard.[103] That is, of course, a fabrication because despite his prowess with a rifle, Christie the busy councilman and family man had no time to follow Bushyhead around.

According to people who claimed they knew him, Zeke Proctor also was bestowed with natural abilities. Berry used a description of Proctor provided by Stanley Clark that appeared in the *Indian-Pioneer Papers* in 1937 and added his own flair. Clark described Proctor's eyes as "keen, black eyes which could look with stern retribution from their depths," and Berry altered that to "perhaps as perfect as any human eyes ever were. He could both see and hear to a superlative degree as almost his entire life was lived dodging real or imagined enemies."[104]

The outlaw-hero frequently outwits and confounds his opponents through a variety of trickster-type tactics. Authorities are unable to catch the outlaw-hero through conventional means.

Christie did have fellow Keetoowahs watch out for possemen, but it appears that most of the time he chased them off by himself. Stories tell of Christie emerging from his home in the forested Cookson Hills, then retreating when the lawmen pursued him.

Some Cherokees say that Christie possessed the ability to shape-shift. Among some tribes, shape-shifting is a witch's ability and is not used for good. Among others, shape-shifting is not an evil maneuver and might be accomplished by those who know how to use medicine and certain ceremonies. Since Christie's brother Goback knew how to heal, and healing is usually associated with spirituality, it could be that Christie learned how to accomplish shifting from his brother, or perhaps from his brother-in-law Seed Wilson. In the context of Christie, the thought is that he managed to elude lawmen not only by shooting them, he could also make them believe he had vanished; that is, he turned into another entity—most likely an animal—and got away.

Roy Hamilton relates two stories told by Ned's widow, Nancy, to her son John (his "Uncle John"): Once a bounty hunter spotted Christie in Wauhillau gathering wild berries. The hunter took aim, intending to shoot, but a gust of wind interrupted him. He took aim again and Christie moved to one side of a large oak tree, but he never reappeared on the other side; rather, a deer appeared and ran off down the hill. The man searched and he saw no human tracks. Uncle

John also said that once a group of lawmen thought they had Christie, but he dropped into the tall grass and thickets, then a dove flew out. There was no sign of Christie.[105]

Jack Kilpatrick wrote in 1969 that while newspapers had engaged in yellow journalism about Bill Pigeon, Cherokees viewed him as "one of the transcendentally great Cherokee medicine men of all time. By reverential general agreement he had the utmost in medicomagical power." When Pigeon lay dying, supposedly those visiting "the great magician" could not stay in the room because flames "blazed out of his eyes and mouth." And, after he died, he appeared to be of normal size, but when his body was viewed, he appeared to be the size of a baby.[106]

Robert Conley also wrote about Pigeon's abilities:

> Now, Bill was an Indian doctor, and some say he was just about the best there ever was. He knew that those federal lawmen would be after him, so he set about making medicine to protect himself right there at his house. Well, they never caught him. They came around looking for him, all right, but they wouldn't even see him. You see, old Bill could make himself invisible. Anyway, that's what they say. He'd be right there looking at them, but they couldn't see him. Another thing he could do, he could turn himself into an owl or a squirrel or just about anything he wanted. A crow maybe. Well, eleven years went by like that. It was 1897 when the federal lawmen finally closed the case.[107]

Most outlaw tales about Christie involve straightforward bullets and dynamite, and a lot of it. The descriptions of his death are among the most dramatic and impressive in all of outlaw lore. Wild West writers cannot tell us about Christie being dispatched by a bullet without first drawing out the final encounter with lawmen that included almost two days of rifle and cannon fire and culminating with a spectacular explosion. As seen in chapter 6, there are multiple dramatic versions of how Christie died and even more claims about who fired the kill shot.

One man in 1937 even asserted that Christie was the only one at his home when the posse arrived, thus making the odds "one man against twenty-seven."[108] In some ways, however, this is true. Charles Hair was only twelve at the time and it remains unknown just how long Arch Wolfe stayed before escaping into the woods. There are no stories about Nancy or Mary shooting in the final melee, so it really could have been just Christie against the entire posse.

The outlaw-hero's death is brought on through a betrayal by a former confederate or friend.

No one betrayed Christie, but several sources claim that someone did just that, namely, the Keetoowah sheriff, Ben Knight. The hole in this theory is that the posse already knew where Christie's home stood and Knight was not the first person to tell them. As already discussed, Knight went with the posse to ensure that Christie understood what the posse leaders had to say. And Yoes does not mention anything in his letter to Miller about Knight firing on Christie.

Our Brother in Red published a letter from B. H. Greathouse, who wrote at length about the violence in the territory, asking, "Have we for years been sowing the wind and just now reaping the whirlwind?" He wrote about political demagogues, train robbers, and murderers, and despite having no knowledge at all about the Christie story, forges ahead to analyze how the treachery of an unnamed neighbor forever changed the once peaceful Ned Christie: "Connivance at or engagement in lesser outlawry leads to the greater. The notorious Ned Christie was once a peaceful citizen. In an evil hour he sold whisky unlawfully and a neighbor reported him to the United States authorities. This enraged him, and when the marshal came to arrest him and the informer was with him, Christie [intended] to shoot the informer, but by mistake shot the marshal. This plunged him into the life of an outlaw."[109]

There also is an accusation that Bub Trainor turned traitor and told authorities where Christie lived. As previously discussed, Speer's claims of Bub Trainor being made a deputy and him guiding the posse to where Christie lived is fabricated in order to fit her narrative.[110] Neither Trainor nor anyone else in a posse would have been highly motivated by a payout. The reward for "capturing" the outlaw was $1,000, according to Yoes, plus $300 supposedly raised by "outside parties," reported by the *Weekly Elevator*.[111] That would be $1,300 divided among sixteen men, or seventeen men if one counts the traitor, making the payment for each around $76.47. Minus the questionable $300, it would only be $58.82 per man.

In order to rationalize how Christie apparently was taken unawares several times, Speer also makes the claim that "as his reputation had grown the sympathy of those in the Keetoowah had lessened."[112] Christie had not lost any sympathy. The issue for him and the Keetoowahs was that no one could stand watch over a vast area every day and night for almost five years. Fellow Keetoowahs did not live right next door to Christie and, in order to keep watch, many of them had to travel and leave their families behind. Crops had to be planted, cultivated, and harvested. Properties had to be maintained and children had to be raised. No one knows exactly who among the Keetoowahs acted as lookouts, nor for how long. We only know that during the time Christie avoided the law, some Keetoowahs attempted to assist him. It also must be remembered that there were lulls in the attempts to accost Christie. There were only four notable sorties on his property in five years, with many months in between in which nothing happened.

The outlaw-hero's death provokes great mourning on the part of his people. The outlaw-hero often manages to "live on" in one or a number of ways.

The Christie family members did not make their feelings about the death of Ned public, and their grieving remained private. Ned had many friends and acquaintances who may have tried to prepare themselves for a bad outcome. The reality of losing him was terrible enough, but those who were aware of the strain his family had endured for five years created bitter feelings. The death of young Jim and the sentencing of Arch Wolfe and Charles Hair made sentiments toward the federal government even more negative.

It was only a few months before Christie's death in 1892, and especially afterward, that newspapers began writing about him in derogatory terms. There were a few news stories that made brief statements questioning his guilt, but it was not until the 1918 *Tulsa World* and *Daily Oklahoman* stories that we see anyone make a public attempt to prove him innocent of killing Maples. Twenty years later, some residents of Indian Territory who knew him, or claimed they knew him, expressed sadness over his killing. Still, Wild West literature, tribute to lawmen websites, and contemporary articles and books still portray him as a vicious killer. Conversely, 124 years later, Cherokees still admire and celebrate the life of Christie.

There is no shortage of men who claimed to have been Christie's friend or witnessed his activities. One says, "I took an active part in the capture of Ned Christie," yet there is no record of his name associated with any engagement of Christie (and he was never "captured");[113] another states in a 1937 interview that he was Christie's brother-in-law, yet that claim is not substantiated in any record.[114] Another, William Hugh Winder, a white man born in Missouri and who settled in the Cherokee Nation in 1884, claimed to have known Christie rather well. In 1937, he testified to a rather fantastical story in which he simultaneously compliments Christie and himself: "I have never forgotten an Indian named Ned Christie, a very honest and honorable Indian who had been a Legislator or Councilman of the Cherokee Nation who had made himself known to me and had proved to me his real admiration for me."[115]

Golda's Mill, once been named Bitting Springs Mill, was a thriving corn-grinding business for owner Golda Unkefer during the 1950s. The mill business was busiest in the spring when the dogwood bloomed. Visitors, including Groucho Marx, watched the old mill grind corn and wandered around in the environment where Ned Christie lived and died, part of the mill's appeal to tourists. Portions of the movie *Where the Red Fern Grows* were filmed at the mill site. The mill burned in October 1983 and only the iron wheel, which had replaced the wooden wheel in 1908, remained. Nearby resident George Dickson purchased the remains of the mill and the land it sat on and for years allowed visitors to view the remains.[116]

In the 1980s, Robert Stoddard, the lead singer for the English rock band Dogs D'Amour, adopted the stage name of "Ned Christie" in honor of Ned, then dropped it when he joined the band L.A. Guns.[117]

In June 2011, the Cherokee Nation Cultural Tourism Group in Tahlequah organized a reenactment of the killing of Dan Maples, then a mock trial for Christie with a jury of his peers; that is, twelve people chosen from the audience. Charlie Soap played Christie and former Cherokee Nation principal chief Chad Smith played his defense attorney. The trial took place at the Cherokee National Capitol. The event included a photo exhibit.[118] In August 2011, Christie was honored during Cherokee Patriot Day, a celebration featuring arts, crafts, food, music provided by the Early Morning High Band, and a fundraiser for Christie's burial site.[119]

The hero's actions and deeds do not always provoke approval and admiration, but may upon occasion elicit mildly stated criticisms, moral warnings, outright condemnation, and refutation of any or all of the previous elements.

The *Indian Chieftain* published a telling story related to Ned Christie in 1894. In this vignette, even though Christie died two years prior, the mere mention of the dead man's name incited dread. We are told that the fearful fellow is a soldier, and a hardened one, yet his reaction reveals that Christie had been tougher and so are his relations:

> Ben Fisher, one of Chouteau's merchants, was in town Monday and had a story to tell about an old soldier he had met recently. This man had been

through most all the battles of the civil war, and longed for more, if his veracity was to be accepted without question. Finally during his conversation with Ben the information was dropped that the latter was a cousin of the late noted Ned Christie. This knowledge fell like a "beck [buck] ague" on the warlike one and he began trembling and got away from there about as quickly as circumstances would permit.[120]

One comment illustrates the ambiguity some people had about Christie. A man interviewed in 1937 stated, "He was always truthful and reliable, never betraying a friend," yet he also said, "His career as an outlaw is known. Nothing I will add or leave off will condone the depredations committed nor will the approval of certain element of sympathizers avail. His deeds are known and we leave it that as it is."[121]

....

While the Christie hunters and killers serve to bolster the cause of the righteous, their images also serve to mold the image of the dead Outlaw Christie, whose full story is never told by those who celebrate the victors. Their Christie Myth, therefore, is a comfort story for those who need to be emotionally reassured about the valor of their heroes. As Wright notes, western movies do not always use star power to draw in business; rather, consumers are attracted to movies with comfortable plots.[122] Just like romcoms (romantic comedies) are comforting because the attractive leads eventually find each other, western stories, headlines, and movies require that the good and bad guys be clearly delineated and the former must defeat the latter. (There have been some exceptions to this, such as the 2007 movie *No Country for Old Men* in which the bad guy, Anton Chigurh, gets away.) Christie lived and died before movies, of course, but readers still hungered to read adventures and about the triumph of good over evil. Details that might cause readers to consider Christie's innocence are not included. Justice needed to be served. And in the case of the deputy U.S. marshals versus Ned Christie, lawmen killed Christie, and all was well. William F. Buckley, Jr., said about the eternal hero John Wayne: "His memory keeps us cheerful."[123] Stories about Christie make people happy, too. Wild West fans are satisfied that the corrupt man perished. Conversely, Cherokees and other Indians who view Christie as the upholder of tribal culture and sovereignty remain inspired by him.

Despite the efforts to offer the innocent version of Christie, the image of Christie as an outlaw continues to influence modern writers. Some, especially lawmen genealogy and obituary pages, and webmasters who manage pages about officers of the law, require that Christie remain a criminal—the more violent the better—in order to bolster the positive images of lawmen. They continue to cherry-pick the most inflammatory descriptions of Christie while eschewing works that discuss Christie's possible innocence.

For example, Brodhead, in his 2003 book on Isaac C. Parker, refers to Christie as "a horse thief, a whiskey seller, and a cold-blooded killer."[124] More recently, in January 2015, Dave Farris composed an editorial headlined "Possee finally nabbed infamous fugitive," a segment of the "Look at Ned Christie" series, in the *Edmond Life and Leisure* online paper. In these stories, he repeats virtually every stereotype and incorrect description of Ned, and even takes the untruths further by adding his own uninformed views, such as "As the years pasted, Cherokee leaders urged their tribe to turn against Christie and perhaps, so did the ancient Cherokee spirits who protected him" and "James Christie was attacked and killed by unknown assassins. His head was severed from his body, demonstrating just how hated his father was by some of the settlers in Indian Territory."[125] Farris did not bother to investigate, else he would have discovered that a murder trial ensued, and the culprit who murdered Christie was found guilty. The killer's reasoning had nothing to do with how he felt about Ned.

Adams further explains these kinds of writers: "they close their minds to anything but the lurid account of a careless earlier author, even though the records may prove he was wrong."[126] What is important to note here is that Adams wrote this concern in 1964, and yet over fifty years later writers continue to parrot every tired and sensational account of Christie that has come before.

The evilness of Christie and his vanquishing are supposed to represent a victory for the good and righteous values so integral to Americans. His death occurred only two years after the superintendent of the U.S. census stated that the frontier line was gone. Frederick Jackson Turner argued a year after Christie's death that the American character had been shaped by the conquest of the western frontier and that included the domination of hundreds of indigenous peoples. From this ordeal, Americans—white Americans, that is—developed certain traits, including individualism, ingenuity, optimism, and adaptability. Writings by newspapermen in the 1890s; by Shirley, McKennon, Rand, and Pride in the 1950s and 1960s; and continuing today with the simplistic columns of Dave Farris reflect the need to clearly identify who was bad and who was good with no analysis or research wanted or needed. Telling stories of a fantastic past in which imagined bad guys lose remains a sure way to feel virtuous.

Newspaper writers and Wild West authors have told us in various ways how villainous outlaws lost. As Michael L. Johnson states about the disappearing frontier, "Thus recalling the wild, America called back in fancy what it had loved and killed."[127] One might say the same about how they felt regarding Ned Christie.

NOTES

ABBREVIATIONS

ARCIA	*Annual Report of the Commissioner of Indian Affairs*
CHN	Cherokee Nation Records
CIA	Canton Asylum for Insane Indians
CLAIT	*The Constitutions and Laws of the American Indian Tribes*
DD	Doris Duke Collection of American Indian Oral History
IA: LT	*Indian Affairs: Laws and Treaties*
IPP	*Indian-Pioneer Papers* (formerly *Indian Pioneer Histories*)
NA	National Archives (other locations than Southwest Region, Fort Worth)
NASW	National Archives, Southwest Region, Fort Worth
OHS	Oklahoma Historical Society, Oklahoma City
WHC	Western History Collections, University of Oklahoma, Norman

INTRODUCTION

Epigraph. Candee, "Oklahoma," 330.

1. Nede Wade means Ned, son of Watt. Although his family referred to him as Nede, popular culture knows him as Ned. I use Ned to avoid confusion. The Christie family tree is complex. Not only do most members have more than one name, but many have the same name (notably Edward, Nede, and Watt), and some are spelled in various ways, such as Greece, Grease, and Greace. "Christie" has been referred to as Guhlaweski, Gotlun-uuski, and Tahlahseeni. For years after their removal to Indian Territory, Christie family members signed their surname as Wakigu.

2. *Chicago Daily Tribune*, November 7, 1892.

3. *Fort Worth Daily Gazette*, November 8, 1890.

4. *Omaha Daily Bee*, November 3, 1890.

5. *Atoka (I.T.) Indian Citizen*, June 6, 1891.

6. *Chicago Daily Tribune*, November 7, 1892.

7. *Arkansas Gazette*, November 5 and 6, 1892.

8. *Kansas City (Mo.) Times*, November 6, 1892.

9. *Muskogee (I.T.) Phoenix*, May 25, 1893.

10. *Wichita (Kans.) Daily Eagle*, March 19, 1895.

11. *Gentry (Ark.) Journal Advance*, June 30, 1899.

12. *Chicago Daily Tribune*, July 20, 1902, and *Rockford (Ill.) Republic*, August 12, 1902.

13. Fischer, "Deputy Marshal Paden Tolbert."

14. *Daily Oklahoman*, March 18, 1906.

15. *Leavenworth (Kans.) Times*, November 5, 1892.

16. *Kansas City (Mo.) Times*, November 6, 1892.

17. *Fort Scott (Kans.) Daily Monitor*, November 10, 1892; *Grand Forks (N.D.) Herald*, November 6, 1892; *St. Louis Republic*, November 5, 1892.

18. *Fort Smith (Ark.) Elevator*, November 11, 1892.

19. *Muskogee (I.T.) Phoenix*, November 10, 1892.

20. *Cleveland Plain Dealer*, June 10, 1900.

21. Phillip Rand, "Blood in the Cookson Hills," 27.

22. Turner cites a 1938 interview in the WPA Writers' Project (presumably the *Indian-Pioneer Papers* oral histories), yet that source cannot be located. Turner, *Rotgut Rustlers*, 19; Smith, *Outlaw Tales of Oklahoma*, 19.

23. Adams, *Burs Under the Saddle* , xi.

24. Ibid.

25. Athearn, *Mythic West in Twentieth-Century America*, 176.

26. For discussions about these issues, see Mitchell, *Westerns*.

27. Hamilton, *Ned Christie*, viii.

28. Baldasty, *Commercialization of News*, 121–25.

29. This notion of "hero" or "legend" by virtue of dispensing with Christie is illustrated in Owens, *Oklahoma Heroes*, 92–93, 130, 139–40.

30. Will Wright, *Sixguns and Society*, 12.

31. Baldasty, *Commercialization of News*, 81–91.

32. *Journalist*, August 14, 1897, p. 134, cited in Baldasty, *Commercialization of News*, 90.

33. For discussions about how newspapers represented Native peoples, see Coward, *Newspaper Indian*.

34. Harmon, *Hell on the Border*, 552.

35. Adams, *Burs Under the Saddle*, xii.

36. William Dellwood Fields interview, June 16, 1937, IPP 29:403–404. See also Martin, "Unsung Heroes," 23, 25.

37. George W. Sorrells interview, November 12, 1937, IPP 85:448. For details about Charles Wilson, his murder, and the subsequent tribal and federal courts murder trials, see Mihesuah, *Choctaw Crime and Punishment*, 21–68.

38. Eli Wilson interview, July 26, 1937, IPP 99:141–49. According to Wilson, Ned told him that he had become drunk while in Tahlequah that night and Maples confronted him. In this rendering, it appears that Wilson is attempting to say that Maples tried to rob Christie or intrude into his home. Christie thought Maples was either a thief or a white intruder and shot him. Wilson also said that "he stated to me that after he had time to realize that he would be charged with murder he thought it no benefit to try to beat a murder case under the existing Cherokee laws. He just decided to die at home fighting."

39. In Speer's *The Killing of Ned Christie*, 100–101, the author uses every aspect of the questionable Eli Wilson testimony and copied much of that Indian and Pioneer transcript

directly into her book. Not surprisingly, the crucial statement she purposefully leaves out is the one about Christie admitting to young Eli Wilson that he killed Maples. She also fabricates a scenario in which Ned and a man named George Wilson have a conversation and then writes that the rifle was purchased from Eli's father, George. The hitch is that the interview clearly states that Eli's father died when he was a week old, his father's name was Wilson Arch, not George, and nowhere in the interview does Eli Wilson state what Speer writes, that Ned came to his house, "entered quietly and sat in a dignified manner as was the custom when visiting. After a respectful period he began to talk."

40. Riggs, "Bits of Interesting History," 149–50; Riggs, August 2, 1937, IPP 76:203. See also "Charles LeFlore," National Park Service, and Burton, "Oklahoma's Frontier Indian Police."

41. Athearn, *Mythic West in Twentieth-Century America*, 171.

42. Prassel, *Great American Outlaw*, xi, 207; Good, "Ned Christie," 39–44. The tone of Good's faulty essay is set at the onset when he writes, "It had been a hot, sticky day and the smothering humidity still lingered," and "the rasping sound of katydids muffled the deputy's footsteps." Maples died on a cool May evening and katydids do not begin "singing" until late summer. The remainder of the article lapses into the same redundant spin as most other pieces about Christie.

43. Shirley, *Law West of Fort Smith*, 54.

44. Rand, "Blood in the Cookson Hills," 27.

45. Pride, "Battle of Tahlequah Canyon," 18–19.

46. Gibson, *Oklahoma*, 134.

47. Walker, "Ned Christie," 30. The Christie family member who gave information to that magazine did not have firsthand knowledge of events and it appears that he gave the editor of *Real West* some newspaper articles and, apparently, a copy of *Iron Men*. Hamilton, personal communication.

48. "Indians Form Talent Guild in Tulsa," *Cherokee Phoenix and Indian Advocate*, December 31, 1979, p. 13.

49. *Galveston Daily News*, May 14, 1978.

50. *America's Most Wanted*, season 3, episode 85, October 8, 1989.

51. Baird, *Story of Oklahoma*, 288. Anderson and Yadon also assert the connection but provide no source, *100 Oklahoma Outlaws, Gangsters, and Lawmen*, 183.

52. Littlefield and Underhill, "Ned Christie and His One-Man Fight," 3–15.

53. Steele, *Last Cherokee Warriors*, 69–72.

54. In addition, Bill Jr. thought Steele was asking about his cousin Nede, not his great- uncle Ned, the subject of this book. On December 16, 1915, an article appeared in the *Standard-Sentinel* about three cousins who were in a "gunfight": William "Bill" Christie (the individual Steele met in the nursing home); another Nede Christie (son of Arch Christie—Ned's nephew—and Nancy Broom); and Joe Christie, the son of Jack Christie and Nancy Grease (Jack was a brother to Ned). In this altercation, Bill Jr. was shot in the leg by his cousin Nede. Steele, however, writes in his book that Ned (the subject of this book) shot him and Bill walked with a limp the rest of his life. Christie family member Roy Hamilton clarified that the "Bill" Christie in that newspaper story was indeed Watt's grandson and lived near him (Roy) in Wauhillau and was sometimes referred to as

"Cripple Bill." Therefore, Steele's book not only includes vignettes about the wrong "Ned Christie," it also includes blatant untruths.

55. Steele, *Last Cherokee Warriors*, 70, 74.

56. McKennon, *Iron Men,* 88.

57. Steele, *Last Cherokee Warriors*, 70–72, 74, 93.

58. Hamilton, *Christie*, 74; Hamilton, personal communication. One can immediately see the nature of the book Speer generated by turning to page 18 of *The Killing of Ned Christie*: the author includes a picture that she copied from the June 9, 1918, issue of the *Daily Oklahoman* and misidentifies the subject as Christie. The man is actually George Jefferson, a member of the posse that ultimately killed Christie. A few more examples: She sensationally titles her January 1983 *True West* essay "Wolf of the Cookson Hills," a descriptor she copies directly from McKennon, who also puts that phrase in quotes but does not attribute it to anyone. McKennon, *Iron Men*, 124. Speer claims to have interviewed a Ned descendant, but that man did not speak English. She also makes the statement that "[Ned] had been heard to say he felt naked without it" (his rifle), when there is no such statement in her citation, p. 30. On page 93, she states that James Padgett was Christie's brother-in-law when there is no documentation to substantiate that claim besides an odd interview with Padgett conducted in 1937. She drops Arch Wolf at 1903, telling us he was sent home after his time at the Government Hospital for the Insane, when in fact he never saw his home again. She liberally copied flawed information from Steele and lifted uncited passages directly from the *Daily Oklahoman* issue. *Strum's Oklahoma Magazine* 11 (September 1910): 25 is listed in her references, but a perusal of that issue reveals nothing related to Christie.

59. Adams, *Burs Under the Saddle*, xiii.

60. The late Robbie McMurtry is the cousin of my Comanche husband, Joshua, on his mother's (white) side of the family and is no relation to the novelist Larry McMurtry nor was he Comanche.

61. Athearn, *Mythic West in Twentieth-Century America*, 175.

62. For example, *Chicago Daily Tribune*, November 7, 1894.

63. Meyer, "The Outlaw," 96.

64. For examples, Choctaws Green McCurtain and Wilson N. Jones, who served as chiefs from 1890 to 1894 and 1896 to 1900, respectively, owned vast acreage. Jones's land encompassed thirty-two square miles, in addition to land in Sherman, Texas. *Caddo Banner*, June 22, 1894 and February 23, 1894. The Cherokee Female and Male Seminaries, schools operated by the Cherokee Nation, offered rigorous curricula that included French, Latin, Shakespeare, and chemistry. See Mihesuah, *Cultivating the Rose Buds*, 100.

65. *Chicago Daily Tribune*, November 7, 1894.

CHAPTER 1

Epigraph. Quoted in Hamilton, *Ned Christie*, viii.

1. Hamilton, personal communication.

2. Valuation 47 for Ned Christie, RG 75, entry 224, Property Valuations, 1835–1939, North Carolina—Box 6, Folder: Welch and Jarrett (BK 14), NA, Washington, D.C. At the time of the valuation in 1839, Edward Nede and Sallie were worth $947.25. Speer also

incorrectly states that Watt is the son of Edward. Speer writes that Ned's grandfather was "also named Edward 'Ned' Christie," but there are two errors in this statement. First, Edward "Ned" Christie was Ned's great-uncle and Ned (the subject of this book) did not go by "Edward." Speer, *Killing of Ned Christie*, 13. Ned's name sometimes appears in error as "Edward" on the National Council records, however.

3. For early Cherokee histories, see Malone, *Cherokees of the Old South* and Mooney, *Myths of the Cherokees and Sacred Formulas of the Cherokees*.

4. See in Kappler, IA: LT: "Treaty with the Cherokee," November 28, 1785, 7 Stat., 18, vol. 2, "Treaties," 9–11; "Treaty with the Cherokee," July 2, 1791, 7 Stat., 39, pp. 29–33; "Treaty with the Cherokee," June 26, 1794, 7 Stat., 43, pp. 33–34; "Treaty with the Cherokee," October 24, 1804, 7 Stat., 288, pp. 73–74; "Treaty with the Cherokee," October 25, 1805, 7 Stat., 93, pp. 82–83; "Treaty with the Cherokee," October 27, 1805, 7 Stat., 95, p. 84; "Treaty with the Cherokee," January 7, 1806, 7 Stat., 101, pp. 90–92; "Treaty with the Cherokee," March 22, 1816, 7 Stat., 138, pp. 124–25; "Treaty with the Cherokee," September 14, 1816, 7 Stat., 148, pp. 133–34; "Treaty with the Cherokee," July 8, 1817, 7 Stat., 156, pp. 140–44.

5. "Treaty with the Western Cherokee," May 6, 1828, 7 Stat., 311, in Kappler, IA: LT, 288–92.

6. For information on the changing social and political Cherokee systems, see Perdue, *Cherokee Women*. See also Mankiller and Wallis, *Mankiller*, 15–29; Strickland, *Fire and the Spirits*; and Anderson, *Cherokee Removal*.

7. Bonnie Speer writes in *The Killing of Ned Christie* that "in later years, Watt Christie would recall how he and his brothers dug for gold" after it was discovered. The citation she uses, however, is not from Watt Christie; rather, it is from Amos Christie and investigation into the latter interview reveals that Watt did no such thing. Speer, *Killing of Ned Christie*, 14, 139n8.

8. Perdue, "The Conflict Within," 467–91; Prucha, *American Indian Policy in the Formative Years*, 231–32. Today, the city of Dahlonega boasts that the town is the site of the country's first gold rush—but with nary a word about the horrors the resident Cherokees faced after they were forced off their lands and marched to Indian Territory.

9. See Moulton, *John Ross, Cherokee Chief*.

10. For information about Boudinot, see Parins, *Elias Cornelius Boudinot*, and Gaul, *To Marry an Indian*.

11. Wilkins, *Cherokee Tragedy*, 235–37, 242–44.

12. Cherokee Nation v. Georgia, 30 U.S. 1 (1831).

13. Worcester v. Georgia, 31 U.S. 1 (1832).

14. "Act Resolved by the Committee and Council, October 26, 1829, CLAIT 5:136–37.

15. McKenney, *Memoirs, Official and Personal*, 261.

16. Thornton, "Demography of the Trail of Tears Period," 75–95.

17. In the words of Cherokee Nannie Buchanan Pierce, "According to the stories told to me by my grandmother when I was a small girl it would be impossible for anyone to graphically portray the horrors and suffering endured by the Cherokees on that journey." Nannie Buchanan Pierce interview, February 24, 1937, IPP 71:373. See also Elizabeth Watts interview, April 27, 1937, IPP 95:530; Eastman Ward interview, May 1, 1937, IPP

95:127; ARCIA, 1886, 149; Mary Cobb Agnew interview, May 25, 1937, IPP 1:290; Lillian Anderson interview, August 20, 1837, IPP 2:337–38; Foreman, *Indian Removal*; King and Evans, "Trail of Tears," 129–90; Perdue and Green, *Cherokee Removal*; Smith, *American Betrayal*; Wilkins, *Cherokee Tragedy*.

18. Thornton, "Cherokee Population Losses During the Trail of Tears," 289–300; Thornton, "Demography of the Trail of Tears Period."

19. Amos Christie interview, June 12, 1969, DD, T-476-1. After arrival, they signed their name as Wakigu, not Christie.

20. In 1840, the tribe created its eight districts: Goingsnake, Illinois, Canadian, Flint, Tahlequah, Delaware, and Saline. The National Council named Goingsnake District in honor of the Eastern Cherokee leader Goingsnake who served as speaker of the National Council in 1827 under Chief John Ross. Goingsnake survived the forced removal, but like many others he died shortly after arrival in Indian Territory. "An Act to Organize the Nation into Eight Districts and for Holding Election," November 4, 1840, CLAIT 1:37–40.

21. Hamilton, *Ned Christie*, 5; Lucinda Sanders Wilhite, April 24, 1969, DD, T-422-3, p. 8.

22. Amos Christie, DD, T-476-1, p. 16.

23. *Tulsa World*, October 26, 1917.

24. *Tulsa World*, February 13, 1916.

25. See for examples, Speer, *Killing of Ned Christie*, 14, 64–66. Speer even devotes the opening pages of chap. 8 to describing the environment of Rabbit Trap. See also Speer, "Ned Christie: Cherokee Outlaw"; Eli Whitmire interview, October 30, 1937, IPP 97:206.

26. Some infer that Ned's father and mother, Watt and Lydia, survived the removal trek together, but that is not correct because Watt was married to Wadaya at the time of removal. See Amos Christie, DD, T-476-1, p. 16; Wiley Wolf interview, January 10, 1969, DD, T-370-2, p. 17.

27. Steele, *Last Cherokee Warriors*, 70.

28. "New Town, Cherokee Nation," November 10, 1825, *Laws of the Cherokee Nation*, 57. See also Perdue, *Cherokee Women*, 174–77.

29. Lucinda Sanders Wilhite cites an elusive trading record book kept by Levi Keys. The whereabouts of the record book is unknown; it is not at the Oklahoma Historical Society or the Cherokee Historical Society. Lucinda Sanders Wilhite, DD, T-422-3, p. 7.

30. See for examples, Lucy Cherry interview, November 26, 1937, IPP 17:370; Agnew, IPP 1:292; William McCleod Patterson interview, September 24, 1937, IPP 69:487; Lula Neighbors interview, January 14, 1938, IPP 66:246; Austin Fite interview, June 16, 1937, IPP 30:104.

31. *Cherokee Advocate*, September 11, 1885.

32. Gould, "Notes on Trees, Shrubs, and Vines," 145–46.

33. Jesse Adair interview, May 17, 1937, IPP 1:125; Zeke Acorn interview, October 4, 1937, IPP 1:115.

34. For discussions about food and health changes among the Five Tribes (Cherokees, Choctaws, Chickasaws, Creeks, and Seminoles), see Mihesuah, "Sustenance and Health among the Five Tribes in Indian Territory," 263–84.

35. Adair, IPP 1:123, 125; Acorn, IPP 1:115.

36. Shirk, *Oklahoma Place Names*, 24; Roy Hamilton, personal communication; Etter, "Water Mill Created Memories." See also National Register of Historic Places Inventory.

37. Hamilton, *Ned Christie*, 1–2; Hamilton, personal communication.

38. Elmira Stevens interview, February 4, 1938, IPP 87:280, 284. Hamilton, personal communication.

39. ARCIA, 1852, p. 407.

40. Bender. *Signs of Cherokee Culture.*

41. Parins, *Literary and Intellectual Life in the Cherokee Nation*, esp. 51–67; Holland *Cherokee Newspapers,* esp. 13–138.

42. "Extracts from the Journal at Dwight," 244; Mooney, *Myths of the Cherokees and Sacred Formulas of the Cherokees*, 319; Skelton, "History of the Educational System of the Cherokee Nation," 74–124. For more information about Dwight Mission, see Foreman, "Cherokee Gospel Tidings of Dwight Mission," 454–69, and Payne and Payne, *Brief History of Old Dwight Cherokee Mission.*

43. McLoughlin, *Cherokee Ghost Dance*, 229, 246.

44. "An Act for the Establishment of two Seminaries or High Schools: one for the education of Males, and the other for Females, and for the erection of buildings for their accommodation," November 26, 1846, CLAIT, 5:146–47; "An Act in Relation to the Male and Female Seminaries, and Establishing Primary Departments Therein for the Education of Indigent Children," November 28, 1873, in *Constitutions and Laws of the Cherokee Nation* (St. Louis: R. and T. A. Ennis Stationers, Printers and Book Binders, 1975), vol. 7 of CLAIT, 267–69. See also Mihesuah, *Cultivating the Rosebuds*; [Abbott], "Out of the Graves of the Polluted Debauches," 503–21.

45. Hamilton, personal communication.

46. Jefferson Tindall interview, February 9, 1970, DD, T-554, p. 3 (second half of transcript beginning after p. 16).

47. *Cherokee Advocate*, May 26, 1882.

48. Amos Christie, DD, T-476 (second interview), 1.

49. George Keys interview, November 5, 1968, DD, T-334-2, pp. 7–8; Wiley Wolf, DD, T-370-2, p. 3.

50. Amos Christie, DD, 1; Wolf, January 10, 1969, 19.

51. Hamilton, personal communication.

52. Amos Christie, DD, pp. 5–6.

53. Confer, *Cherokee Nation in the Civil War*; Gaines, *Confederate Cherokees*, 22, 28; King, "Forgotten Warriors."

54. Muster Roll, Drew's Regiment, November 5, 1861, Watt is listed as Smith Watt Christie (Christy) because of his profession.

55. Speer, however, fabricates a story claiming that Christie helped his father chase away aggressive guerrillas with a shotgun. Speer, *Killing of Ned Christie*, 15. She cites Amos Christie, June 12, 1969, DD, T-476-1, pt. 2, p. 3; but, Ned is not mentioned in this vignette.

56. Gaines, *Confederate Cherokees*, 124.

57. Agnew, IPP 1:294; Watts, IPP 95:537–38; Emma J. Sixkiller interview, June 29, 1937, IPP 84:50; ARCIA, 1863, p. 340; ARCIA, 1865, p. 471; ARCIA, 1865, p. 471; ARCIA,

1872–73, p. 620; *Cherokee Advocate*, June 1, 1872; March 22, 1873; August 23, 1873; December 20, 1873; January 7, 1874; and March 28, 1874.

58. See Miner, *Corporation and the Indian*.

59. Hamilton, personal communication.

60. For detailed instructions on how to play, see [Cherokee] Marbles. "Marbles (di ga da yo s di)."

61. Wright to Council, 1866, in Phillips Collection, WHC.

62. Hamilton, *Ned Christie*, 7.

63. ARCIA, 1884, p. 105.

64. [163 U.S. 612, 613].

65. Brodhead, *Isaac C. Parker*. See also the National Park Service's website on Fort Smith for information about Parker, conviction rulings, history of the courthouse, a list of individuals hung at Fort Smith, etc., at www.nps.gov/fosm/index.htm.

66. Hamilton, *Christie*, 15; Hamilton, personal communication.

67. The best discussion of Zeke Proctor is found in Littlefield and Underhill, "Trial of Ezekiel Proctor," 307–22. See also Mary Jane Green interview, February 26, 1938, IPP 36:36; George T. Candy interview, March 8, 1937, IPP 15:295–96; B. B. Wyne interview, September 16, 1937, IPP 101: 36–37; John H. Connolly interview, May 10, 1937, IPP 20:118–19; Zeke Proctor (son of the subject, Ezekiel Proctor) interview, October 22, 1937, IPP 73:179; Clark, IPP 18:217–18.

68. ARCIA, 1872, pp. 234–35.

69. *Pomeroy's Democrat*, April 27, 1872.

70. A. M. Ryals, September 14, 1937, IPP 79:321–22. His words are "He was once sentenced to be shot for his many crimes but he was never shot because he wore a breastplace and in fact, he wore a steel protection."

71. *Cherokee Advocate*, November 30, 1887; An Act Making an appropriation to pay the current, and contingent expenses of the National Council and Executive Office, for the Regular Session in 1877, and for other purposes; An Act Making an Appropriation to pay the current and contingent expenses of the Extra Session of the National Council in 1878; An Act making an appropriation to pay current and contingent expenses of the National Council and Executive Department, for the Regular Session, for the year 1878, and for other purposes. All in National Council, Letters Sent, 1124–25, 1143–45, 1159, CHN 88, OHS.

72. Steele, in *Last Cherokee Warriors*, tried to justify having both Christie and Proctor on the cover of his book, so he tells us, "Since they lived only some thirty miles apart and both families were active in government and Keetoowa matters, it is the writer's opinion that they most likely were friends." And he also states that Bill Jr. told him that "Ned Christie and Zeke Proctor were great friends." This is a stretch. Thirty miles was not exactly down the road. And Steel claims that Bill Jr. "also recalled that Watt and Ned attended Proctor's trial." There is no evidence, testimony, or witness statement that places the Christies at the trial, not even from the Christie family. Considering Ned's later notoriety, if he had been there, someone in attendance would have said so in later testimonies. Once again, Bill Jr. was only two years old at the time of Christie's death and the previous statements Steele attributes to him are incorrect. Steele, *Last Cherokee Warriors*, 73.

73. Hamilton, *Ned Christie*, 17; Flint District Records, p. 253, CHN 38, OHS.

74. Hamilton, *Christie*, 17.

75. Hamilton, personal communication.

76. Ibid.

77. Ibid.

78. Ibid.

79. ARCIA, 1886, pp. 148–49.

CHAPTER 2

Epigraph. Quoted in Hamilton, *Ned Christie*, 9.

1. ARCIA, 1880, p. 95.

2. ARCIA, 1884, p. 98.

3. ARCIA, 1885, pp. 23, 24.

4. ARCIA, 1886, p. 157.

5. ARCIA, 1881, LIX.

6. ARCIA, 1880, pp. 9–10.

7. Senate Bill 57 (Number One Senate Bill), Regular Session National Council, 1878, 299, in Senate and National Council, 1887–88, CHN, OHS; Members of the Council, 1875, and An Act making appropriations for and for pay of services of members, December 2, 1875, in National Council, Letters Sent, CHN, OHS; National Council, Letters Sent, and others for the year 1876, CHN 12, OHS; *Cherokee Advocate*, August 14, 1885; Cherokee (Tahlequah)–Districts (for example, he served as juror in the case of Cherokee Nation v. Yell Ward in September 1880), 628, CHN 74, OHS; An Act making an appropriation for the current expenses of the National Council for the Regular Session beginning on the first Monday in November 1885 and for other purposes, in National Council, Letters Sent, CHN 88, OHS.

8. *Cherokee Advocate*, August 3, 1883.

9. Ibid., November 20, 1885.

10. Rand, "Blood in the Cookson Hills," 26–27.

11. See Duvall, *Cherokee Nation and Tahlequah*; [Cherokee Female Seminary] Illustrated Souvenir Catalog; issues of *Cherokee Advocate* published in the 1880s.

12. Hamilton, personal communication; Hamilton, *Ned Christie*, 10–11.

13. *Cherokee Advocate,* November 13, 1885.

14. Ibid., December 5, 1884; December 12, 1884; May 1, 1885; May 8, 1885, December 18, 1885. Speer incorrectly identifies George as Ned's brother. Speer, *Killing of Ned Christie*, 12.

15. Hamilton, personal communication, June 11, 2015.

16. Adair, IPP 1:127; Ellis Ketcher interview, January 5, 1938, IPP 50: 420–21.

17. See Nice, "Birds of Oklahoma," 224.

18. Cherokee Nation vs. Ned Christie, Goingsnake District, Cherokee Nation, May 25, 1885, in Going Snake District Records, CHN 40, OHS. See also stories in *Indian Chieftain*, May 21, 1885, and June 11, 1885; *Eufaula (I.T.) Indian Journal*, June 4, 1885; *Cherokee Advocate*, May 21, 1885; *Fort Smith (Ark.) Elevator*, January 16, 1885; Clark, on Ned Christie, IPP 18:140/207.

19. Hamilton, *Ned Christie*, 25.

20. C. H. Taylor to J. M. Bell, April 17, 1885, folder 5785, roll 43, Cherokee Nation papers, WHC.

21. *Cherokee Advocate*, May 26, 1882. On the day of the murder, Blue Duck and Christie left George Scott's house, some three miles from Wyrick's, and went to Hopper's house. Blue Duck was very drunk. Christie claims he went to see Hopper on some trivial matter, but Hopper was not at home. On the road Blue Duck had spoken of killing Wyrick and wanted Christie to take a hand, but he refused. Christie dismounted and said he would wait until Hooper returned, and while Mrs. Hopper was gone to the spring, about 305 yards from the house, lay down on the porch, while Blue Duck rode off in the direction where Wyrick was plowing. Soon five pistol shots were heard, and immediately afterward the horse that Wyrick was plowing with came dashing up to the house, with plow attached. Soon afterward Blue Duck came up on foot with an empty revolver in his hand, and after a trip to get his horse, came back, and refilled his revolver from cartridges in Christie's belt. He next shot at a boy named Billy Wolf, who came riding up about that time, after which he proceeded to the house of Hawkey Wolf and shot at him two or three times. In the meantime, Hopper and Christie had gone to the field where they found the body of Wyrick pierced with five bullets, all of which had passed through him. It was difficult for the law officers to say who committed the murder. Hopper was arrested by which time Christie told the officers Blue Duck's whereabouts and he was arrested and jailed.

22. *Cherokee Advocate*, February 5, 1886.

23. Ibid., April 9, 1886.

24. Case File, Blue Duck, Martin Hopper, and Bill (or William) Christie, criminal jacket 26, NASW.

25. Article 3, sec. 12, *Constitution and Laws of the Cherokee Nation Passed at Tahlequah, Cherokee Nation, 1839,* in CLAIT, vol. 1.

26. See CLAIT, vols. 1–10, which has reprinted those documents, most of which were published in Tahlequah.

27. His name alternately appears in the National Council records as "Ned Christie" and "Edward Christie," possibly because the latter is a more formal name and is his great-uncle's name. Executive Council Records, January 6, 1886, December 16, 1885, pp. 1–52, 138–57. CHN 119, OHS; Executive Council Records, January 12, 1880–May 20, 1886, vol. 710 (this is a different volume from the first with the same title), pp. 138–57 (ledger with pages bound by three small rings); Executive Council Records, July 5, 1886–November 3, 1887, vol. 712, pp.1–56; See also Laws, Extra Session, December 1886, pp. 27–28, 36, in National Council and Senate, 1884–88, CHN 15, OHS; and *Laws and Joint Resolutions of the Cherokee Nation Enacted by the National Council During the Regular and Extra Sessions of 1884–5–6* (Tahlequah, C.N.: E. C. Boudinot, Jr., 1887), vol. 7 of CLAIT.

28. "An Act to legalize Intermarriage with White Men," September 28, 1839, in *Constitution and Laws of the Cherokee Nation passed at Tah-le-quah, Cherokee Nation, 1839* (Washington, D.C.: Gales and Seaton, 1840), vol. 1 of CLAIT, 29–30.

29. "An Act to legalize Intermarriage with White Men," November 15, 1843, CLAIT 1:87–88.

30. For lists of non-Indian men who married Cherokee women, see Murchison, "Intermarried-Whites in the Cherokee Nation," 299–327.

31. Yarbrough, *Race and the Cherokee Nation*, 80.

32. Nat Dickerson interview, June 11, 1937, IPP 24:293.

33. ARCIA, 1881, p. 28.

34. "Dissenting to and protesting against the Act of Congress granting right of way to the Southern Kansas Railway through the Cherokee Nation," April 14, 1886, in *Laws and Joint Resolutions of the Cherokee Nation*, CLAIT 7:33–36.

35. "Construction of the rights of Cherokee Citizenship, as designed to be conferred upon Freedmen and friendly Indians by the 9th and 15th Articles of the Treaty of 1866," CLAIT 7:38–41.

36. "Story of the Capture of Ned Christie with Picture of the Captors," typed and handwritten MS, Charles B. Rhodes Collection, box 1, doc. 66, WHC; Dale, "Cherokee Strip Live Stock Association," 58–78; Savage, *Cherokee Strip Live Stock Association*.

37. "An act to provide for the allotment of lands in severalty to Indians on the various reservations, and to extend the protection of the laws of the United States and the Territories over the Indians, and for other purposes," February 8, 1887, 24 Stat., 388, Acts of Forty-ninth Congress, 2d Sess., in Kappler, IA: LT, vol. 1, Laws, chap. 119, pp. 33–36.

38. *Cherokee Advocate*, February 12, 1886.

39. Senate Bill 8: Making an appropriation for the current expenses of the National Council of April 2, 1886, pp. 50, 53, in National Council, Letters Sent, Docs. 1990–2007, January 24, 1876–June 1900, CHN 88, OHS; Laws, Extra Session, December 1886, pp. 27–28, 36, in National Council and Senate, CHN 15, OHS. The CHN documents have Ned as "Edward." Grease was cousin to Ned Greece, Ned Christie's cousin.

40. Senate Bill No. 8: "An Act making an appropriation for the current expenses of the National Council for the Extra Session beginning on the 12th day of April 1886 and for other purposes," in National Council, Letters Sent, CHN 88, OHS.

41. "To pay the current and contingent expenses of the regular session of the National Council commencing the 1st Monday in November 1886 and ending the 4th day of December 1886," in National Council, Letters Sent, CHN 88, OHS.

42. "An act making an appropriation to pay the current and contingent expenses of the Extra or Special Session of the National Council, convened December 6th 1886, and ending December 21st 1886," in in National Council, Letters Sent, CHN 88, OHS.

43. Prison and High Sheriff, receipt 145, April 11, 1887, CHN 95, OHS.

44. See his signature on page 3 of Criminal Case File for Bub Trainor, Jacket 272. Bonnie Speer writes in *The Killing of Ned Christie* that Bub, "a wild and reckless young man of the town" and one of "Tahlequah's Saturday night outlaws," often visited Tahlequah with his "wild young friends" and "rode along Muskogee Avenue firing their guns and forcing stores to close in self-defense." She puts these descriptions in quotes, thus telling readers she got those descriptors from her source, a ninety-year-old man who did not say any of those things. He actually said, "And when he'd come to town he'd get a little drunk, I guess." Speer, *Killing of Ned Christie*, 23–24, 139n10. The "wild and reckless young man of the town" phrase actually is lifted directly from the June 9, 1918, issue of the *Daily Oklahoman*.

Art Burton copies this passage almost word for word from Speer in an article on his "Art Burton's Frontier" website, http://artburton.com/articles/black_red_deadly2.htm.

45. *Cherokee Advocate*, May 18, 1887.

46. *Eufaula (I.T.) Indian Journal*, Wednesday, March 23, 1887.

47. *Independence (Kans.) Daily Reporter*, April 8, 1887.

48. The version of that event Speer uses is not much more realistic because the ninety-year-old man who claimed in 1968 that he knew every detail of the events eighty-one years in the past—including dialogue between Trainor and Ellis—was only nine at the time of the shooting. Speer, however, changes his age to a more credible seventeen years old. The witness also stated that Trainor wore a "steel, bulletproof vest," reminiscent of the story told by A. M. Ryals about Zeke Proctor in 1937. Ben Hartness interview, April 18, 1968, DD, T-460-2. The document reads that "Ben Hartness was 90 years old at the time of this interview."

49. ARCIA, 1886, p. 156.

50. ARCIA, 1889, p. 210; ARCIA, 1890, p. 92.

51. "An Act to prevent the introduction and Vending of Ardent Spirits," September 28, 1839, CLAIT, 1:29; ARCIA, 1844, 394–95, p. 401.

52. ARCIA, 1880, p. 95; ARCIA, 1883, p. 88; ARCIA, 1884, p. 143.

53. *Arkansas Gazette*, July 19, 1881. Bill Lovett and Deer Track reportedly started a fight and Jim Satterwafte was beheaded.

54. Criminal Case File, Nancy Schell [Shell], jacket 173. Court cases of Fort Smith are located at the National Archives in Fort Worth, Texas. The Oklahoma Historical Society in Oklahoma City houses an index of the cases, arranged in alphabetical order by the last names of the deputy marshals who brought the alleged criminals to Fort Smith, not by the criminals' names. For information about Nancy Scraper Shell, see Joe Scraper, Jr., "From Whiskey Peddler to Sunday School Teacher."

55. *Tulsa World*, June 17, 1917. The *Daily Oklahoman* copied that a year later, writing on June 9, 1918, "Sometimes Christie drank too much whisky," and as a result of that drinking the night of May 4, "he lay in a stupor." In 1937, an unreliable source stated that "he [Ned] had been in session with the Cherokee Council and at the end of the week he had been in the habit of acquiring a pint of good whiskey and starting home. This time he had probably taken a little too much to drink and no doubt it showed in his walk." Wilson, IPP 99:143. These three sources (the latter two copied their information from the first story) have become the foundation for the image of Christie as a drinker who often imbibed to the point of passing out. McKennon then takes it a step further by adding, "It was well known that Ned Christie liked his whiskey and was always on the lookout for choice frontier red-eye." McKennon, *Iron Men*, 88.

56. Foreman, *Park Hill*, 173; Etta Jane Scraper, "Reminiscences of the Cherokee Female Seminary," 2; Foreman, IPP 4:88–89; Isabel Cobb interview, IPP 104:184–85; Rose Gazelle Lane, "Interviews with Pocahontas Club Members/Seminary Graduates," 598.1, Living Legends Collection, OHS; Report of the Joint Committee to investigate the burning of the Cherokee Female Seminary, May 16, 1887, M 9430-1-10, box 9, file 184, in Cherokee Nation Papers: Education, WHC; Ross, *Life and Times of Hon. William Potter Ross*, 138.

57. Derived from the 1880 Cherokee Census and Index, Schedules 1–6, 7RA-07, rolls 1–4; 1890 Cherokee Census (no index), schedules 1–4, 7RA-08, rolls 1–4; Index to the Five Civilized Tribes, the Final Dawes Roll, M1186, roll ; and Enrollment Cards for the Five Civilized Tribes, 1898–1914, M1186, rolls 2–15, cards 1–11132, at NASW. I compiled these stats for my book *Cultivating the Rosebuds* and blood quantums of the graduates are given in Appendix A of that book. For male graduates, see Devon Abbott [Mihesuah], "Out of the 'Graves of the Polluted Debauches'," 503–21.

58. Mihesuah, *Cultivating the Rosebuds*, 95–112; Abbott [Mihesuah], "Out of the 'Graves of the Polluted Debauches.'"

59. Hamilton, personal communication.

60. *Twin Territories*, June 1899.

61. Letters Sent and Received by Principal Chiefs, p. 62, CHN 123, OHS.

> April 11, 1887
> Hon. Edw. Christie
> Executive Councillor
>
> Dear Sir,
>
> I write to request your presence here Thursday next to consider important business. The Female Seminary has burnt down yesterday. The children are all here, and cared for temporarily. I have sent messages to the other members of the Executive Council requesting them to be here Thursday the 14th inst.
>
> > Very truly
> > D. W. BUSHYHEAD
> > pl Chief

62. Letters Sent and Received by Principal Chiefs, pp. 52–4, CHN 123, OHS; Executive Council Records, vol. 710, January 6, 1886, December 16, 1885, pp. 51–52, CHN 119, OHS. Christie was paid sixty-eight dollars for seventeen days. Cherokee Senate Bill 29: Making an appropriation for the current and contingent expenses of the Present Extra Session of the National Council. December 20, 1886, p. 109, in National Council, Letters Sent, CHN 88, OHS. Speer begins her book *The Killing of Ned Christie* with the oft-repeated story about why Ned happened to be in Tahlequah the day Maples was shot. She tells us that Ned attended a council meeting to determine what to do about the destruction of the seminary building. It is true that Christie came to town for a special session about the school, but the destruction of the seminary was covered in the April 16 special session. Maples was shot two and a half weeks later. After the April 16 session, Christie went back home to Wauhillau, then returned for the May 3 National Council session that addressed different topics, such as reviewing an application for a pardon for a man convicted of assault with intent to kill and giving advice to Bushyhead regarding walnut tree-cutting. The council postponed the remainder of its meeting until the second session of the month, May 9. Maples was shot the next evening, the fourth of May; therefore, the destruction of the Cherokee Female Seminary played no role in the

Christie-Maples saga. Speer, *Killing of Ned Christie*, 8–9.

63. Letter from Dennis W. Bushyhead to Senate and Council, May 9, 1887, in Cherokee (Tahlequah)-Schools: Female Seminary, CHN 99, OHS.

64. *Kansas City (Mo.) Times*, December 20, 1885. The paper states that Glover said to Bunch, "I guess we had just as well settle our difficulty now," and brought his shotgun to his shoulder. Bunch was in the act of turning around when Glover fired, the charge taking effect behind the left ear killing him instantly." Only the two men were present so it not known if Glover relayed that story or if the paper created it.

CHAPTER 3

1. *Tahlequah (I.T.) Arrow*, February 2, 1907; Duvall, *Cherokee Nation and Tahlequah* 70; Fullerton, "Story of the Telephone in Oklahoma," 254.

2. *Dallas Morning News*, May 6, 1887.

3. Ibid.

4. *Fort Smith (Ark.) Elevator*, May 13, 1887.

5. *Dallas Morning News*, May 8, 1887.

6. Executive Council Records, vol. 712, p. 58, CHN 119, OHS.

7. *Cherokee Advocate*, May 11, 1887. The group moved and carried that

the Officers of the law empowered to preserve the peace in this vicinity to be requested to exercise such vigilance in the dischage of their duties to that end as the time and circumstance requires, and that the Sheriff of the District be urged to cooperate with the High Sheriff in so doing . . . passed the following resolutions:

Resolved, That we the undersigned citizens of Tahlequah deeply and sincerely deplore the recent death in our midst of Mr. Dan Maples, a citizen of Benton County, State of Arkansas, who, though not personally known to most of us, is represented and recognized as the father of a large family, and a man of sterling character and virtue, and our heartfelt sympathy is hereby expressed for his loved ones and friends at home in the loss they have sustained.

Resolved, further, That we utterly condemn and abhor the commission of the terrible though unusual a crime in our community, though which as stranger, who must have relied, when he came, upon the law-abiding spirit of our people to protect him, and has thus fallen a victim of an assassin; and we ask that the principal chief do use what instruments and means may be in his charge and hands in order to promptly ferret out this crime, discover the perpetrator, and deliver him to the proper authorities to be punished—in conformity with the intercourse laws with the United States, which, by treaty, are made obligatory on us as the laws of this Nation also.

Those who signed the document: D. W. Bushyhead, R. F. Glenn, R. M. French, John Hawkins, Joe Heinrichs, Blue Alberty, T. J. Lyman, G. W. Benge, A. Stevens, Jen Roberson, William Terren, William Campbell, Herbert Kneeland, N. P. Boy, James Gray, Ezekial Crittendon, T. P. Trainer, Geo. Wilkerson, J. W. McSpadden, W. G. Blake, D. W. Wilson, W. N. Evans, S. Richie, D. Ward, Charley Scraper, Jesse Pigion [Pigeon], Jno. M. Taylor,

Cull Thorn, Sam Manus, Jas. Smith, Robt. Fuller, T. J. Adair, R. O. Trent, J. L. Smith, Gideon Morgan, Dr. Willis, W. A. Thompson, Thomas Roach, G. W. Hughes, B. W. Foreman, E. C. Boudinot, Jr., Frank Adair, Than Woflard (?), G. W. Hughes, Jr., Jno. Soears, Johnson Parris, John Lyman, T. W. Foreman, Dr. W. T. Adair, John W. Wolfe, Benj. King, Jas. King, C. C. Lipe, Geo. Butler, P. J. Thomson, John Leosier, Robert B. Ross, Aaron Terrell, Dick Bondinot.

The *Dallas Morning News* (May 8, 1887), claimed to have the resolutions, but the writer altered them:

> Resolved, That we the undersigned citizens of Tahlequah deeply deplore the recent murder in our midst of Dan Maples, of Bentonville, Ark., and our heartfelt sympathy is hereby extended to his friends and loved ones at home in the great loss they have sustained.
>
> Resolved, further, That we bitterly condemn and abhor the commission of so terrible and unusual a crime in our midst, and we ask of the principal chief to use what means he has in his power to arrest the guilty party and deliver him to the proper authority, in conformity with the intercourse laws with the United States, which by treaty are made obligatory on us.

8. Steele, *Last Cherokee Warriors*, 80. Records show that Pigeon, along with Lenny Pigeon, a man named Scruggs, and another named Kagua, were accused of killing Joseph Rogers in October 1882. In July 1885 Pigeon was accused of selling whiskey and in March 1886 he allegedly shot Joseph Richardson in the chest. Pigeon traveled to Fort Smith in February 1886 and swore to the court that he did not sell whiskey. If he was at court at that time, one would surmise that Parker would have attempted to deal with him over the murder charge from four years earlier. Also, there is no conviction listed for anyone named Bill or William Pigeon in the Fort Smith Sentence Books. See also Criminal Case files for Bill Pigeon and William Pigeon, jacket 155 (note four files have the same number) and Fort Smith Sentence Record Book, RG 21, Western District of Arkansas, NASW.

9. Even the *Fort Smith (Ark.) Elevator*, May 13, 1887, stated that he had no writs. There is an oddity in the criminal jacket for Charley Bobtail, however. Within the file is a Writ of Subpoena that was given to Charley Bobtail on July 18, 1887. The curious aspect is that the writ is certified and signed by Dan W. Maples, the man who had been killed more than two months prior. Clearly, either his name was already on the writ and someone else presented the writ and added the date, or the date was wrong to begin with. But the handwriting of the signature and the date that the subpoena was served are the same. Strange errors did appear in these case files and it appears this is one of them. The importance is that some interpret such errors as truth. See Criminal Defendant Case File, Charles Bobtail, Jacket 18, NASW.

10. Whitmire, IPP 97:366. Whitmire claims—without telling us how he knew this information—that "Maples had a warrant for Parris and as soon as Maples halted them, Parris began to shoot and Maples returned fire, as stated by Christie who claimed to have no gun at the time." McKennon writes that John Parris was on a "list of the more persistent

offenders of the federal whiskey law" and that Maples had a copy of that list, while Speer writes that Maples had a warrant for Parris and Trainor. Analysis of those cases shows that there was no warrant for either man and in fact, the charge of whiskey selling for Parris that was closest in time to 1887 clearly has "dismissed" written in the documents. See McKennon, *Iron Men*, 85; Speer, *Killing of Ned Christie*, 34.

11. Example: Looney Coon: Criminal Defendant Case Files for Looney/Loony Coon, 1878, 1884, 1889, 1890, NASW. Also note that for some cases, such as John Parris, there are several files with the same number (Parris has eight files with the same number, 151, and there is no differentiation between them), but events are out of order and pages from separate cases appear to be randomly stapled together. Meg Hacker, Archives Director, National Archives at Fort Worth, explains: "The court used a pigeon-hole system of filing their documents. They started to keep their cases quasi alphabetically by the name of the main defendant and they basically numbered the pigeon hole 1 (held As), 2 (held Bs), 3 (held Cs), and so on. Once they filled up a pigeon hole, they bundled up the files and retired them as Jacket 1, etc. The cases with a defendant's last name starting with A, just got a new pigeon-hole number. If the court had more documents to add to the original case, they didn't open that bundle, they simply placed these new documents into the latest number pigeon hole for that alphabetical number." Personal communication.

12. Criminal Defendant Case File, Charles Bobtail, Jacket 18; Fort Smith Sentence Books, Indictment 1384, NASW.

13. *Kansas City (Mo.) Star*, May 18, 1887.

14. Criminal Case Files for John Parris and James Parris, Jacket 151; John Parris, Jacket 151, NASW.

15. Criminal Case Files for John Parris, George Parris, Jacket 151, NASW.

16. Criminal Case Files for John Parris, Jacket 151, NASW.

17. Criminal Defendant Case Files for John Parris, Jackets 151 (eight jackets) and Jacket 18, NASW. See also Fort Smith Sentence Books, NASW.

18. John Parris, Jacket 231, NASW. Fort Smith Sentence Books, indictment 50, NASW.

19. Speer, *Killing of Ned Christie*, 30, 140n8; John F. Parris interview, October 1, 1937, IPP 69:333. Speer states that he was a half-blood who came over the removal trail, was married to another liquor runner named Kate, had eight children, lived in Dogtown, and was thirty-eight years old. She based all of this information on the nonexistent "Cherokee Census Roll, 1892." Further, she cobbled together a personality named John Parris by using information from various unrelated rolls and interviews that pertain to other men by the same name. She uses an *Indian-Pioneer Papers* interview of an unconnected John F. Parris to create the component of Parris coming from Georgia, the trek being a difficult ordeal, and living in Dogtown. This is the same Parris that the *Daily Oklahoman* states worked as a "printman" for the *Cherokee Advocate* newspaper. If this was the same John Parris involved with Maples, and it is highly doubtful that it is, he would have been twenty-five at the time of Maples's death in 1887 and would have started having his eight children with "Kate" at age twenty-two, provided she had a child every year. The only census that mentions a John and Kate Parris is the 1893 Tahlequah census, but they have two children, who both are his stepchildren. The John and Kate on this census are only

thirty years of age and there is no mention of Dogtown. There is only one John Parris around thirty-eight (thirty-nine in this case) years old on any census, but that person is on the 1880 census and is listed as dead. There is no Kate Parris on the Dawes Roll. John F. Parris states that he was married to a Kate, but they divorced and had no children. And this John F. states that his father's name is Green Parris. Further, while a woman named Kate Parris was indeed convicted of selling whiskey without a license in October 1885 and was accused of the same in November 1886, but not convicted, the only connection between her and the John Parris accused of shooting Maples are their last names and misbehaviors. The John and Kate who were criminals may have been married, but there is nothing to confirm that.

20. John's siblings: Letha, Andrew, Hester, Celia, Nellie, James, George W. (Bud), Polly, Rachel, Sarah, William, and Joe. See siblings on the Guion Miller Roll, Records Relating to Enrollment of Eastern Cherokee, and on Cherokee Census and Index, 1880. With a family this large, however, not all the names appear on every roll; some had died and women married and took their husbands' last names.

21. Criminal Defendant Case File, Charles Bobtail, jacket 18. NASW.

22. Criminal Defendant Case File, Bud Trainor Jacket 187, NASW.

23. Executive Council Records, vol. 712, p. 58, CHN 199, OHS.

24. Criminal Defendant Case File, John Hogshooter Jacket 90, NASW. Also called to testify: Scog Manus, Stephen Vann, Mrs. Triplett, Miss Triplett, Fayette Gunne [Lafayette Guinn], Richard Humphres [Humphrey], Corneleus Boudinot [Elias Cornelius], Dr. Trout, Lewis Walker, Mrs. Sylcox, George French.

25. Criminal Defendant Case File, Kate Parris, Jacket 151, and Criminal Defendant Case File, Kate Parris and Julia Bell, File Unit, RG 21; Criminal Defendant Case File, Nancy Schell [Shell], jacket 173 and Naney [Nancy] Shell, jacket 168. See also Joe Scraper, Jr., "From Whiskey Peddler to Sunday School Teacher"; 1880 Cherokee Census and Index, Schedules 1–6, 7RA-07, rolls 1–4, NASW.

26. Criminal Defendant Case File, John Hogshooter, Jacket 90, NASW.

27. Speer, Killing of Ned Christie, 30, and for the latter statement—that they headed toward Dogtown—there is no citation provided.

28. Steele, Last Cherokee Warriors, 82, 83.

29. Prisoners and High Sheriff, receipt for March 9, 1887, CVHN 95, OHS.

30. Cherokee Advocate, July 6, 1887, September 28, 1887; Eufaula (I.T.) Indian Journal, July 7, 1887; Fort Smith (Ark.) Elevator, July 8, 1887, September 23, 1887. Witnesses were J. Hooper, Johnson Parris, James Smith, Evans Roberson, and William Harnage.

31. Cherokee Advocate, July 6, 1887, September 28, 1887, Fort Smith (Ark.) Elevator, July 8, 1887, September 23, 1887.

32. Speer fabricates some drama by writing, "When Thomas Trainor, Sr., heard about the latest warrant for his son's arrest, he angrily denounced the officers for what he considered the continued harassment of his son. His half-blood friends took up the cry, and the situation in Tahlequah became volatile as rumors spread." While it could be that Trainor was upset about his son, there is no documentation that says he "angrily denounced the officers" and further, his son had been in similar situations before this. And if Trainor had

been so verbally angry, the *Cherokee Advocate* would not have sung his praises after his death. Speer then provides an excerpt from the *Siloam Springs Herald* (reprinted in the *Tahlequah Telephone*) falsely stating that someone "connected with" Maples' death shot into Chief Bushyhead's home. Speer, *Killing of Ned Christie*, 51. See also *Tahlequah (I.T.) Telephone*, May 12, 1887. The editor of the *Tahlequah Telephone* responded by saying this event did not occur, yet Speer includes both statements in her book, thus canceling out her scenario about Thomas Trainor, Sr.

33. John Hawkins to Chief Bushyhead, July 19, 1887, in Cherokee (Tahlequah)-Sheriffs, CHN 103, OHS.

34. Grand Jury Indictment, July 23, 1887; "Grand Jury Cases: A Crimson Docket, List of Murder Cases to be Tried at the Approaching Term of the U.S. Court, Western District of Arkansas"; Criminal Defendant Case File, Ned Christie, 1887, Jacket 38, NASW.

35. Executive Council Records, vol. 712, p. 58, CHN 119, OHS; Executive Council Records, vol. 712, Tuesday, August 23, 1887; Wednesday, August 24, 1887, pp. 58–59; Sec. 51, p. 268, CHN 119, OHS. The council refers to Ned as "Edward."

36. Article 3, Sec. 13, of The Constitution of the Cherokee Nation, in *Constitution and Laws of the Cherokee Nation: Passed at Tahlequah, Cherokee Nation, 1839–51* (Tahlequah: Cherokee Nation, 1852), 8.

37. See *Cherokee Advocate*, January 19, 1883, January 18, 1884, October 26, 1892, April 18, 1894, April 20, 1901; *Indian Chieftain*, March 3, 1887, April 7, 1887; O'Beirne and O'Beirne, *Indian Territory*, 88–89.

38. For an array of issues faced by the Cherokee Nation during the time Christie was wanted for murder, see Federal Relations, CHN 79, OHS. For examples, December 12, 1889, contemptible letter, p. 555, and organizing a delegation to Washington, p. 571. Chief Mayes at odds with Washington, D.C., in wanting to defeat the Oklahoma bill for the territorial government. Agnew, IPP 1:297.

39. Criminal Defendant Case File, George Parris, 151. NASW. Those called to testify: Ned Grease, Mrs. Eva Thom, John Hogshooter, Layfayette [Lafayette] Guinn, Mary Guinn, Josie Schell, and Looney Coon. The next day, G. H. Jefferson, J. M. Peel, George York, Bob Thompson, Ida Triplett, Charlott Triplett, Kate Manus, and Andrew J. Hooper were added to the list.

40. Robin Stann interview, November 12, 1937, IPP 86:472–85.

41. Speer, *Killing of Ned Christie*, 54.

42. *Vinita (I.T.) Indian Chieftain*, December 1, 1887.

43. Criminal Defendant Case File, Bud Trainor, Jacket 187, NASW. Note that most of the documentation in this jacket pertains to the Duckworth Store incident. Speer, however, uses this excuse as fact, stating that the two friends, Christie and Parris, entered Shell's home together, and found Trainor eating. That Trainor was there eating is merely a statement made by Trainor that no one else substantiates. Speer continues by asserting that Christie and Parris "were well acquainted with Trainor, but right now they were more interested in obtaining a drink." This runs counter to Shell's testimony that Christie arrived and left with Grease. See Speer, *Killing of Ned Christie*, 30.

44. Steele states that Christie "sent a message" and even writes, "Upon the messenger's return, Ned surrounded himself with an army of men," giving the impression that a courier came back with an answer and that is when Christie sprang into outlaw action. Steele persists by adding, "He continually denied any knowledge of the crime." Steele, *Last Cherokee Warriors*, 83–84. Speer also states that Christie wrote a letter and showed it to Timothy Brown Hitchcock, clerk of the Cherokee Senate, who in turn gave it to "two prominent Tahlequah citizens" who gave it to Judge Parker, but "everyone had fully decided that Christie was the guilty one and that he positively could expect no bond." Speer, *Killing of Ned Christie*, 56. There are several problems with these assertions. First, she once again cites the questionable voice of Robin Stann. She also cites her 1979 interview with Roberta Hitchcock, and the portion quoting Stann sounds identical to the 1918 *Daily Oklahoman* article. That is not surprising since many later interviewees parrot that old newspaper story. Also, these "prominent Tahlequah citizens" are unnamed and while it is possible they traveled "on two occasions" to Fort Smith to talk to Parker about Christie, the road from Tahlequah to Fort Smith was arduous and quite dangerous; it would not be a trip one took for granted. Further, that "everyone" had already decided Christie's guilt is a broad statement for that time period. Parris, Trainor, and Bobtail were still dealing with the court and no decision had been made about anyone.

45. Hamilton, personal communication.

46. The source Speer uses said "Christy" knew who had killed Maples but would not tell. Speer, *Killing of Ned Christie*, 50. The 1937 interview with C. W. Costen that she uses made dubious claims that the family sent for a doctor from Cincinnati to treat Christie when he was wounded, and the government "made a treaty with him and he died at Shawnee a few years ago." That is, Costen is asserting that Christie did not die until the mid-1930s. C. W. Costen interview, November 10, 1937, IPP 7:389–90. Speer also includes the misspelled citation involving a "Robin Vann," who is actually Robin Stann. In this interview, Stann tells the journalist J. A. Wilson his story. In the story, "Vann" (who is actually Stann) claims that Christie told him that he "absolutely did not shoot Maples." Speer continues, "If Vann believed he had murdered the lawman, [he] would give himself up to the Indian police and stand trial in the Cherokee Nation." Stann's answers were not written down verbatim. There is no passage in the interview that begins with "Stann said." The interviewer clearly edits what Stann told him and interjects his own interpretations and much backstory, such as, "Robin was not unlike other Cherokee boys." There is no way of knowing what Stann actually imparted to the interviewer. Speer, *Killing of Ned Christie*, 42, 141n2. Speer writes that Christie sought advice from Senator Grease at the Greases' "boarding house" and the latter told Christie to "keep his mouth shut." She cites both the 1918 *Daily Oklahoman* article and Ballenger's *Around Tahlequah Council Fires*, but the latter source does not even mention Grease by name. There was no "Grease Boarding House"; it was uncle Nede Grease's home where Christie always stayed when in town. Further, Ballenger is incorrect in his assertion that Maples attempted to arrest Christie after the latter bought whiskey. See Ballenger, *Around Tahlequah Council Fires*, 131.

47. "An act making appropriations for the current and contingent expenses of the Indian Department," March 3, 1885, 23 Stat., 362, sec. 9, Acts of Forty-eighth Congress-Second Session, Kappler, IA: LT, vol. 1, Laws, chap. 341, pp. 32–33; *Telephone*, October 3, 1889.

48. Testimony of Judge Isaac C. Parker, June 4, 1885, in 49th Cong., 1st sess., 2 Senate, *Report of the Committee on Indian Affairs*, pt. 2, p. 399.

49. For discussions of hangings, see Akins, *Hangin' Times in Fort Smith*.

50. Dawes, *A United States Prison*, 143, 214–15.

51. Testimony, William M. Cravens, and comment, Judge Isaac Parker, June 3, 1885, in *Report of the Committee on Indian Affairs*, 390.

52. Dawes, *United States Prison*, 214–15; Testimony, Judge Isaac Parker, June 4, 1885, in *Report of the Committee on Indian Affairs*, 401.

53. See examples in Mihesuah, *Choctaw Crime and Punishment*.

54. Hamilton, *Ned Christie*, 35–36; Hamilton, personal communication.

55. Criminal Defendant Case File, Joe Miller, John Leach, and Bud Trainor, Jacket 221. Criminal Defendant Case File, Joe Miller, John Leach, Bud Trainor, and William Chue, Jacket 134, NASW; *Grand Forks (N.D.) Herald*, October 20, 1887; *Fort Smith (Ark.) Weekly Elevator*, October 21, 1887; *Muskegon (Mich.) Chronicle*, October 20, 1887; *Aberdeen (S.D.) Weekly News*, October 21, 1887.

56. *Topeka (Kans.) Daily Commonwealth*, October 22, 1887; *Lawrence (Kans.) Daily Journal*, October 22, 1887; *Pittsburgh Daily Post*, October 22, 1887; *Manitoba Free Press*, October 24, 1887. Speer, however, recounts the destruction of the buildings and asserts that not only was Trainor guilty, she connects this with yet another false assertion that Trainor became a deputy marshal. Speer, *Killing of Ned Christie*, 73–75.

57. Holland, *Cherokee Newspapers*, 335–42.

58. *St. Louis Post-Dispatch*, December 2, 1887. This story from the Saint Louis paper is cobbled together from reports from Little Rock, Arkansas.

59. *Vinita (I.T.) Indian Chieftain*, November 27, 1887; *St. Louis Post-Dispatch*, December 2, 1887.

60. *Vinita (I.T.) Indian Chieftain*, December 6, 1888; *St. Louis Post-Dispatch*, December 2, 1887, August 20, 1888. There is no Fort Smith case file for Boudinot.

61. Speer writes that the editor of the *Tahlequah Telephone* accused Chief Bushyhead of "openly flouting the federal law and of protecting a murderer, for George Parris could not be found, while Bub Trainor, heavily armed, "can be seen on our streets ever day." Speer, *Killing of Ned Christie*, 50. Her source is the *Tahlequah Telephone*, June 10, 1887. There is no mention of this accusation in this source, nor does the phrase "heavily armed appear." In fact, the paper actually states, "Chief Bushyhead had Parish [Parris] arrested and sent to Fort Smith, and Bub Trainor is on our streets every day."

62. *Fort Smith (Ark.) Elevator*, May 13, 1887.

63. *St. Louis Post-Dispatch*, December 2, 1887.

64. Federal Relations, Book A, p. 263, CHN 79, OHS.

May 11, 1887

Sir:

A letter addressed to the Hon Jos Miller U.S. Commissioner of internal revenue by N. F. Acres, Collector of Kansas, has been forwarded me by the Hon. Attorney General U.S. with the request that I investigate and report upon the matters therein contained as soon as possible. I will therefore than [thank] you to inform me at your earliest opportunity of the manner in which Deputy U.S. Marshals have conducted themselves in the Cherokee Nation since November 1886. The writer says "I have never heard of a square Reliable Officer in the Indian Territory as a Deputy Marshal or Indian Police, as a rule they are desperate characters, they protect crime and criminals and are generally understood to be engaged in the whiskey business or some other questionable transaction, and an honest Officer cannot live among them criminals who stand in with such men are defiant as you may guess.

The foregoing quotation is sufficient to advise you of the changes to which I am required to respond. I have concluded that the most satisfactory information as to the conduct of my deputies could be obtained by a correspondence with the Chief Executive Officers of the different Indian Nations and hence I have written a like communication to the Chief officers of the Chickasaw, Choctaw, Creek & Seminole Nations.

The sweeping changes made by our Kansas neighbor would if true, Justify, and even demand the immediate withdrawal of all my deputies from the Indian Country and hence I have determined to make a thorough and searching examination in order that the truth may be established upon a more solid foundation than a mere sweeping declaration from Mr. Acres.

I am respectfully your obedient servant.

JOHN CARROLL, U.S. Marshal.

65. *Tahlequah (I.T.) Telephone*, July 22, 1887. For example, "The National party is jealous of the white man's intelligence. . . . The party who ignores a white man in its nominations and will show its preference for the colored over the white, does not deserve to carry a white voter in its ranks."

66. *Atoka (I.T.) Indian Citizen*, July 28, 1887.

67. Ibid., July 21, 1887. The laws were taken from Mankiller Catcher, a candidate for the council on the National ticket and a Tahlequah lodge captain.

68. *Daily Arkansas Gazette*, October 30, 1887.

69. *Fort Worth Daily Gazette*, November 20, 1887.

70. *Cherokee Advocate*, January 4, 1888.

71. Ibid., January 16, 1889.

72. *Cherokee Advocate*, March 13, 1889.

73. *Fort Smith (Ark.) Elevator*, March 22, 1889.

74. *Chicago Daily Inter Ocean*, September 21, 1887.

75. *Cherokee Advocate*, January 11, 1888.

76. *Fort Smith (Ark.) Elevator*, June, 25, 1889.

77. *Cherokee Advocate*, January 25, 1888, March 28, 1888, July 18, 1888; William Christie Jacket 38; Fort Smith Sentence Record Books, RG 21, Western District of Arkansas, NASW.

78. *Vinita (I.T.) Indian Chieftain*, March 29, 1888.

79. Roach married Katie Christie, daughter of the aforementioned George Christie (son of Arch Christie and Katie Wolf) and Lucy Young.

80. *Cherokee Advocate*, June 19, 1889.

81. *Vinita (I.T.) Indian Chieftain*, September 5, 1889.

CHAPTER 4

1. Criminal Defendant Case File, Ned Christie, Jacket 38 NASW.

2. *Fort Smith (Ark.) Weekly Elevator*, November 1, 1889.

3. *Vinita (I.T.) Indian Chieftain*, October 3, 1889.

4. *Cherokee Advocate*, May 18, 1887. See also Flint District Records, pp. 248–49, 256–85, CHN 38, OHS.

5. *Cherokee Advocate*, June 29, 1887.

6. Ibid., January 25, 1888.

7. *Vinita (I.T.) Indian Chieftain*, February 2, 1888, April 26, 1888, May 10, 1888; *Cherokee Advocate*, March 21, 1888; April 25, 1888.

8. Jerry Akins at the Fort Smith National Historic Site confirms that the difference, besides the length, is the way the magazine is attached to the barrel. A carbine has a band that goes around the mag and barrel. The gun in the case has bands up near the sight. The weapon in Christie's left hand has a different attachment farther down the barrel. This rifle came from the elusive [Cecil] "Atchison Collection" (that is not in any archive) and Atchison did not state where he acquired the weapon. Personal communication.

9. McKennon, *Iron Men*, photo section after p. 104; Hamilton, personal communication.

10. Prison and High Sheriff, Receipt for April 11, 1887, CHN 95, OHS; Hamilton, *Ned Christie*, 8, 21.

11. Hamilton, personal communication.

12. Kilpatrick, "Cherokees Remember Their Badmen," 64.

13. Densmore, "Chippewa Customs," 43.

14. *Cherokee Advocate*, June 26, 1889, July 24, 1889.

15. Hamilton, *Ned Christie*, 38.

16. *Dallas Morning News*, February 19, 1888, February 25, 1888.

17. *Leavenworth (Kans.) Times*, February 25, 1888; *New Orleans Times-Picayune*, February 25, 1888; *St. Louis Post-Dispatch*, February 24, 1888. That latter described Christie as "the head of a gang of ruffianly outlaws who terrified that country."

18. *Cherokee Advocate*, March 1, 1888.

19. Prison and High Sheriff, receipt 137, CHN 95, OHS.

20. Flint District Records, CHN 38, OHS.

21. Speer, *Killing of Ned Christie*, 74; Shirley, *Law West of Fort Smith*, 59.

22. *Fort Smith (Ark.) Elevator*, January 31, 1890.

23. Shirley also discusses Starr's death in *Belle Starr and Her Times*, 248, 250, and uses the same citations: *Fort Smith (Ark.) Elevator*, January 24 and 31, 1890, and *Vinita (I.T.) Chieftain*, January 30, 1890.

24. Anderson and Yadon, *100 Oklahoma Outlaws, Gangsters, and Lawmen*, 28, 95.

25. Speer, *Killing of Ned Christie*, 74; Shirley, *Law West of Fort Smith*, 59. Criminal Case file, Thomas Trainor, jacket 187, NASW. Speer writes about how a list of prominent Cherokee men served as sureties for Trainor's bond for the four charges of arson, "assault with the intent to kill in the Indian Country," "murder in the Indian Country," and "introducing liquors into the Indian Country." The men who signed for him included Rogers, along with Joel B. Mayes, Lucien B. Bell, Elias C. Boudinot, Richard F. Boudinot, John H. Coody, and Jesse B. Mayes. Anderson and Yadon, however, use only Clem Rogers since he is the personality most likely to be recognized by their readers. There is nothing in the court docket about Trainor becoming a deputy marshal, but Speer says he becomes one. Anderson and Yadon also use the same source that Speer uses. Unfortunately for these writers, the timeline does not fit.

26. The fountainhead of misinformation Glenn Shirley uses sources from 1890, yet Speer retroactively uses them as 1889 data. Several papers refer to Trainor and Hutchins as "Deputy Marshals" and others call them members of Bruner's "posse," which is not the same thing. Other papers describe the two men as being more like bounty hunters, not deputies or possemen. *New Ear*, February 5, 1890; *Eufaula (I.T.) Indian Journal*, January 30, 1890; *Chicago Daily Tribune*, February 2, 1890; *Galveston Daily News*, February 6, 1890.

Making this false claim of Trainor becoming a deputy U.S. marshal even more problematic is that Speer conveniently uses it as yet another tie-in to the Christie saga: "Parker's idiosyncrasy and the hiring of Bud Trainer were soon to have a disastrous effect on the life of Ned Christie." What she means by that is found in her chapter 10, in which she states that Heck Thomas and I. P. Isbell recruited Trainor to join them on the 1889 attack on Christie's home. She writes about Judge Parker and his occasional use of men with shady (that is, violent) histories as his lawmen in words that she lifts directly from Shirley. Then she misquotes Shirley: "for a man could 'be highly moral but he did not have what it took to be a marshal in the Indian Country,'" when Shirley actually wrote, "A coward could be highly moral, but 'he could not serve as a marshal in the Indian Country.'"

The June 10, 1918, issue of the *Daily Oklahoman* ran a story about Christie, and within the story is a heading "Trainor Helped in Pursuit," but oddly, the story that follows includes nary a sentence about Trainor. It appears that the misleading headline is all it took to give Shirley the idea to make Trainor a lawman. Speer, *Killing of Ned Christie*, 78; Shirley, *Law West of Fort Smith*, 59; *Daily Oklahoman*, June 10, 1918.

27. Lucinda Sanders Wilhite, December 23, 1968, DD, T-360-1, p. 23; Catherine Wilhite, DD, T-135.

28. Hamilton, *Ned Christie*, 38.

29. *Fort Smith (Ark.) Elevator,* May 31, 1889. Yoes to Steven Wheeler, December 4, 1888, letter at Fort Smith Archives.

30. *Fort Smith (Ark.) Elevator,* May 31, 1889.

31. *Journal* (April 1979), pp. 18–19; Albert W. Bishop, Adjutant General of Arkansas, 1867. "First Arkansas Cavalry Historical Memoranda," Report of the Adjutant General of the State of Arkansas, list of pension applications, n.p., Fort Smith Archives.

32. Shirley, *Heck Thomas, Frontier Marshal,* 47.

33. *Daily Oklahoman,* January 8, 1911.

34. Candee, "Oklahoma," 330.

35. *Cherokee Advocate,* September 18, 1889.

36. *Vinita (I.T.) Indian Chieftain,* October 3, 1889. Another account in the *Muskogee Phoenix,* October 3, 1889, says that the outhouse was a "smokehouse."

37. *Cherokee Advocate,* October 30, 1889.

38. *Fort Smith (Ark.) Elevator,* October 4, 1889; *Cherokee Advocate,* October 23, 1889; *Fort Smith (Ark.) Weekly Elevator,* November 1, 1889; Jacob Yoes to Hon. W. H. H. Miller, Attorney-General, U.S., November 12, 1892. In his letter to Miller, Yoes states that this incident took place in October 1889, but newspapers report the activity as September 26. General Records, Department of Justice, NA, College Park, Md.

39. *Atoka (I.T.) Indian Journal,* October 3, 1889.

40. *Fort Worth Daily Gazette,* September 28, 1889.

41. *Muskogee (I.T.) Phoenix,* October 3, 1889. The paper also asserts that Christie killed eight men besides Maples.

42. *Muskogee (I.T.) Phoenix,* January 23, 1890.

43. *Cherokee Advocate,* October 23, 1889.

44. John Henry Pedford interview, IPP 60:192.

45. Saugee Grigsby, May 2, 1969, DD, T-426-2, p. 7.

46. Wilson, IPP 99:146, 147. Wilson fabricates more about this particular shooting: "This time they had shot him through the head and Arch, his son, had kept up a pretty good stall for him so that after about an hour he began to see a spot of light about the size of a pin head. It got larger and larger very slowly, and after so long he could see everything. All this time his mind was perfectly clear, but he was unable to speak or see. After several hours his son, Arch, got a couple of fellows squarely down on the ground dead, and the gang loaded them up and left."

47. Walker, "Ned Christie," 32.

48. McKennon, *Iron Men,* 95.

49. *Milwaukee Journal,* June 30, 1967.

50. *Fort Smith (Ark.) Elevator,* November 1, 1889.

51. Wilson, IPP 99:142–44.

52. *Fort Smith (Ark.) Weekly Elevator,* November 1, 1889.

53. Clark, "Ned Christie," IPP 18: 148/215.

54. Pedford, IPP 60:191; Hamilton, *Ned Christie,* 44.

55. Pride, "Battle of Tahlequah Canyon."

56. *Muskogee (I.T.) Phoenix,* July 2, 1891.

57. *Omaha Daily Bee*, November 3, 1890.

58. McKennon, *Iron Men*, 99. He provides no endnotes in his book and his bibliography does not contain any issue of the *Cherokee Advocate*. Speer copies this scenario in her *Killing of Ned Christie*, 105, as does the *Milwaukee Journal*, June 30, 1967.

59. *Atoka (I.T.) Indian Citizen*, June 6, 1891; Going Snake District Records, vol. 115, p. 122, CHN, OHS.

60. *St. Louis Republic*, October 15, 1891.

61. *Omaha World Herald,* December 10, 1891, *Washington (D.C.) Evening Star,* December 10, 1891.

62. McKennon, *Iron Men*, 99–100.

63. Kirchner, "Ned Christie," 58–60.

64. This incident is discussed in chap. 4. *Fort Smith (Ark.) Weekly Elevator,* October 21, 1887; *Muskegon (Mich.) Chronicle*, October 20, 1887; *Aberdeen (S.D.) Weekly News*, October 21, 1887.

65. Criminal Defendant Case File, Miller, Leach, and Trainor, Jacket 221, NASW.

66. Rand, "Blood in the Cookson Hills," 27.

67. *Vinita (I.T.) Indian Chieftain*, June 7, 1888.

68. *Muskogee (I.T.) Phoenix*, December 31, 1891.

69. Thomas J. Welch, Sheriff of Goingsnake, to Harris, Cherokee Chief, April 7, 1892, in Cherokee (Tahlequah)–Depredations, CHN 74, OHS.

70. *Fort Smith (Ark.) Elevator*, November 7, 1890; *Fort Worth Daily Gazette*, November 8, 1890.

71. *Vinita (I.T.) Indian Chieftain*, November 27, 1890.

72. For example, see Burton, "Bass Reeves (1838–1910)."

73. *Boston Herald*, January 27, 1891.

74. *Mansfield (Ohio) News-Journal*, January 27, 1891; *Waukesha (Wis.) Journal*, January 31, 1891.

75. *Muskogee (I.T.) Phoenix*, January 29, 1891.

76. Ibid., February 5, 1892.

77. Ibid., June 11, 1891.

78. Joel B. Mayes did not even mention Christie's name in his fourth annual message to the Cherokee Nation delivered just a month later. Fourth annual message of Chief J. B. Mayes, November 4, 1890, in folder 7834, roll 50, Cherokee Nation Papers, WHC.

79. The *Cherokee Advocate* ran a story about criminals in Indian Territory. The paper rightly pointed out that many criminals enter the nation without invitation, then proceed to rob, steal, and kill. The paper defended Native residents of Indian Territory by stating that "previous to the advent of such characters no one ever heard of a mail robbery, the rifling of banks or the wholesale murder of innocent and law abiding people. Loyalty to one another and integrity in tribal relations are characteristic of the Red Man." The paper bemoaned the impressions that non-Indians have of Indians: "A day never passes but that we are pictured as an indolent and ravenous set of cannibals—brothers and sisters, fathers and mothers." The paper did concede, "though with a high degree of sadness, that such as base contamination of the Indian with renegades of justice from the states—after a

generation has passed away—is beginning to assert itself." See *Cherokee Advocate*, August 3, 1892. And the paper had a point. In 1894 the U.S. Census Office published its findings about Indian Territory in 1890. Among the statistics it found were the following: "Few murders are committed by citizens. The intruder or noncitizen population contributes 80 of the murders." U.S. Census Office, *Five Civilized Tribes in Indian Territory*, 4, 9.

80. Order of the Court, November Term 1892, signed by Stephen Wheeler, Clerk of the District Court of the U.S. for Western District of Arkansas, November 12, 1892, Fort Smith Archives.

81. *Fort Worth Daily Gazette*, November 8, 1890.

82. Criminal case file, John Hogshooter, jacket 368, NASW.

83. Criminal Defendant Case Files, Charles Bobtail, jacket 240, NASW.

84. Criminal case file, John Parris, Jacket 231; Fort Smith Sentence Books, indictment 50, both NASW.

85. Criminal case file, George Parris, Jacket 151, NASW.

86. *Muskogee (I.T.) Phoenix*, June 4, 1891.

87. *Cherokee Advocate*, September 7, 1892.

88. *Evening Kansan*, October 12, 1892.

89. Yoes to Miller, November 12, 1892.

90. *Tulsa Daily World*, October 5, 1952.

91. *Cherokee Advocate*, December 9, 1891.

92. *Atoka (I.T.) Indian Citizen*, June 6, 1891.

93. Ibid., June 27, 1891; *Kansas (Mo.) City Star*, June 20, 1891.

94. *Cherokee Advocate*, July, 1891.

95. Criminal Defendant Case Files, Tom Wolf and Arch Wolfe [Wolf], 479, NASW; Letter and Adair's sworn testimony, capreas and subpoena (270), and other records (2881) pertaining to the incident, Fort Smith Archives.

96. Going Snake District Records, p. 122, vol. 115, CHN 40, OHS.

97. *Galena (Kans.) Times*, July 10, 1891.

98. *Cherokee Telephone*, December 10 and 17, 1891.

99. *Muskogee (I.T.) Phoenix*, December 10, 1891. The *Omaha World Herald*, December 10, 1891, printed a different story, in which the men planned to accompany John Brown to the whiskey camp. Instead, they arrived at the camp and Brown instructed them to proceed further into "a dismal swamp." Around ten o'clock, they ran into a group of men who proceeded to shoot at the officers numerous times. According to the papers, "great excitement prevails here today and all the Cherokees join in denouncing the murderers and stand ready to volunteer their services to crush the bloodthirsty outlaws out of existence."

100. *Toledo Bee*, February 4, 1892.

101. *Watertown (N.Y.) Daily Times*, December 11, 1891. One paper asserted that Waco had killed five men by December 1891. See *Muskogee (I.T.) Phoenix*, December 17, 1891.

102. *Cherokee Telephone*, December 10, 1891. The *Muskogee Phoenix* also asserts that Waco was the nephew of Christie. *Muskogee (I.T.) Phoenix*, December 17, 1891.

103. *Our Brother in Red*, December 10, 1891.

104. *Dallas Morning News*, December 15, 1891.

105. Steele, *Last Cherokee Warriors*, 88–89.

106. *Tahlequah (I.T.) Telephone*, October 3, 1889.

CHAPTER 5

1. Steele, *Last Cherokee Warriors*, 95.

2. Yoes to Miller, November 12, 1892.

3. Steele, *Last Cherokee Warriors*, 95.

4. See Mihesuah, *Choctaw Crime and Punishment*, 108–37.

5. *Pittsburg (Kans.) Daily Headlight*, October 12, 1892.

6. See for example, *Fort Smith (Ark.) Weekly Elevator*, October 14, 1892.

7. *Omaha World*, October 12, 1892.

8. *Saginaw (Mich.) News*, October 15, 1892. Taken from Tahlequah newspaper October 15.

9. *Fort Smith (Ark.) Weekly Elevator*, October 14, 1892; *Washington (D.C.) Evening Star*, October 12, 1892.

10. *Sacramento Record-Union*, October 12, 1892; Stanley A. Clark, on Ned Christie, October 20, 1937, IPP 18:140/207. Jacob Yoes refers to Bowers as "Powers" in Yoes to Miller, November 12, 1892.

11. Yoes to Miller, November 12, 1892; *Dallas Morning News*, October 13, 1892; *Cherokee Advocate*, October 19, 1892; *Fort Smith (Ark.) Weekly Elevator*, October 14, 1892; *Washington (D.C.) Evening Star*, October 12, 1892; *Leavenworth Times*, October 13, 1892.

12. *Cherokee Advocate*, October 11, 1892.

13. *Muskogee (I.T.) Phoenix*, October 27, 1892.

14. *Cherokee Advocate*, October 19, 1892.

15. *Rockford (Ill.) Morning Star*, October 13, 1892.

16. *New Haven (Conn.) Register*, October 14, 1892.

17. *Dallas Morning News*, October 16, 1892.

18. Criminal Defendant Case File, George Christi [Christie], Arch Wolf, Jack Wolf, Jackson Wolf, Jim Christi [Christie], jacket 286, NASW.

19. Hamilton, *Ned Christie*, 51.

20. Abbe, "Dates of First Killing Frosts," 328.

21. Caelti, *Adventure, Mystery and Romance*, 233–34.

22. McKennon, *Iron Men*, 135–36.

23. Steele, *Last Cherokee Warriors*, 98; Speers, *Killing of Ned Christie*, 109.

24. Turner, *Rotgut Rustlers*, 23.

25. Benjamin Knight interview, July 23, 1937, IPP 51:267–73.

26. McKennon, *Iron Men*, 135. An undated online version of the *Tombstone News* copies this statement almost verbatim from McKennon: "a full-blooded Cherokee with an athletic build and a well-worn six-gun strapped to his thigh." Fischer, "Deputy Marshal Paden Tolbert."

27. Newspaper article enclosed with Yoes letter to Miller, November 12, 1892; Kraus, "Research Report: Allen, U.S. Marshal."

28. See, for example, Rhodes, IPP 75:343, and Ellis interview, IPP 8:377, 33:120, 92:254; *Fort Smith (Ark.) Weekly Elevator*, October 14, 1892.

29. Pedford, IPP 60:192.

30. *Allentown (Pa.) Morning Call*, November 5, 1892.

31. Ellis, IPP 8:377; 33:120; 92:254; C. B. Rhodes interview, n.d., IPP 75:343. Walker probably got his name from those two sources for his sensationalistic "Terror of the Cookson Hills," 58.

32. Rhodes, IPP 75:343.

33. Walker, "Terror of the Cookson Hills," 58.

34. S. R. Lewis interview, September 29, 1937, IPP 53:481–82.

35. *Salina (Kans.) Daily Republican*, October 14, 1892.

36. Yoes to Miller, November 12, 1892.

37. *Fort Smith (Ark.) Elevator*, November 11, 1892.

38. *St. Louis Republic*, November 4, 1892.

39. McKennon, *Iron Men*, 137.

40. Hamilton, personal communication. See also Enrollment Cards for the Five Civilized Tribes, 1898–1914, Cherokee Nation Enrollment 20710, Cherokees by Blood, M1186, NASW.

41. Yoes to Miller, November 12, 1892.

42. *Arkansas Gazette*, November 5, 1892; Yoes to Miller, November 12, 1892.

43. R. Y. Nance interview, March 12, 1937, IPP 66:78.

44. Yoes to Miller, November 12, 1892.

45. Hamilton, *Ned Christie*, 59.

46. Yoes to Miller, November 12, 1892.

47. Hamilton, personal communication. A sound also mastered by Ned's cousin J. P. Johnson.

48. Rand, "Blood in the Cookson Hills," 30. Cagney actually said "you dirty, yellow-bellied rat" in the 1932 movie *Taxi!*

49. Kirchner, "Ned Christie," 61.

50. Walker, "Ned Christie," *Real West*, 33.

51. *Allentown (Pa.) Morning Call*, November 5, 1892. This is same as stated by Rhodes, IPP 75:343, who obviously got the statistics from the newspaper.

52. Drago, *Outlaws on Horseback,* 190–91.

53. *Tulsa Daily World*, October 5, 1952. The projectiles were not cannonballs, but were oblong, shaped like shells.

54. Yoes to Miller, November 12, 1892.

55. *Arkansas Gazette*, Sunday November 6, 1892; Pedford, IPP 60:192; Yoes to Miller, November 12, 1892; *Daily Oklahoman*, June 9, 1918; *Stilwell Democrat-Journal*, January 14, 1971.

56. Rhodes, "Lest We Forget," IPP 75:343–44.

57. *Arkansas Gazette*, Sunday November 6, 1892.

58. William Ballard interview, July 20, 1937, IPP 4:382; Rhodes, IPP 343–44.

59. *Guthrie (O.T.) Daily Leader*, May 23, 1900.

60. *Chicago Daily Tribune*, November 7, 1894.

61. Rand, "Blood in the Cookson Hills," 62.

62. Gilbert Fallin interview, October 8, 1968, DD, T-316-3, p. 14.

63. Dickerson, IPP 24:304–305.

64. Ballard, IPP 4:382.

65. Walker, "Ned Christie," 58.

66. Stanley A. Clark, on Ned Christie, October 20, 1937, IPP 18:146/213.

67. *Arkansas Gazette*, November 6, 1892.

68. *Chicago Daily Tribune*, November 7, 1894.

69. Yoes to Miller, November 12, 1892.

70. Dickerson, IPP 24:304–305.

71. Ballard, IPP 4:382.

72. Nance, IPP 66:78.

73. Pedford, IPP 60:192. Wiley Wolf copies that assertion in his interview of January 10, 1969, T-370-2, p. 18.

74. Rhodes, IPP 75:342.

75. *Tulsa Daily World*, October 5, 1952.

76. *Milwaukee Journal*, June 30, 1967.

77. McKennon, *Iron Men*, 159, 162, 164, 210. McKennon probably got this information from Bowman's wife and son, both of whom are listed in his references (but not cited).

78. Yoes to Miller, November 12, 1892; *Cherokee Advocate*, November 9, 1892.

79. "Ned Christie, Justice Gone Wrong," *Grand Lake News Online*.

80. *Daily Illinois State Register*, November 5, 1892.

81. *Allentown (Pa.) Morning Call*, November 5, 1892.

82. *Muskogee (I.T.) Phoenix*, November 10, 1892, reporting November 5 news from Tahlequah; *Fort Smith (Ark.) Weekly Elevator*, November 17, 1893.

83. *Fort Smith (Ark.) Weekly Elevator*, November 17, 1893. During his arraignment Wolf stated that as he ran away he encountered one of the deputies, a "tall man." After they saw each other, both turned and ran in opposite directions. The alleged tall deputy remains unidentified and there is no other documentation that Wolf actually said this.

84. *Fort Smith (Ark.) Weekly Elevator*, November 11, 1892.

85. Yoes to Miller, November 12, 1892.

86. *Muskogee (I.T.) Phoenix*, December 1, 1892. Parker had authorized Yoes to pay a reward of one thousand dollars for the arrest and delivery of Ned Christie to the jail at Fort Smith. Order of the Court, November Term 1892, signed by Stephen Wheeler, Clerk of the District Court of the U.S. for the Western District of Arkansas, November 12, 1892, Fort Smith Archives.

87. Newspaper article attached to letter Yoes to Miller, November 12, 1892; *Vinita (I.T.) Indian Chieftain*, September 26, 1895.

88. Statement signed by McCabe, et al., November 7, 1892, and subscribed by Stephen Wheeler, document at Fort Smith, Arkansas.

89. McKennon, *Iron Men*, 163.

90. Pride, "Battle of Tahlequah Canyon," 46.

91. *Muskogee (I.T.) Phoenix*, November 10, 1892.

92. *Huron (S.D.) Daily Plainsman*, November 9, 1892.

93. Hamilton, *Ned Christie*, 2.

94. Pride, "Battle of Tahlequah Canyon," 46.

95. LaRue, *He Was a Brave Man*, 39.

96. *Kansas City (Mo.) Times, Evening Kansan, Muskogee (I.T.) Phoenix*, all April 27, 1893.

97. *Muskogee (I.T.) Phoenix*, May 25, 1893.

98. Cherokee (Tahlequah)–Depredations: "Relative to a suit in the circuit court," CHN; *Cherokee Advocate*, April 29, 1893; July 22, 1893; August 12, 1893; August 19, 1893; September 23, 1893; November 18, 1893; February 21, 1894; December 14, 1895, *Vinita (I.T.) Indian Chieftain*, January 2, 1896.

99. For examples, *Tacoma Daily News*, July 5, 1893, used the headline, "A Bad Man Murdered." See also *Watonga (O.T.) Republican*, July 12, 1893; *Grand Forks (N.D.) Herald*, July 7, 1893; *Aberdeen (S.D.) Daily News*, July 6, 1893; *Kansas City (Mo.) Times*, July 5, 1893.

100. *Cherokee Advocate*, July 8, 1893, July 29, 1893; August 26, 1893; October 7, 1893.

101. Resignation letter dated April 3, 1893 in Yoes file: "Ark. W. Dist. 1893–1897," Fort Smith Archives.

102. "Yoestown."103. Mihesuah, *Choctaw Crime and Punishment*, 159–70.

104. Criminal case file, Bud [Bub] Trainor, jacket 445, NASW.

105. *Daily Oklahoman*, June 9, 1918.

106. Oath of Office, November 12, 1895, Archives, Fort Smith Archives.

107. Owens, *Oklahoma Heroes*, 54.

108. *Fort Smith (Ark.) Elevator*, August 28, 1896; Keen, "Thomas, Henry Andrew."

109. *Kansas City (Kans.) Daily American Citizen*, August 17, 1899.

110. "Lose Their Hair Never," *Kansas City (Mo.) Star*, January 24, 1906.

111. *Kansas City (Mo.) Star*, April 15, 1903.

112. *Muskogee (I.T.) Daily Phoenix*, April 14, 1903.

113. Schmid, *Cherokee Mounted Rifles Muster Rolls*, 31; U.S. Civil War Records, File C2537426, U.S. War Dept. General Services Administration, Records and Pension Office, U.S. Department of the Interior, Bureau of Pension Records, NA, Washington, D.C; Shirk, *Oklahoma Place Names*, 197; Writers' Project, *Oklahoma*, 257–58.

114. *Tulsa World*, July 27, 1913.

115. *Stilwell (Okla.) Democrat-Journal*, March 28, 1968.

116. Shirk, *Oklahoma Place Names*, 51.

117. Hamilton, personal communication.

118. Jack Christie, Census number 9363, Native American Applications for Enrollment in the Five Civilized Tribes, 1898–1914, NASW. According to a Christie family member, "He just didn't know what he was talking about and he always stretched truths and gossiped."

119. Hamilton, personal communication.

CHAPTER 6

Epigraph. Oscar A. Gifford, Superintendent of Canton Asylum for Insane Indians to commissioner of Indian affairs, 1903.

1. Criminal Defendant Case Files, Tom Wolf and Arch Wolf, 1892, jacket 479, NASW.

2. Goingsnake District Records,, p. 122, CHN. Original Title: Sheriff Reports, 1892.

3. Steele does not state where he accessed information for either scenario and there are no newspaper or court reports stating that marshals found Arch in Illinois. Nor are there any Christie family stories about his journey and there are no stories about a person named Bear Paw. Nevertheless, Speer writes the same thing in *Killing of Ned Christie*, citing Steele. Steele, *Last Cherokee Warriors*, 103; Speer, *Killing of Ned Christie*, 126.

4. *Muskogee (I.T.) Phoenix*, January 26, 1893.

5. Criminal Defendant Case Files, Tom Wolf and Arch Wolf, 1892, jacket 479, NASW. See also United States v. Arch Wolf, indictment 2881, November 9, 1894, Common Law Record Books, 1855–1959, p. 394, WAR16, file unit from RG 21, Records of the District Courts of the United States, U.S. District Court for the Fort Smith Division of the Western Division of Arkansas, NASW. On the other matter of being charged with attempting to kill Gideon White, see United States v. Arch Wolf, indictment 2898, November 9, 1893, Common Law Record Books, 1855–1959, p. 395, WAR16, NASW.

6. Testimony of Sam Six Killer, May 26, 1885, in 49th Cong., 1st sess., 2 Senate, Report 1278, *Report of the Committee on Indian Affairs*, pt. 2, p. 217.

7. Lane, "Choctaw Nation," 57; *Atoka (I.T.) Indian Citizen*, December 6, 1900; James T. McDaniel interview, May 5, 1938, IPP 58: 22.

8. *Fort Smith (Ark.) Elevator*, May 13, 1887.

9. Criminal Defendant Case File, John Hogshooter, 1887, no. 90, File Unit from RG 21, ARC 223400. Nancy Schell (Shell), Sam Manus, R. S. Gragan, and Cull Thorne all lived in Tahlequah. Criminal Defendant Case File, Charles Bobtail, 1887, no. 18. J. M. Peel, J. F. Stokes, and George York all lived in Bentonville, Arkansas. ARCIA, 1881, 103–104. Online at http://digital.library.wisc.edu/1711.dl/History.AnnRep91p1.

10. ARCIA, 1880, 103–4.

11. United States v. Arch Wolf, indictments 2898 and 2881, February 8, 1894, Common Law Record Books, 1855–1959, WAR16, file unit from RG 21, p. 9, NASW.

12. Ibid., pp. 10, 395.

13. Criminal Defendant Case File, Arch Wolf, indictments 3196, 3197, Liquor Jacket 479, file unit from RG 21, Records of the District Courts of the United States, U.S. District Court for the Fort Smith Division of the Western Division of Arkansas, NASW.

14. Criminal Defendant Case Files, Charles Hair, 1892, no. 365, Indictment 2898; United States v. Chas. Hair, indictment 2898, May 25, 1893, Common Law Record Books, 1855–1959, WAR16, NASW, ARC Identifier 1157516, p. 483; A. J. Falls, President of the Board of Trustees of the Reform School of the District of Columbia to Hon. J. H. Gallinger, Chairman, Subcommittee on the District of Columbia, January 21, 1893, in *Reports of Committees of the Senate of the United States*, 1:4–5; Pisciotta, "House Divided," 169, 170.

15. Personal communication, John Reinhardt, Supervisor of the Operations Section of the Illinois State Archives, November 2, 2015. Robert Ellis, archivist of the federal judicial records, also confirms that there is no record of Charles Hair or Hare on any of the lists of committed children between 1884 and 1912. Robert Ellis to Meg Hacker, November 12, 2015, personal communication from Hacker, November 19, 2015.

16. *Vinita (I.T.) Indian Chieftain*, September 26, 1895.

17. Enrollment Cards for the Five Civilized Tribes, 1898–1914, M1186, Cherokee Nation 20710, Cherokees by Blood, NASW.

18. Dawes, *A United States Prison*, 143; Testimony, William M. Cravens, and comments, Judge Isaac Parker, June 3 and 4, 1885, in *Report of the Committee on Indian Affairs*, 390, 401.

19. United States v. Arch Wolf, indictment 2881, February 8, 1894, Common Law Record Books, 1855–1959, WAR16, pp. 491, 492, 493, NASW,.

20. Criminal Defendant Case Files, Tom Wolf and Arch Wolf, 1892, defendant jacket 479, Indictment 2898, NASW.

21. United States v. Arch Wolf, indictment 2898, March 30, 1894, Common Law Record Books, 1855–1959, WAR16, pp. 491, 492, 493, NASW,.

22. Yoes to Miller, November 12, 1892; *Fort Smith (Ark.) Elevator*, November 11, 1892.

23. *Brooklyn (N.Y.) Daily Eagle*, July 6, 1877.

24. Ibid., September 16, 1888.

25. Arch Wolf, Record Group 418, Case File 9653 in 418.4.1, Records of the Medical Records Branch, Records of St. Elizabeths Hospital, Federal Records, NA, Washington, D.C.

26. *Brooklyn (N.Y.) Daily Eagle*, August 29, 1895.

27. *Cherokee Advocate*, November 18, 1893. For a summary article about the asylum, see Steen, "Home for the Insane, Deaf, Dumb and Blind of the Cherokee Nation," 402–19.

28. *Cherokee Advocate*, October 12, 1887.

29. Minutes of the Board of Trustees, No. 686, p. 167.

30. Otto, *St. Elizabeths Hospital*; *Washington Post*, May 20, 2014.Otto's book offers much information about the administration of the school, but it contains nothing about how patients were admitted or how they or their families perceived the institution.

31. *New York Times*, June 30, 1896.

32. William C. Endicott, Jr., to Dr. W. W. Godding, June 29, 1896, in Arch Wolf, Case File 9653.

33. Young to Godding, February 3, 1898, in Arch Wolf, Case File, 9653.

34. Young to Godding, January 2, 1900, in Arch Wolf, Case File, 9653.

35. Young to A. B. Richardson, M.D., March 12, 1900, in Arch Wolf, Case File, 9653.

36. See discussion of this issue in Mihesuah, *Cultivating the Rose Buds*, 67.

37. Records of the Superintendent, Letters Sent Executive Series, NA and Record Administration, RG 418, Entry 9, February 27, 1885, p. 430.

38. For discussions about the malady, see Gant, *Constipation and Intestinal Obstruction*, 207–208, and Whorton, *Inner Hygiene*, esp. 29–54.

39. Hirschlorn, Feldman, and Greaves, "Abraham Lincoln's Blue Pills," 315–32.

40. Spitum Exam in Arch Wolf, Case File 9653.

41. Susan Burch, personal communication, November 30, 2015.

42. Asylum for Insane Indians. U.S. Senate Report 567 on S 2042, 55th Cong., 2d sess., February 11, 1898.

43. Ibid.

44. "Asylums and Insanity Treatments."

45. Asylum for Insane Indians. U.S. Senate Report 567 on S 2042. 55th Cong., 2d sess., February 11, 1898.

46. Riney, "Power and Powerlessness," 47–48.

47. ARCIA, 1903, 325.

48. See Quarterly Sanitary Reports, CIA, 1905–1906, Letters Received, and O. S. Gifford to CIA, March 20, 1903, Letters Received, 18929, RG 75, NA, Washington, D.C.

49. ARCIA, 1903, 325.

50. RG 75, CIA, CCF 1907–39, Box 2, NA, Washington, D.C.

51. Campbell, *Campbell's Psychiatric Dictionary*, 967.

52. CIA, "Annual Report for Fiscal Year 1910," August 4, 1910, p. 3.

53. Putney, "Canton Asylum for Insane Indians," 9–10.

54. RG 75, CIA, CCF 1907–39, Box 19, NA, Washington, D.C.

55. Soule and Soule, "Death at the Hiawatha Asylum for Insane Indians," 17–18.

56. Records of the Superintendent, Letters Sent Executive Series, NA and Record Administration, RG 418, Entry 9, February 27, 1885, p. 429.

57. Bureau of Indian Affairs, Canton Asylum for Insane Indians, Canton, S.D., decimal correspondence file, 1914–1934; letters received from the commissioner, 1916–1930, RG 75, NA, Kansas City, Mo.

58. See Quarterly Sanitary Reports, CIA, 1905–1906, Letters Received, and O. S. Gifford to CIA, March 20, 1903, Letters Received, 18929, RG 75, NA.

59. Lewis, *Problem of Indian Administration*; Putney, "Canton Asylum for Insane Indians," 23.

60. "Memorandum for the Press," October 15, 1933, Canton Asylum RG 75, CCF, 1907–39, Box 3, PI-163-E-121, HM2003, NASW.

61. Philp, *John Collier's Crusade for Indian Reform*, 130–31.

62. Soule and Soule, "Death at the Hiawatha Asylum," 16–17; Records Relating to the Department of the Interior, 1902–1943, Records of St. Elizabeths Hospital, RG 418, NA, Washington, D.C., 325–27.

63. Records Relating to the Department of the Interior, 1902–43, Records of St. Elizabeths Hospital, RG 418, NA, Washington, D.C., 325–27.

64. Hummer paper read at the American Medico-Psychological Association in Atlantic City, New Jersey, May 28, 1912, at South Dakota State Archives.

65. *Huerfano World Journal*, September 8, 2011.

66. *Argus (S.D.) Leader*, August 30, 1957.

CHAPTER 7

Epigraph. "Outlaw Index: Ned Christie," *Legends of America.*

1. *Tulsa World*, March 5, 1917.

2. *Vinita (I.T.) Indian Chieftain*, November 10, 1892; Criminal Defendant Case File, Charles Bobtail, jacket 18.

3. *Tulsa World*, June 17, 1917.

4. *Daily Oklahoman*, June 9, 1918.

5. Steele, *Last Cherokee Warriors*, 84–85. Steele writes that the story appeared in 1922 and on the same page, 1992—the latter obviously an error. His notes on page 109: "Tulsa (Okla.). Tulsa World, Fred E. Sutton, editorial, 1922." A perusal of 1922 issues does not turn up this story.

6. Alex Laney of the Oklahoma Climatology Survey confirms that records did not start until 1900. Personal communication, December 21, 2015.

7. Speers, *Killing of Ned Christie*, 126.

8. Steele, *Last Cherokee Warriors*, 84.

9. Wallace Roll of Cherokee Freedmen in Indian Territory, 76, NA.

10. *Cherokee Advocate*, December 4, 1889.

11. *Vinita (I.T.) Indian Chieftain*, January 2, 1896; *Vinita (I.T.) Leader*, January 9, 1896.

12. *Daily Oklahoman*, June 9, 1918.

13. Speer, *Killing of Ned Christie*, 6.

14. Speer, *Killing of Ned Christie*, 44–45, 142n12. Personal communication with the American Heritage Center (AHC) at the University of Wyoming reveals that there is no evidence of her source that supposedly is housed at UW. The *Fayetteville (Ark.) Democrat*, May 13, 1887, which she cites, does not mention a broken bottle, nor does it mention Marshals Carroll and Curtis:

> Dan Maples, a highly respected citizen of Bentonville and a U.S. Deputy Marshal, went to the Territory last week to serve some writs, being accompanied by his son, J. M. Peel and a Mr. Jefferson. They camped near Tahlequah on the 5th-inst and just after dark Maples and Jefferson were returning from town to camp when they were confronted at the crossing of the branch by an unknown party who drew a pistol but was told by Maples not to shoot. He fired, however, mortally wounding Maples. Both returned the fire and several shots passed. Maples died the next day and his body was shipped to Bentonville for burial. The cause of the killing is unknown and the affair has created considerable excitement among the citizens of Bentonville.

15. *Cherokee Advocate*, July 6, 1887.

16. "Necrology: Mrs. Anna C. Trainor Matheson," 101. The biography for Anna's son Albert Clifford Stidham has slightly different information about Anna and the end of her marriage. Although he was told his father had died, in fact, he had been committed to Fulton State Hospital in Missouri, where he finally died in 1904. The family does not know whether Anna and Stidham were ever divorced. See Stidham, "My Genealogy Home Page"; Calhoun, "Whatever Happened to Miss Indian Territory?"

CHAPTER 8

Epigraph 1. Maria Kunnikova, "How Stories Deceive," *The New Yorker*, December 29, 2015.

Epigraph 2. D. C. Gideon, *Indian Territory, Descriptive, Biographical and Genealogical, Including the Landed Estates County Seats, with a General History of the Territory* (New York: Lewis, 1901), 108.

1. Marsden, "Popular Western Novel as a Cultural Artifact," 205.

2. Johnson, *Hunger for the Wild*, 211.

3. *Fort Smith (Ark.) Weekly Elevator*, October 4, 1889, November 1, 1889; *Kansas City (Mo.) Star*, June 20, 1891.

4. *Chicago Daily Tribune*, November 7, 1894.

5. *Waukesha (Wis.) Journal*, January 31, 1891.

6. *Deadwood (S.D.) Daily Pioneer Times*, January 4, 1891.

7. *Spearfish (S.D.) Queen City Mail*, December 31, 1890.

8. For example, *Atoka (I.T.) Indian Citizen*, June 6, 1891, and *Omaha World Herald*, October 15, 1892.

9. *Fort Smith (Ark.) Weekly Elevator*, November 17, 1893.

10. *Cherokee Telephone*, December 17, 1891.

11. McKanna. *Court-Martial of Apache Kid*; Hutton, *Apache Wars,* esp. 388–414.

12. For example, the Apache Kid is described as "the notorious Indian outlaw" in the *Sacramento Record-Union*, June 17, 1892; he grew from "a little naked savage with all the venom of a young rattler to a villainous buck whose mission is that of a human butcher" in *Princeton Union*, April 5, 1894; he is "the educated Devil," in the *Philadelphia Times*, November 11, 1894; and "a pest that has long menaced the safety of mountaineers," in *Coconino Sun*, February 14, 1895.

13. *Newton (Kans.) Daily Republican*, October 13, 1892. The two articles are repeated in the *Kingman (Kans.) Leader Courier*, November 10, 1892.

14. *Salina (Kans.) Daily Republican*, November 7, 1892. Repeated in *Wellington (Kans.) People's Voice*, November 11, 1892.

15. *Muskogee (I.T.) Phoenix*, November 10, 1892.

16. Reprinted in *Vinita (I.T.) Indian Chieftain*, November 27, 1890. For discussion about the animosities between newspaper editors, see Holland, *Cherokee Newspapers*.

17. Marsden, "Popular Western Novel as a Cultural Artifact," 205.

18. *Cherokee Advocate*, July 8, 1893.

19. *Tahlequah (I.T.) Telephone*, October 3, 1889.

20. Repeated in *Omaha World Herald*, December 10, 1891, *Washington (D.C.) Evening Star*, December 10, 1891.

21. *Salina (Kans.) Daily Republic*, October 14, 1892.

22. *Chicago Daily Tribune*, July 20, 1902.

23. Speer, *Killing of Ned Christie*, 109; Steele, *Last Cherokee Warriors*, 98.

24. McKennon, *Iron Men*, 90.

25. Steele, *Last Cherokee Warriors*, 88–89.

26. Kirchner, "Ned Christie," 58.

27. Berkhofer, *White Man's Indian*, 98.

28. McMahon and Csaki, *Philosophy of the Western*, 2.

29. Frederick Jackson Turner, "Significance of the Frontier."

30. Johnson, *Hunger for the Wild*, 190.

31. *Chicago Daily Tribune*, November 7, 1894.

32. Rizzo, "Showdown at a Mountain Fortress

33. Rand, "Blood in the Cookson Hills," 27.

34. *Washington (D.C.) Evening Star*, October 12, 1892; *Arkansas Gazette*, October 12, 1892, and November 5, 1892; *Daily Illinois State Register*, November 5, 1892.

35. Anderson and Yadon, *100 Oklahoma Outlaws, Gangsters, and Lawmen*, 186.

36. Forbes, "Mose Miller," 10–12, 52–53. Turpin followed that in 2011 with an even more turgid chapter on Miller called "Mad Killer of Cookson Hills" in *Hot Lead and Cold Steel*, 9–27. Turpin appears to have liberally borrowed from Forbes, but does not provide any references.

37. *Muskogee (I.T.) Phoenix*, December 10, 1891.

38. See Will Wright, *Sixguns and Society*, 57, for discussion about "wilderness" in westerns.

39. Meyer, "Outlaw," 94–124.

40. *Northwest Arkansas Times*, November 16, 1964.

41. *St. Louis Republic*, January 30, 1894.

42. *Cleveland Plain Dealer*, June 10, 1900, p. 31.

43. Rhodes, "Lest We Forget," n.d., IPP 75:342.

44. Deputy Marshal A. B. Allen: 27; Deputy Marshal James Birkett (Poteau); Oscar Blackard (Clarksdale): 23; Tom Blackard (Clarksdale); Deputy Marshal James Wesley Bowman: 23; Eli Hickman "Heck" Bruner: 33; Deputy Marshal Harry Clayland (Clarksville): 17; Deputy Marshal Charles E. Copeland (Siloam Springs): 26; William Ellis; Vint Gray (Clarksville); George Jefferson (Bentonville); Deputy Marshal Thomas "Tom" B. Johnson (Fayetteville); Cherokee sheriff Ben Knight; Mack Peel (Bentonville); Cook Frank "Becky" Polk; Deputy Marshal Edward Burton "E. B." "Coon" Ratteree (Hartshorne, Poteau): 40; Deputy Marshal Dave V. Rusk: 53; Frank Sarber (Clarksville): 18; Deputy Will Smith (Fayetteville); John Tolbert (Clarksville); Paden Tolbert (Clarksville): 29; Captain Gideon "Cap" S. White: 48.

45. *Daily Oklahoman*, January 8, 1911.

46. Abernathy, *"Catch 'em Alive Jack,"* xv. See also "Old West Lawmen: John R. Abernathy," Legends of America website.

47. *Ironwood (Mich.) Times*, October 27, 1894

48. *St. Louis Post-Dispatch*, July 9, 1899.

49. Rand, "Blood in the Cookson Hills," 62.

50. *Kansas City (Kans.) Daily American Citizen*, August 17, 1899.

51. Will Wright, *Sixguns and Society*, 48.

52. See also the numerous repetitive works by Art T. Burton, such as *Black, Red and Deadly; Black Gun, Silver Star;* and "Christie, Ned"; Fisher and O'Reilly, *Bill O'Reilly's Legends and Lies*; Littlefield and Underhill, "Negro Marshals in Indian Territory," 81; Finkelman, *African Americans and the Legal Profession*, 203; in addition to dozens of websites devoted to lawmen and outlaws such as Bennett, "Legendary Lawman Bass Reeves," Officer.com.

53. *Wichita (Kans.) Beacon*, July 27, 1897.

54. "Bowden, Charles L. D.U.S. Marshal, 1889–1890–1891–1895–1896–1897," on the Oklahoma United States Marshals Deputy United States Marshals and Possemen list, http://www.okolha.net/dusm_usm_A.htm.

55. *Muskogee (I.T.) Phoenix*, October 27, 1892. The paper refers to him as "L. C. Bowden."

56. Rhodes, IPP 75:342.

57. *Denver Post*, December 17, 1921.

58. *Tulsa Daily World*, October 5, 1952.

59. *Southwest Times Record*, September 26, 1982; McKennon, *Iron Men*, 88. See also the biography of "James Wesley 'Wes' Bowman, U.S. Deputy Marshal" at http://freepages. genealogy.rootsweb.ancestry.com, which makes no mention of him having to choose between the life of a lawman or criminal.

60. *Cherokee Advocate*, April 10, 1895.

61. *St. Louis Republic*, November 5, 1892, *Dallas Morning News*, November 5, 1892, *Cincinnati Post*, November 5, 1892.

62. Edward Hines interview, August 16, 1937, IPP 43:469.

63. *Chicago Daily Tribune*, July 20, 1902.

64. Ibid.

65. C. H. McKennon, *Iron Men*, 88.

66. *Southwest Times Record*, September 26, 1982; Steele, *Last Cherokee Warriors*, 74; Dorman, "Dead or Alive, Preferably Dead," 41; Good, "Ned Christie," 40.

67. Anderson and Yadon, *100 Oklahoma Outlaws, Gangsters, and Lawmen*, 187.

68. Bederman, *Manliness and Civilization*, 15.

69. McKennon, *Iron Men*, 159; *Milwaukee Journal*, June 30, 1967.

70. See Edmunds, *Tecumseh and the Quest for Indian Leadership*.

71. *Atoka (I.T.) Indian Journal*, January 30, 1890.

72. *Arkansas Gazette*, October 18, 1890.

73. *Philadelphia Times*, November 13, 1882.

74. Meyer, "Outlaw," 94–124. Frey also discusses characteristics of a hero in his book *The Key*, 46–47, and Christie also fits the bill of this type of hero who has courage, a special talent, is clever and resourceful, is an "outlaw" living by his or her own rules, is good at what he or she does for a living, is a protagonist (takes the lead in a cause or action), has been wounded or is wounded (that is, maimed, disgraced, grieving, etc.), is motivated by idealism, and is sexually potent.

75. *Cherokee Advocate*, March 6, 1885.

76. Steele, *Last Cherokee Warriors*, 55–56.

77. See for examples, *New York Times*, November 7, 1897, *Sacramento Record-Union*, December 3, 1897, *Stilwell (Okla.) Standard-Sentinel*, March 7, 1907, *Arkansas City (Kans.) Daily Traveler*, March 11, 1907; *Springfield (Mass.) Union*, February 20, 1983. Note that newspapers often republished the same stories years after they first appeared.

78. *Arkansas Gazette*, November 5, 1892.

79. Steele, *Last Cherokee Warriors*, 11, 76.

80. *Fort Smith (Ark.) Elevator*, November 11, 1892.

81. Pride, "Battle of Tahlequah Canyon," 18.

82. Speer, "Ned Christie." 32.

83. Anderson and Yadon, *100 Oklahoma Outlaws, Gangsters, and Lawmen*, 187; O'Neal, *Encyclopedia of Western Gunfighters*, 59. They got this tidbit from Burton, *Red, Black and Deadly*, 35, but neglect to cite this source.

84. Stann, IPP 86:482–83.

85. Wilson, IPP 99:145.

86. Berry, "Uncle Sam's Treaty with One Man," 228.

87. Clark, IPP 18:207.

88. Whitmire, IPP 97:366.

89. "Spell of the West."

90. Hogan Markham interview, February 2, 1972, DD, T-663, DDC, p. 7.

91. Hamilton, *Ned Christie*, 14.

92. Wilson, IPP 99:145.

93. Clark, IPP 18:207.

94. Hamilton, *Ned Christie*, viii.

95. *Our Brother in Red*, May 31, 1894.

96. Kilpatrick, "Cherokees Remember Their Badmen," 63.

97. Tindall, DD, T-554-1.

98. Whitmire, IPP 97:371.

99. Steele, *Last Cherokee Warriors*, 80.

100. Shirley, *Law West of Fort Smith*, 54.

101. McKennon, *Iron Men*, 99–100.

102. Steele, *Last Cherokee Warriors*, 72.

103. Good, "Ned Christie," 40.

104. Clark, IPP 18:217; Berry, "Uncle Sam's Treaty with One Man," 227. The IPP interview notes that Jas. S. Buchanan is the "interviewer" and Stanley A. Clark is the interviewee; however, Clark prefaces his answers with "Two of his most Interesting stories of tragical nature that happened in the Cherokee Nation during the life of Mr. Whitmore [Whitmire] were of Ned Christie and the Proctor fight or better known as the Going Snake tragedy," which might be Clark's recollection of what Eli H. Whitmire told him about the two men. In an example of copying from another source, Virgil Berry steals a line about Ned from Stanley Clark, calling him "straight as an arrow" and "rather tall" (Clark, IPP 18:207). Clearly, Berry juxtaposed Clark's commentary about Ned and Proctor. John F. Parris said he was "a low heavy set Indian" (John F. Parris interview, October 1, 1937, IPP 69:337), and Proctor described himself as being five feet seven on his Civil War pension application.

105. Hamilton, *Ned Christie*, 65–66.

106. Kilpatrick, "Cherokees Remember Their Badmen," 21, 62.

107. Conley, "End of Old Bill Pigeon," 49.

108. Clark, on Ned Christie, IPP 18:145/212.

109. *Our Brother in Red*, February 14, 1895.

110. Speer, *Killing of Ned Christie*, 74–75, 78.

111. Yoes to Miller, November 12, 1892; *Fort Smith (Ark.) Weekly Elevator*, November 1, 1889.

112. Speer, *Killing of Ned Christie*, 79. That awkward sentence may be missing the word "society" after "Keetoowah."

113. Louis Taylor interview, May 24, 1937, IPP 89:259.

114. There are two interviews with Padgett in vol. 60 and both appear only as "Interview" in the index. Interview/Padgett, IPP 69:5, 10, and Interview/Padgett IPP 69:15. This

is a particularly odd set of interviews. The first one tells us on page 5 that he is a white man from Georgia who married Eliza Sixkiller and had twelve children, then on page 10 states that "he and Ned Christie were brothers-in-law." The second interview says the same in addition to a discussion about how Christie told him about the night Maples was killed.

115. William Hugh Winder interview, November 5, 1937, IPP 99:298–302. The full diatribe:

I have never forgotten an Indian named Ned Christie, a very honest and honorable Indian who had been a Legislator or Councilman of the Cherokee Nation who had made himself known to me and had proved to me his real admiration for me. Once upon a time he sent me word to come to Daniel Gritts' place right away as he wanted to see me; the man bringing the message was Sam Manus.

So I said to my wife, "Well, I guess I had better go hadn't I?" and she said, "Why Hugh, he may be just wanting to kill you." And I said, "Why, no, I haven't done him any harm; Ned is my friend."

Anyway I went down there and when Ned saw me he jumped up and shook my hand and seemed to be very glad to see me. Ned said, "Mr. Winder I hear that a new United States Marshal has been appointed at Muskogee and he has promised the Government that he will catch me. Now, Mr. Winder, please get him word that I don't want to hurt him but he had better stay with his loving wife and children and I also wanted to tell you that I am coming up to your saw mill and kill Alex Holt for talking too much and snitching on me to the U.S. Marshals."

I said, "Ned, I am not your enemy, not in any sense of the word and you know I never have and never will meddle in your business, but on account of this fellow Holt being there at my saw mill I want to beg you to please let him go and I will get him to leave tomorrow if I can, but give me a few days to get him out of the country, besides you will scare my wife to death if you do that."

Ned Christie said, "Mr. Winder, on account of your plea and for your wife's sake, I give you a few days to get him gone, but about this new Marshal, Mr. Creekmore; I intend to shoot at his head the first glimpse I get of him." I said, "That's all right Ned, I haven't a word to say against that, but I will tell him what you said if I get the chance." I left him with a smile on his face; he seemed to be pleased with his interview with me.

I told Mr. Creekmore the news, but he scorned it and took no heed and only said "Augh, I am not afraid of Old Ned." In about a week Ned took a shot at Creekmore from a distance a week later. The bullet narrowly missed Creekmore's head and he ran into the woods and he never was heard of again in that country.

The United States Marshal knocked on my door one morning just before daylight and wanted to come in, so I let him in and he searched all through my place for Ned Christie and after he got through, I said, "Mr. Creekmore, I want you to sit down a minute. I want to talk to you." I told him all that Ned had said and he got up and gave me the horse laugh and said, "Nonsense I am after old Ned and aim to get him the first time I come upon him."

Now Creekmore was a tall blond curly-headed man and a very over confident sort of fellow. About three days afterward I heard some shooting down from below in the hollow and I recognized Ned's big forty-four Winchester talking and other guns were of lesser report, probably high powered army caliber rifles. In about thirty minutes a couple of men came running through the woods, hats off and all excited to death.

I met them in the yard and one of them was this tall blonde curly-headed man and I said, "Now what's happened?" and Curley said, "We been fighting the real Ned Christie. My God! He shot our horses dead in their tracks and before we could find a real good place to hide to do our shooting, he had killed our horses and look at these holes in my hat, in my pocket and my ear sure is bleeding isn't it? What seems to be left of it, and look at my partner, he is shot two or three times. I don't know how bad."

I said, "Come in here let me wash your ear." After I had washed them up I found that his deputy had only several flesh wounds about the body and Curley had the prettiest letter U cut out of the end of his ear you ever saw. This man Curley left out of those forests and never came back that I ever knew of.

116. Etter, "Water Mill Created Memories."

117. "Robert Stoddard (musician)."

118. *Tahlequah (Okla.) Daily Press*, July 23, 2014.

119. *Cherokee Phoenix*, August 15, 2011.

120. *Vinita Indian Chieftain,* September 13, 1894.

121. Clark, IPP 18:140/207, 149/216–50/17.

122. Will Wright, *Sixguns and Society*, 13–14.

123. Quoted in Eyman, *John Wayne*, 562.

124. Michael J. Brodhead, *Isaac C. Parker*, 43.

125. Farris, "Possee Finally Nabbed Infamous Fugitive." See also his book, *Oklahoma Outlaw Tales*. We see the same thing happen to Zeke Proctor. Recent publications persist in describing him as a drunk and "downright mean." "Transformation of Ezekiel Proctor," *Grand Lake News*, December 26, 2013.

126. Adams, *Burs Under the Saddle*, xiii.

127. Johnson, *Hunger for the Wild*, 212.

BIBLIOGRAPHY

MANUSCRIPT AND ARCHIVAL SOURCES

FORT SMITH ARCHIVES. FORT SMITH HISTORIC SITE. FORT SMITH, ARKANSAS.

GOVERNMENT DOCUMENTS

The Constitutions and Laws of the American Indian Tribes. Vols. 1–10. Wilmington, Del.: Scholarly Resources, 1973, 1975.

Kappler, Charles J., ed. *Indian Affairs: Laws and Treaties.* Vols. 1–4. Washington, D.C.: Government Printing Office, 1902.

Lane, John W. "Choctaw Nation." In *The Five Civilized Tribes in Indian Territory: The Cherokee, Chickasaw, Choctaw, Creek, and Seminole Nations.* Washington, D.C.: Census Printing Office, 1894.

Report of the Committee on Indian Affairs, United States Senate, on the Condition of the Indians in the Indian Territory and Other Reservations, etc. In two parts. U.S. congressional serial set 2363, S. rep. 1278, pt. 2, Friday, January 1, 1886. Washington, D.C.: Government Printing Office, 1886.

Reports of Committees of the Senate of the United States for the Second Session of the 52d Congress and the Special Session Convened March 4, 1893, U.S. congressional serial set 3072, rep. 1213, Vol. 1. Washington, D.C.: Government Printing Office, 1893.

Sixth Annual Report of the Commissioner to the Five Civilized Tribes to the Secretary of the Interior for the Fiscal Year Ended June 30, 1899. Washington, D.C.: Government Printing Office, 1899.

United States Congress. House Executive Documents.

United States Office of Indian Affairs. *Annual Report of the Commissioner of Indian Affairs.* 1840, 1844, 1845, 1852, 1863, 1872, 1880, 1881, 1883, 1884, 1885, 1886, 1889, 1890, 1898.

Wallace Roll of Cherokee Freedmen in Indian Territory. Dept. of the Interior, Office of Indian Affairs. National Archives Catalog. NA Identifier 300345. https://research.archives.gov/id/300345.

HISTORICAL SOCIETY OF THE CHEROKEE NATION. TAHLEQUAH, OKLAHOMA.
Photographic collection.

NATIONAL ARCHIVES. COLLEGE PARK, MARYLAND.
General Records, Department of Justice. Letters Received. RG 60.3.2.

NATIONAL ARCHIVES, SOUTHWEST REGION, FORT WORTH, TEXAS.

Canton Asylum, CCF, 1907–39. RG 75, Box 2.

Cherokee Census, Schedules, 1890. 7RA-08.

Cherokee Census and Index, 1880. 7RA-07.

Common Law Record Books, 1855–1959. Records of the District Courts of the United States, U.S. District Court for the Fort Smith Division of the Western Division of Arkansas. RG 21, WAR16.

Criminal Record Jackets, 1866–96. Records of District Courts of the United States, U.S. District Court for the Fort Smith Division of the Western Division of Arkansas. RG 21.

Enrollment Cards, Five Civilized Tribes, 1898–1914. M1186.

Fort Smith Sentence Record Book, Western District of Arkansas. RG 21.

Fort Smith Subpoena Record Book, Western District of Arkansas. RG 21.

Henderson Roll of Eastern Cherokees, 1835, and Index. M1773.

Index to the Five Civilized Tribes, the Final Dawes Roll. M1186.

Miller, Guion, Roll. Records Relating to Enrollment of Eastern Cherokee, 1908–10. M-685.

Mullay Roll of North Carolina Cherokees, 1848. M1186.

Native American Applications for Enrollment in the Five Civilized Tribes, 1898–1914. M1301.

Roster, First Cherokee Mounted Rifles. M258, rolls 77–79.

NATIONAL ARCHIVES, WASHINGTON, D.C.

Canton Asylum, CCF 1907–39. RG 75.

Muster Roll, Drew's Regiment, November 5, 1861. Compiled Service Records of Confederate Soldiers Who Served in Organizations Raised Directly by the Confederate Government. Microcopy 258, rolls 77, 78.

Property Valuations, 1835–1939, North Carolina. RG 75, entry 224.

Records of the Medical Records Branch. Records of St. Elizabeths Hospital, Federal Records. RG 418.

U.S. Civil War Records. File C2537426. U.S. War Dept. General Services Administration, Records and Pension Office, U.S. Department of the Interior. Bureau of Pension Records.

NORTHEASTERN STATE UNIVERSITY. ARCHIVES. JOHN VAUGHAN LIBRARY. TAHLEQUAH, OKLAHOMA.

Ballenger, Thomas Lee, Collection.

Bushyhead, Chief Dennis. Annual Messages.

[Cherokee Female Seminary] Illustrated Souvenir Catalog, 1850–1906.

OKLAHOMA HISTORICAL SOCIETY (OHS), INDIAN ARCHIVES DIVISION, OKLAHOMA CITY.

Cherokee Female Seminary. Vertical File 10.

Cherokee National Records (CHN).

   Cherokee (Tahlequah)–Depredations. Letters Sent and Letters Received, and Other Documents, March 19, 1872–January 21, 1897. CHN 74.

   Cherokee (Tahlequah)–Districts. Letters Sent and Letters Received, and Other Documents, November 8, 1943–December 27, 1885. CHN 74.

Cherokee (Tahlequah)–Schools: Female Seminary, undated, and December 5, 1874–January 16, 1909. CHN 99.

Cherokee (Tahlequah)–Sheriffs. Letters Sent and Letters Received, and Other Documents, April 4, 1884–March 4, 1902. CHN 103.

Executive Council Records, January 12, 1880–May 20, 1886, 1885–87. CHN 119, vol. 710.

Executive Council Records, July 5, 1886–November 3, 1887. CHN 119, vol. 712.

Federal Relations, July 12, 1886–December 23, 1898. CHN 79.

Flint District Records: Supreme, Circuit and District Courts, May 15, 1877–January 7, 1898. CHN 38, vol. 103.

Going Snake District Records: Supreme, Circuit and District Courts, July 11, 1890–January 13, 1896. CHN 40, vol. 115. Original title: Sheriff Reports, 1892.

Letters Received and Documents Regarding Cherokee Enrollment and Census Matters, November 30, 1866–January 21, 1911. CHN 1.

Letters Sent and Received by Principal Chiefs and other Executive Documents, March 23–July 18, 1887. CHN 123.

National Council, Letters Sent and Letters Received, and Other Documents, undated and September 19, 1839–December 20, 1899. CHN 88.

National Council and Senate, 1884–88. CHN 15, vol. 284.

Officials' Reports, 1880–85. CHN 125, vol. 403.

Prison and High Sheriff, April 16, 1880–March 20, 1909. CHN 95.

Senate, 1886. CHN 16, vol. 290.

Senate and National Council, 1887–88. CHN 12, vol. 273.

Senate and National Council, 1800–83. CHN 13, vol. 278.

Senate and National Council, 1892–95, 1900–1902. CHN 18, vol. 302.

Choctaw National Records [CTN].

Choctaw, Sheriffs and Rangers. Documents 22522–23088. April 21, 1857–May 29, 1909. CTN 87.

Duke, Doris, Collection of American Indian Oral History.

Foreman, Grant, ed. *Indian-Pioneer Papers* (originally *Indian Pioneer Histories*).

WESTERN HISTORY COLLECTIONS. UNIVERSITY OF OKLAHOMA, NORMAN.

Ballenger, Thomas Lee, Collection.

Boudinot, E. G., Papers.

Bushyhead, Dennis Wolfe, Papers.

Cherokee Nation Papers.

Phillips Collection.

Rhodes, Charles B., Collection.

NEWSPAPERS

Aberdeen (S.D.) Weekly News

Ada (Okla.) Evening News

Allentown (Pa.) Morning Call

Argus (S.D.) Leader

Arkansas City (Kans.) Daily Traveler
Arkansas Democrat
Arkansas Gazette
Atoka (I.T.) Indian Citizen
Biloxi (Miss.) Daily Herald
Boston Herald
Brooklyn (N.Y.) Daily Eagle
Brooklyn (N.Y.) Standard Union
Caddo (I.T.) Banner
Cherokee Advocate (I.T.)
Cherokee Phoenix (Okla.)
Cherokee Phoenix and Indian Advocate (Cherokee Nation)
Cherokee Telephone (I.T.)
Chicago Daily Inter Ocean
Chicago Daily Tribune
Cincinnati Enquirer
Cleveland Plain Dealer
Coconino Sun (Flagstaff, Ariz.)
Daily Arkansas Gazette
Daily Illinois State Journal
Daily Illinois State Register
Daily Oklahoman
Dallas Morning News
Deadwood (S.D.) Daily Pioneer Times
Denver Post
Detroit Free Press
Eufaula (I.T.) Indian Journal
Evening Kansan
Fayetteville (Ark.) Democrat
Fort Gibson (I.T.) Post
Fort Scott (Kans.) Daily Monitor
Fort Smith (Ark.) Democrat
Fort Smith (Ark.) Elevator
Fort Smith (Ark.) Weekly Elevator
Fort Worth Daily Gazette
Fort Worth Star Telegram
Galena (Kans.) Evening Times
Galveston Daily News
Galveston Daily Tribune
Gentry (Ark.) Journal Advance
Grand Forks (N.D.) Herald
Guthrie (O.T.) Daily Leader
Huerfano World Journal (Walsenburg, Colo.)

Huron (S.D.) Daily Plainsman
Independence (Kans.) Daily Reporter
Ironwood (Mich.) Times
Journalist
Kansas City (Kans.) Daily American Citizen
Kansas City (Kans.) Daily Citizen
Kansas City (Mo.) Star
Kansas City (Mo.) Times
Kingman (Kans.) Leader Courier
Lawrence (Kans.) Daily Journal
Leavenworth (Kans.) Times
Louisville Courier-Journal
Manitoba Free Press
Mansfield (Ohio) News-Journal
Milwaukee Journal
Muskegon (Mich.) Chronicle
Muskogee (I.T.) Daily Phoenix
Muskogee (I.T.) Phoenix
Muskogee (Okla.) Times-Democrat
New Ear
New Haven (Conn.) Register
Newton (Kans.) Daily Republican
New York Herald
Northwest Arkansas Times
Omaha Daily Bee
Omaha World Herald
Our Brother in Red (Muskogee, I.T.)
Pittsburg (Kans.) Daily Headlight
Pittsburgh Daily Post
Pomeroy's Democrat (New York, N.Y.)
Princeton (Minn.) Union
Richmond (Va.) Times
Rockford (Ill.) Daily Gazette
Rockford (Ill.) Morning Star
Rockford (Ill.) Republic
Sacramento Record-Union
Saginaw (Mich.) News
Salina (Kans.) Daily Republican
Southwest Times Record (Fort Smith, Ark.)
Spearfish (S.D.) Queen City Mail
Springfield (Mass.) Union
St. Louis Post-Dispatch
St. Louis Republic

Stilwell (Okla.) Democrat Journal
Stilwell (Okla.) Standard-Sentinel
Tacoma Daily News
Tahlequah (I.T.) Arrow
Tahlequah (I.T.) Telephone
Tahlequah (Okla.) Daily Press
Toledo Bee
Topeka (Kans.) Daily Commonwealth
Tulsa Daily World
Tulsa World
Vinita (I.T.) Chieftain
Vinita (I.T.) Indian Chieftain
Vinita (Okla.) Leader
Washington Evening Star
Washington Post
Watertown (N.Y.) Daily Times
Watonga (O.T.) Republican
Waukesha (Wis.) Journal
Wichita (Kans.) Beacon
Wichita (Kans.) Daily Eagle

BOOKS AND ARTICLES

Abbe, Cleveland, ed. "Dates of First Killing Frosts." *Monthly Weather Review* 22, no. 8 (July 1894): 328–30.

Abbott, Devon I. "Out of the 'Graves of the Polluted Debauches': The Boys of the Cherokee Male Seminary." *American Indian Quarterly* 15 (Fall 1991): 503–21.

Abernathy, John R. *"Catch 'em Alive Jack": The Life and Adventures of an American Pioneer.* Lincoln: University of Nebraska Press, 2006. First published 1936 by General Board of Young Men's Christian Association.

Adams, Ramon F. *Burs Under the Saddle: A Second Look at Books and Histories of the West.* Norman: University of Oklahoma Press, 1964.

Akins, Jerry. *Hangin' Times at Fort Smith: A History of Executions in Judge Parker's Court.* Little Rock: Butler Center for Arkansas Studies, 2012.

Anderson, Dan, and Laurence Yadon. *100 Oklahoma Outlaws, Gangsters, and Lawmen, 1839–1939.* Edited by Robert Barr Smith. Gretna, La.: Pelican, 2007.

Anderson, William L., ed. *Cherokee Removal: Before and After.* Athens: University of Georgia Press, 1991.

Athearn, Robert G. *The Mythic West in Twentieth-Century America.* Lawrence: University Press of Kansas, 1986.

Baird, W. David. *The Story of Oklahoma.* Norman: University of Oklahoma Press, 1994.

Baker, Elmer LeRoy. *Gunman's Territory.* San Antonio, Tex.: Naylor, 1969.

Baldasty, Gerald J. *The Commercialization of News in the Nineteenth Century*. Madison: University of Wisconsin Press, 1992.

Ballenger, Thomas Lee. *Around Tahlequah Council Fires*. Muskogee, Okla.: Motter Bookbinding, 1935.

Bederman, Gail. *Manliness and Civilization: A Cultural History of Gender and Race in the United States, 1880–1917*. Chicago: University of Chicago Press, 1996.

Bender, Margaret. *Signs of Cherokee Culture: Sequoyah's Syllabary in Eastern Cherokee Life*. Chapel Hill: University of North Carolina Press, 2002.

Benedict, John Downing. *Muskogee and Northeastern Oklahoma*. Chicago: S. J. Clarke, 1922.

Berkhofer, Robert F. *The White Man's Indian: Images of the American Indian from Columbus to the Present*. New York: Random House, 1978.

Berry, Virgil. "Uncle Sam's Treaty with One Man." Notes and Documents. *Chronicles of Oklahoma* 32 (Spring 1954): 227–29.

Breihan, Carl W., with Charles A. Rosamond. *The Bandit Belle*. Seattle, Wash.: Hangman / Superior, 1970.

Brodhead, Michael. *Isaac C. Parker: Federal Justice on the Frontier*. Norman: University of Oklahoma Press, 2003.

Brown, John. *Old Frontiers*. Kingsport, Tenn.: Southern, 1938.

Brown, Richard Maxwell. "Desperadoes and Lawmen: The Folk Hero," *Media Studies Journal* (Winter 1992): 151–62.

Burch, Susan. "'Dislocated Histories': The Canton Asylum for Insane Indians." *Women, Gender, and Families of Color* 2, no. 2 (Fall 2014): 141–62.

Burton, Art T. "Bass Reeves (1838–1910)." *The Encyclopedia of Arkansas History and Culture*. Last updated May 29, 2012. www.encyclopediaofarkansas.net/encyclopedia/entry-detail.aspx?entryID=1747.

———. *Black, Red and Deadly: Black and Indian Gunfighters of the Indian Territory, 1870–1907*. Austin, Tex.: Eakin, 1991.

———. *Black Gun, Silver Star: The Life and Legend of Frontier Marshal Bass Reeves*. Lincoln: University of Nebraska Press, 2008.

———. "Christie, Ned (1852–1892)." *Encyclopedia of Oklahoma History and Culture*. Accessed June 7, 2015. www.okhistory.org.

Calhoun, Nancy. "Whatever Happened to Miss Indian Territory?" *Muskogee Phoenix*, November 24, 2007.

Campbell, Robert J. *Campbell's Psychiatric Dictionary*. New York: Oxford University Press, 2009.

Candee, Helen Churchill. "Oklahoma." *Atlantic Monthly*, 86, no. 515 (September 1900): 328–36.

Carselowey, James Manford. *Cherokee Pioneers*. Adair, Okla.: published by author, 1961.

Clines, Peter Clines. *The Fold*. NY: Crown, 2015.

Collier, Peter. *When Shall They Rest? The Cherokees' Long Struggle with America*. New York: Holt, Rinehart, and Winston, 1973.

Confer, Clarissa W. *The Cherokee Nation in the Civil War*. Norman: University of Oklahoma Press, 2012.

Conley, Robert J. *Cherokee Thoughts: Honest and Uncensored.* Norman: University of Oklahoma Press, 2008.

———. "The End of Old Bill Pigeon, Just the Way It Was Told to Me—More or Less." *Appalachian Heritage* 38, no. 2 (Spring 2010): 49–51.

———. "Ned Christie." In *Songs from This Earth on Turtle's Back: Contemporary American Indian Poetry*, edited by Joseph Bruchac, 53. Greenfield Center, N.Y.: Greenfield Review Press, 1983.

———. *Ned Christie's War.* New York: St. Martin's Paperbacks, 2002.

———. *The Witch of Goingsnake and Other Stories.* Norman: University of Oklahoma Press, 1988.

Coward, John M. *The Newspaper Indian: Native American Identity in the Press, 1820–90.* Urbana: University of Illinois Press, 1999.

Dale, Edward Everett. "The Cherokee Strip Live Stock Association." *Chronicles of Oklahoma* 5, no. 1 (March 1927): 58–78.

Davis, Mace. "Chitto Harjo." *Chronicles of Oklahoma* 13 (June 1935): 139–45.

Dawes, Anna. *A United States Prison.* Philadelphia: Indian Rights Association, 1886.

Debo, Angie. *And Still the Waters Run: The Betrayal of the Five Civilized Tribes.* Norman: University of Oklahoma Press, 1989.

Densmore, Frances. "Chippewa Customs." *Smithsonian Institution Bureau of American Ethnology Bulletin* 86. Washington, D.C.: U.S. Government Printing Office, 1929.

Dewitz, Paul W. H., ed. *Notable Men of Indian Territory at the Beginning of the Twentieth Century, 1904–1905.* Muskogee, Indian Territory: Southwestern Historical, 1905.

Dilenschneider, Anne, "An Invitation to Restorative Justice: The Canton Asylum for Insane Indians." *Northern Plains Ethics Journal* (2013): 105–28.

Doran, Michael. "Population Statistics of Nineteenth-Century Indian Territory." *Chronicles of Oklahoma* 35 (Winter 1975–76): 492–515.

Dorman, Robert L. "Dead or Alive, Preferably Dead: 1892, Rabbit Trap." In *It Happened in Oklahoma*, 41. Billings, Mont.: TwoDot, 2006.

Drago, Harry Sinclair. *Outlaws on Horseback: The History of the Organized Bands of Bank and Train Robbers Who Terrorized the Prairie Towns of Missouri, Kansas, Indian Territory, and Oklahoma for Half a Century.* Lincoln, Neb.: Bison Books, 1998.

Duvall, Deborah L. *The Cherokee Nation and Tahlequah.* Charleston, S.C.: Arcadia, 1999.

Eaton, Carolyn Rachel. *John Ross and the Cherokee Indians.* Menasha, Wis.: George Banta, 1914.

Edmunds, R. David. *Tecumseh and the Quest for Indian Leadership.* New York: Longman, 2006.

Etter, Jim. "Water Mill Created Memories Along with Bags of Cornmeal." *NewsOK*, June 20, 1993. http://newsok.com/article/2434035.

Etulain, Richard. *Re-imagining the Modern American West: A Century of Fiction, History, Art.* Tucson: University of Arizona Press, 1996.

———. *Telling Western Stories: From Buffalo Bill to Larry McMurtry.* Albuquerque: University of New Mexico Press, 1999.

"Extracts from the Journal at Dwight." *Missionary Herald* 21 (August 1825): 244.

Eyman, Scott. *John Wayne: The Life and Legend*. New York: Simon and Schuster, 2014.

Farris, David. *Oklahoma Outlaw Tales*. Edmond, Okla.: Little Bruce, 1999.

———. "Possee Finally Nabbed Infamous Fugitive." *Edmond Life & Leisure*, January 22, 2015. http://edmondlifeandleisure.com/mdetail.asp?hn=edmondlifeandleisure&l=possee -finally-nabbed-infamous-fugitive-p10872-76.htm.

Felter, Harvey Wickes. *The Eclectic Materia Medica, Pharmacology and Therapeutics*. Cincinnati: John K. Scudder, 1922. Reprint, Bisbee, Ariz.: Southwest School of Botanical Medicine, 2001.

Fernald, Walter E. "The Imbecile with Criminal Instincts." *Journal of American Psychiatry* 65, no. 4 (April 1, 1909): 731–49.

Finkelman, Paul. *African-Americans and the Legal Profession in Historical Perspective*. New York: Garland, 1992.

Fischer, Ron W. "Deputy Marshal Paden Tolbert: 'Bane of the Badmen.'" *Tombstone News*, n.d. (Two installments.) http://thetombstonenews.com/deputy-marshal-paden-tolbert- bane-of-the-badmen-p1025-84.htm; http://thetombstonenews.com/deputy-marshal -paden-tolbert-bane-of-the-badmen-p1067-84.htm.

Fisher, David, and Bill O'Reilly. *Bill O'Reilly's Legends and Lies: The Real West*. New York: Henry Holt, 2015.

Forbes, Jack. "Mose Miller: Mad Killer of the Cookson Hills." *The West: True Stories of the Old West* 1 (September 1964): 10–12, 52–53.

Foreman, Carolyn Thomas. "The Cherokee Gospel Tidings of Dwight Mission." *Chronicles of Oklahoma* 12 (December 1943): 454–69.

———, ed. "Journal of a Tour in the Indian Territory." *Chronicles of Oklahoma* 10 (June 1932): 256.

———. "The Lighthorse in Indian Territory." *Chronicles of Oklahoma* 34 (Spring 1956): 17–43.

———. *Oklahoma Imprints*. Norman: University of Oklahoma Press, 1936.

———. *Park Hill*. Muskogee, Okla.: Star Printery, 1948.

Foreman, Grant. *Advancing the Frontier, 1830–1860*. Norman: University of Oklahoma Press, 1933.

———. *Five Civilized Tribes*. Norman: University of Oklahoma Press, 1934.

———. *Fort Gibson: A Brief History*. Norman: University of Oklahoma Press, 1936.

———. *Indian Removal: The Emigration of the Five Civilized Tribes of Indians*. Norman: University of Oklahoma Press, 1932.

———. *A Traveler in Indian Territory: The Journal of Ethan Allen Hitchcock*. Norman: University of Oklahoma Press, 1996.

Freeman, Charles R. "Rev. Thomas Bertholf, 1810–1817." *Chronicles of Oklahoma* 11, no. 4 (December 1933): 1019–24.

Frey, James N. *The Key: How to Write Damn Good Fiction Using the Power of Myth*. New York: St. Martin's, 2000.

Fullerton, Eula E. "The Story of the Telephone in Oklahoma." *Chronicles of Oklahoma* 12, no. 3 (September 1934): 251–57.

Gaines, W. Craig. *The Confederate Cherokees: John Drew's Regiment of Mounted Rifles*. Baton Rouge: Louisiana State University Press, 1989.

Gant, Samuel Goodwin. *Constipation and Intestinal Obstruction (Obstipation)*. Philadelphia: W. B. Saunders, 1909.

Gardner, Mark Lee. *To Hell on a Fast Horse: The Untold Story of Billy the Kid and Pat Garrett*. New York: William Morrow Paperbacks, 2011.

Gaul, Theresa Strouth, ed. *To Marry an Indian: The Marriage of Harriett Gold and Elias Boudinot in Letters, 1823–1839*. Chapel Hill: University of North Carolina Press, 2005.

Gibson, Arrel. *Oklahoma: A History of Five Centuries*. Norman: University of Oklahoma Press, 1965; reprint 1981.

Gideon, D. C. *Indian Territory, Descriptive, Biographical and Genealogical: Including the Landed Estates County Seats a General History of the Territory*. Lewis, 1901.

Goins, Charles R., and Danney Goble, *Historical Atlas of Oklahoma*. 4th ed. Norman: University of Oklahoma Press, 2006.

Goldschmidt, Henry. *Race and Religion Among the Chosen People of Crown Heights*. New Brunswick, N.J.: Rutgers University Press, 2006.

Good, Clyde. "Ned Christie: Determined Cherokee Renegade," 39–44. In *Guns and the Gunfighters*, edited by editors of *Guns & Ammo*. New York: Crown, 1975.

Gould, Charles N. "Notes on Trees, Shrubs, and Vines in the Cherokee Nation." *Transactions of the Kansas Academy of Science* 18 (1903): 145–46.

Green, John. "Recollections of the Kings County Penitentiary Two Decades Ago." *Brooklyn Standard Union*, 1906. http://fultonhistory.com/Newspaper%2014/Brooklyn%20NY%20Standard%20Union/Brooklyn%20NY%20Standard%20Union%201906/Brooklyn%20NY%20Standard%20Union%201906%20-%201961.pdf.

Hamilton, Roy. *Ned Christie: Cherokee Warrior*. Stilwell, Okla.: Sugartree, 2004.

Hammond, Sue. "Socioeconomic Reconstruction in the Cherokee Nation, 1865–1870." *Chronicles of Oklahoma* (Summer 1978): 158–70.

Harmon, S. W. *Hell on the Border: He Hanged Eighty-Eight Men*. Lincoln: University of Nebraska Press, 1992. First published Fort Smith, Ark.: Phoenix, 1898.

Herring, Sidney L. "Crazy Snake and the Creek Struggle for Sovereignty: The Native American Legal Culture and American Law." *American Journal of Legal History* 34, no. 4 (October 1990): 365–80.

Hirschlorn, Norbert, Robert G. Feldman, and Ian Greaves. "Abraham Lincoln's Blue Pills: Did Our 16th President Suffer from Mercury Poisoning?" *Perspectives in Biology and Medicine* 44, no. 3 (Summer 2001): 315–32.

Holland, Cullen Joe. *Cherokee Newspapers, 1828–1906: Tribal Voice of a People in Transition*. Edited by James P. Pate. Tahlequah, Okla.: Cherokee Heritage, 2012.

Hutton, Paul Andrew. *The Apache Wars: The Hunt for Geronimo, the Apache Kid, and the Captive Boy Who Started the Longest War in American History*. New York: Crown, 2016.

Institute for Government Research. *The Problem of Indian Administration*. Studies in Administration. Baltimore, Md.: Johns Hopkins Press, 1928.

Jackson, Cathy Madora. "The Making of an American Outlaw Hero: Jesse James, Folklore and Late Nineteenth-Century Print Media." Ph.D. diss., University of Missouri–Columbia, 2004.

Johnson, Michael L. *Hunger for the Wild: America's Obsession with the Untamed West.* Lawrence: University Press of Kansas, 2007.

Joinson, Carla. *Grim Shadows: The Story of the Canton Asylum for Insane Indians.* Lincoln: University of Nebraska Press, 2016.

Keen, Patrick. "Thomas, Henry Andrew (1850–1912)." *The Encyclopedia of Oklahoma History and Culture.* www.okhistory.org.

Kilpatrick, Jack F. "Cherokees Remember Their Badmen: Who Can Better Evaluate a Man than His Own People?" *True West* 16 (July–August, 1969): 63.

King, Duane K., and E. Raymond Evans, eds. "The Trail of Tears: Primary Documents of the Cherokee Removal." *Journal of Cherokee Studies* 3 (1978): 129–90.

King, Patricia Jo Lynn. "The Forgotten Warriors: Keetoowah Abolitionists, Revitalization, the Search for Modernity and the Struggle for Autonomy in the Cherokee Nation, 1800–1866." Ph.D. diss., University of Oklahoma, 2013.

Kirchner, Paul. "Ned Christie." In *The Deadliest Men: The World's Deadliest Combatants Throughout the Ages.* Boulder, Colo.: Paladin, 2001.

Knight, Oliver. "Cherokee Society under the Stress of Removal, 1820–46." *Chronicles of Oklahoma* 32 (Winter 1954–55): 414–28.

Kunnikova, Maria. "How Stories Deceive." *New Yorker,* December 29, 2015. www.newyorker.com/science/maria-konnikova/how-stories-deceive.

Lane, John W. "Choctaw Nation." In *The Five Civilized Tribes in Indian Territory: The Cherokee, Chickasaw, Choctaw, Creek, and Seminole Nations.* Washington, D.C.: Census Printing Office, 1894.

LaRue, Lisa C. *He Was a Brave Man: The Story of an Indian Patriot.* CreateSpace, 2010.

Lewis, Meriam, comp. *The Problem of Indian Administration: Report of a Survey Made at the Request of Honorable Hubert Work, Secretary of the Interior, and Submitted to Him February 21, 1928.* Baltimore: Johns Hopkins Press, 1928.

Libke, Aileen Stroud. "The Man Who Killed Ned Christie." *Orbit Magazine* (February 27, 1977).

Littlefield, Jr., Daniel F., and Lonnie E. Underhill. "Ned Christie and His One-Man Fight with the United States Marshals." *Journal of Ethnic Studies* 1, no. 4: 3–15.

———. "Negro Marshals in Indian Territory." *Journal of Negro History* 56, no. 2 (April 1971): 77–87.

———. "The Trial of Ezekiel Proctor and the Problem of Judicial Jurisdiction." *Chronicles of Oklahoma* 48, no. 3 (1970): 307–22.

Malone, Henry Thompson. *Cherokees of the Old South: A People in Transition.* Athens: University of Georgia Press, 1956.

Mankiller, Wilma, and Michael Wallis, *Mankiller: A Chief and Her People.* New York: St. Martin's, 1993.

Marsden, Michael D. "The Popular Western Novel as a Cultural Artifact." *Arizona and the West* 20, no. 3 (Autumn 1978): 203–14.

Martin, Amelia. "Unsung Heroes: Deputy Marshals of the Federal Court for the Western District of Arkansas, 1875–1896." *Journal of the Fort Smith Historical Society,* 3, no. 1 (April 1979).

McKanna, Jr., Clare V. *Court-Martial of Apache Kid: The Renegade of Renegades*. Lubbock: Texas Tech Press, 2009.

McKenney, Thomas L. *Memoirs, Official and Personal; with Sketches of Travels among the Northern and Southern Indians; Embracing a War Excursion, and Descriptions of Scenes Along the Western Borders*. New York: Paine and Burgess, 1846.

McKennon, C. H. *Iron Men: A Saga of the Deputy United States Marshals Who Rode the Indian Territory*. New York: Doubleday, 1967.

McLoughlin, William. *Champions of the Cherokees: Evan and John B. Jones*. Princeton, N.J.: Princeton University Press, 1990.

McMahon, Jennifer L., and B. Steve Csaki, eds. *The Philosophy of the Western*. Lexington: University Press of Kentucky, 2010.

McMurtry, Larry, and Diana Ossana, *Zeke and Ned: A Novel*. New York: Simon and Schuster, 1997.

McMurtry, Robby. *Native Heart: The Life and Times of Nede Christie, Cherokee Patriot and Renegade*. CreateSpace, 2009.

Meserve, John Bartlett. "Chief John Ross." *Chronicles of Oklahoma* 8 (December 1935): 421–37.

Meyer, Richard E. "The Outlaw: A Distinctive American Folktype," *Journal of the Folklore Institute* 17, no. 2–3 (May–December 1980): 94–124.

Meyers, Olevia. "Zeke Proctor—Outlaw or Lawman?" *The West* 4, no. 6 (May 1966): 30–33, 49–52.

Mihesuah, Devon A. *Choctaw Crime and Punishment*. Norman: University of Oklahoma Press, 2010.

———. *Cultivating the Rose Buds: The Education of Women at the Cherokee Female Seminary, 1851–1909*. Urbana: University of Illinois Press, 1993.

———. "Out of the 'Graves of the Polluted Debauches': The Boys of the Cherokee Male Seminary." *American Indian Quarterly* 15 (Fall 1991): 503–21.

———. "Sustenance and Health among the Five Tribes in Indian Territory, Post-Removal to Statehood." *Ethnohistory* 62, no. 2 (April 2015): 263–84.

Miner, Craig H. *The Corporation and the Indian: Tribal Sovereignty and Indian Civilization in Indian Territory, 1867–1907*. Columbia: University of Missouri Press, 1976.

Mitchell, Lee Clark. *Westerns: Making the Man in Fiction and Film*. Chicago: University of Chicago Press, 1996.

Mooney, James. *Myths of the Cherokees and Sacred Formulas of the Cherokees*. Nashville: Charles and Randy Elder-Booksellers, 1982. Originally published in *Nineteenth Annual Report of the Bureau of American Ethnology, 1897–98*, pt. 1. Washington, D.C. Government Printing Office, 1900.

Morris, John Wesley. "Mayes." In *Ghost Towns of Oklahoma*. Norman: University of Oklahoma Press, 1978.

Moulton, Gary E. *John Ross, Cherokee Chief*. Athens: University of Georgia Press, 2004.

Murchison, A. H. "Intermarried-Whites in the Cherokee Nation." *Chronicles of Oklahoma* 6 (September 1928): 302–27.

Nebitt, Paul. "J. J. McAlester." *Chronicles of Oklahoma* 11 (June 1933): 758–64.

"Necrology: Mrs. Anna C. Trainor Matheson, 1872–1938." *Chronicles of Oklahoma* 18 (March 1940): 101.

"Ned Christie, Justice Gone Wrong," *Grand Lake News Online,* n.d. Accessed February 4, 2016. http://grandlakenewsonline.com/ned-christie-justice-gone-wrong-p1627–126. htm.

Nice, Margaret Morse. "Birds of Oklahoma" *Publication of the University of Oklahoma Biological Survey* 3, no. 1 (April 15, 1931).

O'Beirne, H. F., and E. S. O'Beirne. *The Indian Territory: Its Chiefs, Legislators and Leading Men.* St. Louis: C. B. Woodward, 1892.

"Officer Down! The Death of Ike Gilstrap." *Grand Lake News Online,* n.d. http://grandlakenewsonline.com/officer-down-the-death-of-ike-gilstrap-p1343–126.htm.

Oklahoma Almanac. Oklahoma City: Oklahoma Department of Libraries, 2005–2006.

O'Neal, Bill. *Encyclopedia of Western Gunfighters.* Norman: University of Oklahoma Press, 1991.

Otto, Thomas J. *St. Elizabeths Hospital: A History.* Washington, D.C.: U.S. General Services Administration, 2013. http://dcpreservation.wpengine.netdna-cdn.com/wp-content/uploads/2013/05/0-COMPLETE-St.-Elizabeths-Hospital-A-History.pdf.

Owens, Ron. *Oklahoma Heroes: The Oklahoma Peace Officers Memorial.* Nashville, Tenn.: Turner, 2000.

Parins, James W. *Elias Cornelius Boudinot: A Life on the Cherokee Border.* Lincoln: University of Nebraska Press, 2005.

———. *Literacy and Intellectual Life in the Cherokee Nation, 1820–1906.* Norman: University of Oklahoma Press, 2013.

Payne, Betty, and Oscar Payne. *A Brief History of Old Dwight Cherokee Mission, 1820–1953.* Tulsa: Dwight Presbyterian Mission, 1954.

Payne, Ruth Holt. "One-Man Peace Treaty." Nuggets. *Frontier Times* (September 1965): 39.

Perdue, Theda. *Cherokee Women: Gender and Culture Change, 1700–1835.* Lincoln: University of Nebraska Press, 1998.

———. "The Conflict Within: The Cherokee Power Structure and Removal." *Georgia Historical Quarterly* 73 (Fall 1989): 467–91.

Perdue, Theda, and Michael D. Green. *The Cherokee Removal: A Brief History with Documents.* New York: Bedford / St. Martin's, 2005.

Philp, K. R. *John Collier's Crusade for Indian Reform, 1920–1954.* Tucson: University of Arizona Press, 1977.

Pisciotta, Alexander W. "A House Divided: Penal Reform at the Illinois State Reformatory, 1891–1915." *Crime and Delinquency* 37 (April 1991): 165–85.

Prassel, Frank Richard. *The Great American Outlaw: A Legacy of Fact and Fiction.* Norman: University of Oklahoma Press, 1996.

Pride, Joe. "The Battle of Tahlequah Canyon." *True West* (October 1963): 18–19.

Prucha, Francis Paul. *American Indian Policy in the Formative Years: The Indian Trade and Intercourse Acts, 1790–1834.* Lincoln: University of Nebraska Press, 1962.

Putney, Diane T. "The Canton Asylum for Insane Indians, 1902–1934." *South Dakota History* 14 (1984): 1–30.

Rand, Phillip Rand. "Blood in the Cookson Hills." *True West* (January 1958): 26–28.

Reid, John Philip. *A Law of Blood*. New York: New York University Press, 1970.

Riggs, W. C. "Bits of Interesting History." *Chronicles of Oklahoma* 7, no. 2 (June 1929): 149–50.

Riney, Scott. "Power and the Powerlessness: The People of the Canton Asylum." *South Dakota History* 27, nos. 1–2 (1997): 41–64.

Ross, Mrs. William Potter Ross, ed. *The Life and Times of Hon. William P. Ross*. Fort Smith, Ark.: Weldon & Williams, 1893.

Sanders, J. G. *Who's Who Among Oklahoma Indians*. Oklahoma City: Trave, 1928.

Savage, William W., Jr. *The Cherokee Strip Live Stock Association: Federal Regulation and the Cattleman's Last Frontier*. Columbia: University of Missouri Press, 1973.

Schmid, Vernon. *Cherokee Mounted Rifles Muster Rolls*. CreateSpace, 2012.

Scraper, Etta Jane. "Reminiscences of the Cherokee Female Seminary." *Tsa-La-Gi Columns* 8 (Spring 1984): 1–2.

Sewell, Steven L. "Choctaw Beer: Tonic or Devil's Brew?" *Journal of Cultural Geography* 23 (Spring–Summer 2006): 105–16.

Shirk, George H. *Oklahoma Place Names*. Norman: University of Oklahoma Press, 1974.

Shirley, Glenn. *Belle Starr and Her Times: The Literature, the Facts and the Legends*. Norman: University of Oklahoma Press, 1983; reprint 1990.

———. *Heck Thomas, Frontier Marshal: The Story of a Real Gunfighter*. Norman: University of Oklahoma Press, 1981.

———. *Last of the Badmen*. New York: David McKay, 1965.

———. *Law West of Fort Smith: A History of Frontier Justice in the Indian Territory, 1834–1896*. New York: Henry Holt, 1957.

———. *Toughest of Them All*. Albuquerque: University of New Mexico Press, 1953.

Skelton, Robert H. "A History of the Educational System of the Cherokee Nation, 1801–1910." Ph.D. diss., University of Arkansas, 1970.

Smith, Daniel Blake. *An American Betrayal: Cherokee Patriots and the Trail of Tears*. New York: Henry Holt, 2011.

Smith, Robert Barr. "A Matter of Honor." *Wild West* (n.d.): 58–89.

———. *Outlaw Tales of Oklahoma: True Stories of the Sooner State's Most Infamous Crooks, Culprits, and Cutthroats*. Helena, Mont.: TwoDot, 2008.

Smith, W. R. L. *The Story of the Cherokees*. Cleveland, Tenn.: Church of God Publishing House, 1928.

Soule, Bradley, and Jennifer Soule. "Death at the Hiawatha Asylum for Insane Indians." *South Dakota Journal of Medicine* 56, no.1 (January 2003): 15–18

Spaulding, John M. "The Canton Asylum for Insane Indians: An Example of Institutional Neglect." *Hospital and Community Psychiatry* 37, no. 10 (October 1986): 1007–11.

Speer, Bonnie. *The Killing of Ned Christie, Cherokee Outlaw*. Norman: Reliance, 1990.

———. "Wolf of the Cookson Hills." *True West* (January 1983): 26–29.

Starr, Emmet. *History of the Cherokee Indians and Their Legends and Folk Lore*. Oklahoma City: Warden, 1979. First published 1922.

Starr, Henry. *Thrilling Events, Life of Henry Starr: Famous Cherokee Outlaw Narrates His Many Adventures from Boyhood to Date, Written in the Colorado Penitentiary by Himself.* Tulsa, Okla.: R. D. Gordon, 1914.

Steele, Phillip. *The Last Cherokee Warriors.* Gretna, La.: Pelican, 1987.

Steen, Carl T. "The Home for the Insane, Deaf, Dumb and Blind of the Cherokee Nation." *Chronicles of Oklahoma* 21 (December 1943): 402–19.

Strickland, Rennard. *Fire and Spirits: Cherokee Law from Clan to Court.* Norman: University of Oklahoma Press, 1975.

Thomas, Howard K. "Origin and Development of the Redbird Smith Movement." Master's thesis, University of Oklahoma, 1933.

Thoburn, Joseph H. *A Standard History of Oklahoma.* Vol. 3. Chicago: American Historical Society, 1916.

Thornton, Russell. "Cherokee Population Losses During the Trail of Tears: A New Perspective and a New Estimate." *Ethnohistory* 31 (1984): 289–300.

———. *The Cherokees: A Population History of a People.* Lincoln: University of Nebraska Press, 1992.

———. "The Demography of the Trail of Tears Period: A New Estimate of Cherokee Population Losses." In *Cherokee Removal: Before and After,* edited by William L. Anderson. Athens: University of Georgia Press, 1991.

"The Transformation of Ezekiel Proctor." *Grand Lake News,* December 26, 2013. http://www.grandlakenews.com/article/20131226/NEWS/312269919/?Start=1.

"The Trial of Stand Watie." *Chronicles of Oklahoma* 12, no. 3 (September 1934): 305–309.

Turner, Erin H. *Rotgut Rustlers: Whiskey, Women, and Wild Times in the West.* Helena, Mont.: 2009.

Turner, Frederick Jackson. "The Significance of the Frontier in American History." Paper read at the meeting of the American Historical Association, Chicago, July 12, 1893, during World Columbian Exposition.

Turpin, Robert F. "Cherokee Bill Pigeon." *Great West: True Stories of Old Frontier Days* 5 (June 1971): 20–21.

———. "Mad Killer of Cookson Hills." In *Hot Lead and Cold Steel,* 9–27. Grove, Okla.: Bob Turpin, 2010.

Tyner, Howard Q. "The Keetoowah Society in Cherokee History." Master's thesis, University of Tulsa, 1949.

U.S. Census Office, Department of the Interior. *The Five Civilized Tribes in Indian Territory: The Cherokee, Chickasaw, Choctaw, Creek and Seminole Nations.* Extra Census Bulletin. Washington, D.C.: U.S. Census Printing Office, 1894.

Walker, Wayne T. "Ned Christie: Terror of the Cookson Hills." *Real West* 21, no. 160 (November 1978): 30

Wardell, Morris J. *Political History of the Cherokee Nation, 1830–1907.* Norman: University of Oklahoma Press, 1938.

Washburn, Wilcomb E. *The Assault on Indian Tribalism: The General Allotment Law (Dawes Act) of 1887.* Philadelphia: Lippincott, 1975.

Watts, J. W. *Cherokee Citizenship and a Brief History of Internal Affairs in the Cherokee*

Nation with Records and Acts of the National Council from 1871 to Date. Muldrow, Indian Territory: Register Print, 1895.

Whorton, James C. *Inner Hygiene: Constipation and the Pursuit of Health in Modern Society*. New York: Oxford University Press, 2000.

Wilkins, Thurman. *Cherokee Tragedy: The Story of the Ridge Family and the Decimation of a People*. New York: Macmillan, 1970.

Woodward, Grace Steele. *The Cherokees*. Norman: University of Oklahoma Press, 1963.

Wright, Muriel Hazel. *Springplace: Moravian Mission and the Ward Family of the Cherokee Nation*. Guthrie, Okla.: Cooperative Publishing, 1940.

Wright, Will. *Sixguns and Society: A Structural Study of the Western*. Oakland: University of California Press, 1977.

Writers' Project of Work Projects Administration, comp. *Oklahoma: A Guide to the Sooner State*. American Guide Series. Norman: University of Oklahoma Press, 1941.

Yarbrough, Fay A. *Race and the Cherokee Nation: Sovereignty in the Nineteenth Century*. Philadelphia: University of Pennsylvania Press, 2007.

Young, Steve. "A Shameful Past: Indian Insane Asylum." *Tulalip News*, May 5, 2013. www.tulalipnews.com/wp/2013/05/06/a-shameful-past-indian-insane-asylum/.

WEBSITES

"Arkansas Executions." http://users.bestweb.net/~rg/execution/ARKANSAS.htm.

"Asylums and Insanity Treatments, 1800–1935: Canton Asylum's First Patients." *Indians, Insanity, and American History Blog*. April 15, 2010. http://cantonasylumforinsaneindians.com/history_blog/canton-asylums-first-patients/.

Bennett, Charles. "Legendary Lawman Bass Reeves." December 22, 2010. Officer.com. www.officer.com/article/10232183/legendary-lawman-bass-reeves.

Burton, Art T. "Black, Red and Deadly, Part II." *Art Burton's Frontier*. June 16, 2010. http://artburton.com/articles/black_red_deadly2.htm.

———. "Oklahoma's Frontier Indian Police: Indian Police." 1996. Lest We Forget. http://lestweforget.hamptonu.edu/. Originally published *Oklahoma State Trooper Magazine*.

"Charles LeFlore." National Park Service. Fort Smith National Historic Site. www.nps.gov/fosm/historyculture/charles_leflore.htm.

[Cherokee] Marbles. "Marbles (di ga da yo s di)." Cherokee Nation website. www.cherokee.org/AboutTheNation/Culture/General/Marbles%28digadayosdi%29.aspx.

"Executions in the U.S., 1608–2002: Executions by Name." The Espy File. Death Penalty Information Center website. www.deathpenaltyinfo.org/ESPYname.pdf.

"The Gateway to Oklahoma History." Oklahoma Historical Society. http://gateway.okhistory.org/.

"James Wesley 'Wes' Bowman, U.S. Deputy Marshal." http://freepages.genealogy.rootsweb.ancestry.com/~rkinfolks/stories/jameswesbowman.html.

"Judge Isaac Charles Parker." RootsWeb. http://freepages.genealogy.rootsweb.com/~rkinfolks/deputies.html.

Kraus, Larry. "Research Report: Allen, U.S. Marshal?" www.larkcom.us/ancestry/allen/reports/allen_us_marshal_display.htm.

Legends of America website. www.legendsofamerica.com/.

"The Marshals: Violent Deaths of U.S. Marshals." Silverstar Collectables. www.silverstarcollectables.com/killed.htm.

National Register of Historic Places. State Listings. Oklahoma, Latimer County. List of Registered Historic Places. /www.nationalregisterofhistoricplaces.com/OK/Latimer/state.html.

National Register of Historic Places Inventory–Nomination Form. Golda's Mill (Bitting Springs Mill), November 9, 1972. http://focus.nps.gov/pdfhost/docs/NRHP/Text/72001049.pdf.

"Ned Christie." *The Spell of the West.* www.jcs-group.com/oldwest/outlaws/christie.html.

"Oklahoma United States Marshals, Deputy United States Marshals and Possemen." www.okolha.net/oklahoma_united_states_marshals_WI-WY.htm.

OKOLHA (Oklahoma, Outlaws, Lawmen, History Association). www.okolha.net/index.html.

"Old West Lawmen: John R. Abernathy, aka: Wolf Catcher, Catch 'em Alive Jack (1876–1941)." *Legends of America.* www.legendsofamerica.com/we-lawmenlist-a.html#John R. Abernathy.

"Outlaw Index: Ned Christie." *Legends of America.* http://www.legendsofamerica.com/we-outlawindex-c.html.

Rizzo, Tom. "Showdown at a Mountain Fortress." http://tomrizzo.com/showdown-at-a-mountain-fortress/.

"Robert Stoddard (musician)." www.liquisearch.com/robert_stoddard_musician.

Scraper, Joe, Jr. "From Whiskey Peddler to Sunday School Teacher." http://scraperhistory.com/pdfs/Nancy_Gritts.pdf.

Speer, Bonnie. "Ned Christie: Cherokee Outlaw." *HistoryNet*, June 12, 2006. www.historynet.com/ned-christie-cherokee-outlaw.htm. Originally appeared in February 2000 issue of *Wild West.*

Stidham (Hodgden), Dayna Lynne. "My Genealogy Home Page: Information about Albert Clifford Stidham." Genealogy.com. www.genealogy.com/ftm/h/o/d/Dayna-L-Hodgden-MO/WEBSITE-0001/UHP-0002.html.

"U.S. Deputy Marshal in the Federal District Court for the Western District of Arkansas and Indian Territory at Fort Smith, Arkansas, Circa 1872–1896." Fort Smith National Historic Site Publication. Living the Legacy. www.nps.gov/fosm/forteachers/upload/legacy%20part%204.pdf.

"Vaughn Cemetery." LeFlore County, Oklahoma. www.rootsweb.com/~oklefcem/vaughn5.html.

Williams, Kerah. "Ned Christie's Last Stand." Porter Briggs.com: The Voice of the South, n.d. http://porterbriggs.com/ned-christies-last-stand/.

"Yoestown," 410–11. In *History of Crawford County, Arkansas.* Van Buren, Ark.: Press-Argus 1950. Excerpt posted by Diron Ahlquist, February 9 2005, under title "U.S. Marshal Jacob Yoes." Oklahombres. http://oklahombres.org/eve/forums/a/tpc/f/5176036794/m/74310347121.

INDEX